Gesher

Studies on Themes and Motifs in Literature

Horst S. Daemmrich
General Editor

Vol. 77

PETER LANG
New York • Washington, D.C./Baltimore • Bern
Frankfurt am Main • Berlin • Brussels • Vienna • Oxford

Olga Gershenson

Gesher

Russian Theatre in Israel—
A Study of Cultural Colonization

PETER LANG
New York • Washington, D.C./Baltimore • Bern
Frankfurt am Main • Berlin • Brussels • Vienna • Oxford

Library of Congress Cataloging-in-Publication Data

Gershenson, Olga.
Gesher: Russian theatre in Israel—a study of cultural colonization / Olga Gershenson.
p. cm. — (Studies on themes and motifs in literature; vol. 77)
Includes bibliographical references and index.
1. Gesher (Theater company: Tel Aviv, Israel). 2. Theater—Israel—
Tel Aviv—History—20th century. 3. Russian drama—
History and criticism. I. Title. II. Series.
PN2919.6.T45G47 792'.095694'8—dc22 2005002297
ISBN 0-8204-7615-3
ISSN 1056-3970

Bibliographic information published by **Die Deutsche Bibliothek**.
Die Deutsche Bibliothek lists this publication in the "Deutsche Nationalbibliografie"; detailed bibliographic data is available on the Internet at http://dnb.ddb.de/.

The paper in this book meets the guidelines for permanence and durability of the Committee on Production Guidelines for Book Longevity of the Council of Library Resources.

275 Seventh Avenue, 28th Floor, New York, NY 10001
www.peterlangusa.com

Printed in Germany

To Alik Loevsky
and to all other theatre-makers
in Russia and abroad

Contents

Figures

Tables

Acknowledgments

This book, and the doctoral dissertation on which it is based, would have been impossible without the support of my mentors, Anne Ciecko, Vernon Cronen, Briankle Chang, and Rajagopalan Radhakrishnan. I would like to thank them for their thoughtful comments and suggestions on all stages of this project.

I also want to extend my gratitude to the Gesher troupe members for their participation in this project. Their friendship and selfless contribution to my research have been invaluable and will forever be appreciated. Special thanks to Michal Savel, the publicist of the Gesher theatre, for helping with data collection and for contributing the photographs (which were taken by Sergey Fishbach, Gadi Dagon, Nicolay Adani-Tarkanov, Eldad Baron, and Gil Hadani).

I also wish to express my gratitude to the Graduate School of the University of Massachusetts at Amherst, the Jewish Endowment Foundation of Springfield, and the Community Foundation of Western Massachusetts for funding this research and providing travel expenses during the fieldwork.

A special thank you to my husband, Jonathan Schaffer, whose love, friendship, and support made the writing process fun.

• CHAPTER ONE •

Gesher Theatre and the Making of Israeli Culture

A bridge is not a road. A bridge has no destination. A bridge merely connects, right and left, one side and another. It is built because the two sides need to be connected. The bridge itself forms a space in-between, on neither side. Thus, a bridge becomes a metaphor for connection, for difference, and for the space in-between. A bridge is a metaphor for hybridity.

I am not sure that the Soviet immigrants had these metaphors in mind when they chose a name for their brainchild, a Russian-language theatre in Israel. But they called it Gesher, Hebrew for bridge. Whether they made this choice consciously or intuitively, the name aptly describes the theatre, and its position in the Israeli social landscape. Today, it is one of the major Israeli public theatres. Like a prism, Gesher refracts issues of interethnic relations, cultural and immigration policy, and the status of media discourse in Israel. This book is a history of the theatre in the 1990s, and an analysis of its critical reception in the mainstream Israeli media.

What's Wrong with This Picture?

During the nineties, the Israeli social landscape was transformed by the arrival of over 900,000 Soviet Jewish immigrants (about 15% of the Israeli population). This new wave of Soviet immigration turned into a tsunami that hit Israeli society dead on. It led not only to unemployment and lack of housing, but also to the clash of mutual expectations between many new immigrants and veteran Israelis. The new Soviet immigrants did not fit the Zionist expectations, according to which they should be earnestly learning Hebrew while working in the kibbutz field. Fed up with ideology in their

Soviet past, and coming from successful professional backgrounds, these immigrants were not in a rush to leave behind their diasporic past and plunge into a new cultural reality. This new wave of immigration, neither quite Israeli nor quite Soviet, neither quite complicit nor quite resistant, inhabited the borderlands of the Israeli cultural landscape.

This mass migration led to vast changes in Israeli society, culture, and politics, adding a new ethnic minority with a distinct cultural voice. In the early nineties, different organizations and advocacy groups were formed in order to represent the interests of the immigrants. This nascent political movement voiced the demands of this population: creation of jobs, separation of religion from state, and strengthening of civil rights law.

Already at the 1996 elections, the 'Russian' party, *Israel b'Aliyah*, headed by Nathan Scharansky[1] gained 7 out of 120 seats in the Fourteenth Knesset [Israeli parliament] and was awarded two Cabinet Ministers upon joining the coalition. As a result of the 1999 elections, two of the 'Russian' parties gained enough votes to be represented in Knesset: *Israel b'Aliyah* and *Israel Beiteinu*. Some other parties (*Israel Ahat, Shinui*, and *Habhira Hademocratit*) had Soviet immigrants as their Knesset representatives. However limited, the Soviet immigrant community had received political representation. Yet, throughout the nineties, the community remained unrecognized in Israeli culture.[2]

The voices of immigrants, with their accents and foreign intonation, were never heard on Israeli radio; the characters of immigrants almost never appeared on TV or in film. There were no recent Soviet immigrants among Israeli public cultural producers. Media coverage of immigration was always given from the veteran Israeli vantage point. A thriving industry of Russian-language media and culture existed separately from the mainstream Hebrew media, and thus was rendered invisible for Israeli audiences. Later, this situation started gradually changing: in 1998, Russian subtitles were introduced on some cable channels (by the company *Yes*); in 2001, Russian subtitles were introduced in movie theatres. In 2002, a Russian-language cable TV channel (*Israel Plus*) was launched. These steps towards recognition of the Russian-speaking audience in Israel, however, have not resolved the problem of under-representation of immigrants in the mainstream cultural production

1 Nathan Scharansky was a recent *refusnik* and an Israeli national hero. In the early 90s he served as a president of Zionist Forum of the Soviet Jewry, a non-profit organization that helped to integrate new Soviet immigrants in Israel.

2 In my claim that Soviet immigrants were unrecognized, I rely on Nancy Fraser's (1998) definition of "politics of recognition" as social practices of representation, interpretation, and communication.

in Israel. Journalists and actors with Russian accents still make only cameo appearances in Hebrew-language media.

But throughout the 90s, one of the few places in the Israeli cultural scene where the Soviet immigrants were seen and heard was Gesher Theatre. The Russian accent, usually relegated to the cultural margins, sounded there in the context of a major artistic production.

Gesher's history stands in contrast to the history of Habima, the first national theatre in pre-Israel Palestine. Habima, originally created in Moscow as the Hebrew-speaking theatre, was driven by the idea of Hebrew language revival (Levy 1979a). In contrast to this Zionist mission, Gesher has a cultural vocation. In 1990, it was founded to be a bridge (*gesher*) between the Russian culture of the actors and the Israeli culture of audiences.

However, already by 1992 Gesher was forced to switch from Russian to Hebrew since Israeli audiences were not interested in shows with simultaneous translation. At first the actors, who were new immigrants, did not know Hebrew and had to learn their parts phonetically. In spite of these challenges, the company proved to be both a box-office and critical success, and received recognition from the international theatre community. In the late nineties, the Gesher troupe, comprised of Soviet immigrants and veteran Israelis, performed mostly in Hebrew and only occasionally in Russian. However, in the Israeli public sphere Gesher was still perceived as a "theatre of Russian immigrants."

Some Israeli critics say that the theatre of immigrants is always a political theatre (Y. Shahal, personal communication, June 11, 2001). Since its early stages, Gesher has opposed this claim. The founders did everything to position the new theatre as an aesthetic endeavour devoid of an overt political or ideological agenda.[3] In various interviews Gesher's co-founders, Yevgeny Arye and Slava Maltzev, resist the narrow reading of the theatre as an "ethnic phenomenon" and insist on its artistic value. Gesher defines itself as a professional Israeli theatre: its productions are in Hebrew; they are geared towards the general theatre-going audience in Israel; its repertoire is similar to that of other major Israeli companies. Gesher shows never deal with the topic of Soviet immigration to Israel; its government funding comes from the same sources as that of other public theatres. Besides the cultural identity of Gesher troupe members and their accents, this theatre is seemingly not different from any other company in Israel. And yet, it is.

3 To distinguish between ideological and political, "ideology" here refers to Zionism, the dominant ideology in Israel, and "politics" refers to the ongoing negotiation of balance of power in a society.

The decision to be "beyond politics" is itself a political decision, and both critics and audiences are aware of it. Despite its egalitarian mythology, Israeli society is highly politically and ethnically divided, each group with its own agenda. Under these circumstances, Gesher becomes a political card that critics, politicians, and cultural producers consistently play in order to showcase their support for, or critique of, the immigrant minority. Despite Gesher's efforts to be 'just a theatre', and to be represented by its artistic productions, the Israeli critics consistently frame the theatre as a phenomenon of immigrant absorption and interethnic relations.

Critical acclaim, popular success, and official recognition on the one hand, and a condescending view of the theatre as an "ethnic" or "immigrant" venue on the other, lead to Gesher's ambivalent position in Israeli culture and politics. The theatre's media reception reflects this ambivalence. For these reasons, Gesher Theatre is an interesting site for this research, which aims to analyze the processes of cultural production and exchange that emerge in the Israeli discourse surrounding Gesher. This theoretical goal defines the structure of this book.

In the first chapter, I give an introduction to the social and cultural contexts in Israel in which Gesher Theatre was founded. In the second chapter, I lay out the theoretical tools that I use in my analysis of Gesher's media reception. I draw parallels between the discursive conditions of immigration and colonization and suggest a model of Mutual and Internal Colonization. I explain this model and its application to the specific context of immigration in Israel.

In the third chapter, I report on my methods of collecting and interpreting data. In chapters four to ten, I tell the history of Gesher Theatre and its media reception in Israel over the 90s. Each one of these chapters answers two sets of questions. First, how is Gesher situated within the Israeli social and cultural contexts? And how did this situation change over the years? Second, how is this situation reflected in Gesher's media reception of the time? And what are the main issues at stake in this reception?

In the last chapter, I place Gesher's history and its media reception in the contexts of Russian and Israeli cultures. I also draw conclusions about the processes of cultural production and exchange operative within the discourses surrounding Gesher Theatre.

The Social Context: Politics of Immigration in Israel

The politics of immigration in Israel is best understood in the context of Zionism, the movement whose goal was the return of the Jewish people to the Land of Israel. From its very appearance at the end of nineteenth century, the ideology of Zionism was hybrid and discordant, with different religious and historical traditions woven into it. It became an umbrella term for several school of thoughts, among them Messianic, Spiritual, Labor (or Socialist), and Revisionist Zionism.

However different in their visions and objectives, these versions of Zionism have three important commonalities. Firstly, all versions of the Zionist ideology are based on the assumption that the Jews in different ages and countries constitute a nation.[4] This assumption allows for the claim of the historic national home and leads to the choice of Palestine, rather than any other place (such as Uganda in an earlier scheme) for the creation of the modern Jewish state. The second commonality is commitment to the revival of Hebrew language as a national language of the state. Finally, the third commonality is a commitment to *aliyah* [immigration to the national state, see Glossary]. This commitment, backed up by the Law of Return (which confers Israeli citizenship on any diaspora Jew), became *raison d'être* of the state of Israel. These common assumptions in many ways define politics of immigration and immigrant absorption in Israel.

In 1949 David Ben-Gurion, the first prime-minister, called the citizens of the newly formed state to "speed and make more powerful the stream of immigration to the utmost of our power, for the ingathering of the exiles is the purpose of our existence and also a precondition of it" (quoted in Gitelman 1982, p. 36). Later, Golda Meir claimed that immigration is "the essence of our life" and that "there is no State of Israel without a large and powerful *aliyah*" (Gitelman 1982, p. 37). Moshe Dayan also emphasized the importance of immigration and even called for personal sacrifices in order "to fulfill needs of those Jews who are ready to come here" (Gitelman 1982, p. 37). These quotes demonstrate a reflexive connection between the ideology of Zionism and the politics of immigration: Zionism justifies immigration, whereas immigration reinforces the Zionist idea. Even though throughout the

4 For an opposing view, claiming that there is no such historical entity as Jewish people see Koestler (1976) and Wexler (1993).

history of Israel the politics of immigration and absorption have changed, this connection remained present.[5]

In the early days of the state of Israel, the Zionist ideology led to adoption of a "melting pot" model of absorption, according to which new immigrants let go of their ethnic-cultural differences and acquired new Israeli identity. This model was reinforced by political parties and the Jewish Agency that fulfilled quasi-governmental functions in respect to immigrants. The parties provided public and welfare services and thus connected immigrants to national institutions. Such politicization of immigrants' absorption resulted in a paternalistic system leaving immigrants (especially immigrants from Asia and North Africa) completely dependent on the political powerholders of the society.

The changing profile of immigrants after the Six-day War necessitated different absorption mechanisms. Most of the immigrants were of Western origin, possessing higher education and economic power. In the late 60s and early 70s a series of benefits for new immigrants was designed, including lower taxation, favorable mortgage rates, and professional retraining. (These benefits though made some Israelis jealous of the immigrants and act hostile towards them.) At that time, immigrants also received more freedom to choose their place and mode of residence. In contrast to the party system, the newly established Ministry of Absorption administered immigrant absorption, and the semi-governmental Jewish Agency had limited functions.

Soviet immigration during the 90s (that started strictly speaking in 1989) opened a new chapter in the Israeli immigration and absorption policies and practices. In 1989, the US immigration policy that previously granted a status of political refugees to Soviet Jews, had been changed. The democratization of the political regime and loosening emigration restrictions by the Soviet authorities increased the potential scale of immigration. The threat of mass Jewish Soviet immigration along with pressure from the Israeli government put a stop to rerouting Soviet emigrants to the US. As the scholar of Soviet immigration Clive Jones reports, "By reinterpreting, and stringently applying the definition of who was a political refugee, Washington effectively sanctioned Israel as the only viable destination for those Jews who wished to leave Soviet Union" (1996 p. 52). As a result, he continues, "the decision was made for them."

5 For further discussion of immigration and absorption in Israel, see Leshem and Shuval (1998) and Shuval (1998).

The new American policy began to take effect from October 1989. By the end of that year a vanguard of the new immigration wave arrived in Israel. By mid-1992, the number of immigrants already reached 400,000.

For the right-wing Likud coalition government, the new wave of immigration became a political card in a conflict over occupied territories. The Prime Minister at the time, Yitzhak Shamir, declared the successful absorption to be a major national priority. However, the Israeli absorption machine nearly collapsed under the incredible pressure. The local centers of absorption responsible for paperwork, referrals to language courses and subsidies were so overcrowded that immigrants had to keep a night vigil in the lines if they wanted to speak with a social worker in the morning.

The situation with both housing and employment was critical. Lack of housing was the first problem. So called "direct absorption" [placement of immigrants directly into existing communities] failed because of the lack of apartments available for rent. The scarce market resulted in inflated prices, which forced immigrants to share overcrowded apartments with family or roommates. By the end of 1990, about 30% of the 185,000 Soviet immigrants lived in such shared apartments (Jones 1996, p. 129). The settlement pattern of immigrants also changed the demographic balance in Israel. Given the option of a "direct absorption," secular, non-Zionist, urban, academically educated Soviet immigrants flocked to the bigger cities in expectation to find work corresponding to their status. And that is where they faced the second problem—unemployment.

Israel faced a high national unemployment rate even before the immigration wave. In 1991, it reached 10.6%, whereas amongst immigrants the rate of unemployment was as high as 50%. Of those immigrants who were employed only 20% worked in their chosen profession (Jones 1996, p. 126). The under- or unemployment of Soviet immigrants had not only financial but also social implications—they felt isolated and devalued.

A lack of housing and the increasing unemployment led to the growing discontent among both new immigrants and veteran Israelis. Aside from competition over jobs and housing, the immigration profile also "exacerbated tensions among Israel's disparate interest groups and communities, raising questions concerning the citizenship and loyalty of the Soviet *olim* [immigrants] towards the Jewish State" (Jones 1996, p. 119). First, the Mizrahi (North-African and Middle-Eastern Jews) community saw the Soviet immigrants as reinforcing Ashkenazi (European Jews) dominance in Israeli society. Second, ultra-religious groups who represented the establishment in absorption policies expressed doubts about the Judaism of immigrants and thus presented Israel as a theocratic state to Soviet immigrants (Jones 1996).

The attitudes of the religious groups caused feelings of resentment towards Judaism and Israeli culture and encouraged defensive ethnocentrism. As the immigrants bitterly observed: "We were Jews in Russia, we became Russians in Israel."

In contrast to the immigrants of the 70s who aspired to "become Israelis," the immigrants of the 90s yearned to retain their own cultural identity and heritage. Clive Jones explains:

> Regarding themselves as the standard bearers of a rich intellectual heritage that encompassed the writings of Tolstoy and Pushkin, these immigrants expressed considerable antipathy towards a society that was viewed as brash, aesthetically barren, and unduly influenced by synthetic American culture. (1996, p. 140)

The fact that Israeli society also presented itself to the immigrants as an ultra-orthodox theocracy only added to their disappointment. Not surprisingly, these sentiments were accompanied by a low motivation to learn Hebrew, which threatened the established linguistic hegemony.

As a result, Jones comments, "the new immigrants did not conform to the 'we' identity of the recipient society" (1996, p. 119). Moreover, they put it at risk. The emergent stereotype of Soviet immigrants as a threat to national identity was reflected in the media. In the early 90s, media portrayed the immigrants as alcoholics, children- and wife-beaters, and as a community of criminals, drug-dealers, and prostitutes. Soviet Jews were conveniently blamed for social problems that existed in the society prior to their arrival. These attitudes are expressed by the old Israeli folk wisdom: "Israelis love immigration, but hate immigrants." In this way, Zionist ideology shaped both the official immigration policies and public cultural attitudes towards immigrants. In their turn, the cultural attitudes of the Soviet immigrants led them to believe Israelis to be blunt, uncivilized, and shallow.

The Cultural Context: Theatre Production and Reception in Israel

The ideology of Zionism was instrumental in shaping the scene of cultural production as well. In Israel, theatre is subject to pressures from both right and left. From the left, it is subject to pressure from the critics holding an antiquated idea of *agitprop* art and aligning with the Zionist ideology. From the right, it is subject to commercial pressure.

Israeli critics act as gatekeepers of the dominant ideology, placing national values high on their priority list. Their position is explained by the cultural specificity of theatre history in Israel. For centuries Jewish religious tradition was hostile to theatre (except for Purim performances), as well as to other figurative arts. The basis for this hostility is in the biblical commandment: "Thou shalt not make unto thee any graven image..." (Exod. 20:4; Deut. 5:8). The emergence of Hebrew theatre was possible only with the establishment of Hebrew secular culture, which evolved alongside with the ideology of Zionism.

In this context, Hebrew theatre was assigned an ideological rather than an aesthetic value. The critics, committed to politically-oriented art, insisted that the theatre should perform first and foremost ideological functions (Levy 1988; Rokem 1988). The two main functions were to disseminate Zionist ideology and to popularize the Hebrew language. Some authors observe that in the post-state era the role of critics underwent a transformation, and their judgment became more specialized and professional (Levy 1979b; Weitz 1996d). But the pervasive view of theatre as a national institution, and the role of critics as ideological gatekeepers are still deeply embedded in Israeli popular culture.

This view results in a tension between ideology and aesthetics in Israeli theatre criticism. Of course, it is difficult to speak of such a tension, because the ideological and the aesthetic shade into each other. Art is always political, and aesthetic values are deeply grounded in social and historical contexts. Yet still, Levy's definitions of ideology and aesthetics prove useful for understanding Israeli theatre criticism. According to Levy, *aesthetic* criteria include "various aspects of the play's dramatic structure, plot, and characters" and "aspects of the production of the play (staging, acting, sets, costumes, etc.)" (1979b, p. 176). *Ideological* criteria include "discussion of the cultural and political significance of the play in terms of its ideological message and the timing of its presentation" (1979b, p. 177).

Using Levy's definitions, I would say that the problem of Israeli criticism is a complete substitution of aesthetic with ideological criteria of judgment. In other words, the problem is that Israeli critics only focus on whether the production and its creators feed into the dominant ideology.

The Israeli critics do not oppose their position as ideological gatekeepers, but rather make it their *modus operandi*. They rarely, if ever, give a resistant (to dominant ideology) interpretation of a production. Instead, critics, in Bourdieu's terms, mobilize themselves to maintain "symbolic capital" (1986) setting the same priorities as the political establishment. The gains of such position for critics are clear: their reputation is created and continued through their participation in hegemonic discourse. Indeed, "'theatre is called to order' whenever it stepped out of line in terms of the national consensus" (Weitz[6] 1996d, p. 105). Thus, the important function of theatre to criticize social reality and to suggest alternatives is lost; instead, theatre critics become a means of replicating the dominant ideology.

Theatre in Israel is also subject to pressure from the right. Like theatre in the West, Israeli theatre is coming increasingly under the influence of the market economy and conservative values of theatre audiences. Public theatres in Israel receive governmental support on the level of 40–60% (from the budget of the Ministry of Education and Culture and from municipal funds). The other part of the budget is expected to come from ticket sales. The marketing system in Israel relies mainly on a subscription system and collective sales to union workers. Only 9% of the tickets are purchased individually from the box-office (Avigal 1996). The result of this marketing system is that theatres inadvertently start catering to the tastes of conservative audiences: "State-supported theatres, which in theory receive subsidies in order to be able to create art in a context disconnected from commercial constraints of supply and demand, began adapting their repertoire and artistic standards to the expectations of the subscribers and to large-scale collective buyers" (Avigal 1996, p. 19). Thus theatres become "production agencies in a commercial field, operating according to the dictates of supply and demand in the theatrical marketplace" (p. 21).

This marketing system shapes the patterns of theatre going in Israel. Since tickets are sold in advance to large-scale collective buyers, "theatre attendance is thus detached from the process of artistic evaluation and aesthetic selection" (Avigal 1996, p. 19). Theatre attendance is increasingly adherent to the petit-bourgeois and popular norm.

Theatres that don't use a subscription system (such as Gesher) are less subjected to influence from the right. But that seeming freedom comes at the price of increasing pressure from the left, as the box-office sales of their productions are highly dependent on critical opinion. For such theatres, critic's position as a "tastemaker" is endowed with significant financial power, defining the popular success or failure of a production.

---

6 Ironically enough, this is the same Weitz, who (as the reader will see later) wrote multiple reviews of Gesher, 'calling it to order'.

• CHAPTER TWO •

Rethinking Colonization and Immigration

My focus here is discourse. Following Foucault, I understand discourse as a system of statements, which contain social knowledge. Discourse is a capillary form of power—a way of constituting knowledge, social practices, forms of subjectivity, and power relations. In this sense, culture, national identity, and ideology are all forms of discourse. These forms of discourse operate through such channels as law, education, and mass media. But in any form, discourse is not homogeneous; it is woven of different voices that both constitute and challenge it. Even the dominant discourse contains within it multiple voices, some of them affirming and some resisting each other. These voices do not exist in the simple opposition of 'empowered' versus 'powerless' discourse, but rather are "blocks operating in the field of force relations" (Foucault 1981, p. 101).

Contemporary Israeli discourse is not an exception: in addition to the dominant Zionist discourse, other voices, such as those of traditional Jews, Mizrahi Jews, and post-Zionist scholars are woven into it.[1] New Soviet immigrants have added one more voice to this polyphony, a voice that both resists and affirms the dominant Zionist discourse.

My project is to understand the complex relationships between the Soviet immigrant and Zionist discourses. To this end, it will prove useful to borrow from the theoretical toolbox of post-colonial discourse analysis. Following Ella Shohat and Robert Stam, I use "colonization" as "the infantilizing trope, which projects colonized people as embodying an earlier stage of individual human or broad cultural development, a trope which posits the cultural

1 For further discussion of traditional Jewish discourse in the context of Zionism see Kimmerling (2001). For further discussion of Mizrahi discourse in the context of Zionism see Shohat (1999). For further discussion of post-Zionism (critical approach to Israeli history and ideology) see Silberstein (1999) and Nimni (2003).

immaturity of colonized...peoples" (1998, p. 28). Relying on this definition, I understand colonial discourse in a broad sense, as a discourse under the conditions of inequity of power, such as the dominance of hegemonic ideology.

In order to account for complex discursive relations, I propose a model of Mutual and Internal Colonization. This model, emerging out of a tradition of post-colonial discourse analysis, is intended to analyze the relations between colonizer and colonized within the discursive realm. It reflects the cultural politics of difference rather than the social politics of equality.

In the traditional understanding of the colonial discursive operation (such as in Said 1978), the colonial relations were modeled as a one-way street: the colonizer subjugates the colonized, and that is possible because the colonized adulates the colonizer (see Figure 1). This process is best described by Frantz Fanon: "The colonized is elevated above his jungle status in proportion to his adoption of the mother country's cultural standards" (1952, p. 18).

The liberatory prospects are quite clear in this model—to remove the colonizer. However, post-colonial history shows that this model does not give adequate answers to the questions of the colonial relationship. Robert Young critiqued such a model claiming that cultural exchange is never a one-way process, whatever the power relations involved. Young suggested to talk about cultural exchange as a two-way process where cultures are not "destroyed but rather layered on each other, giving rise to struggles that themselves only increase imbrication of each with the other" (1995, p. 174).

Homi Bhabha describes cultural exchange as a two-way process. Combining Foucaldian approach to discourse with psychoanalysis, Bhabha shows that colonial discourse operates not only on the conscious level of the construction of knowledge, but also on the ambivalent protocols of fantasy and desire. In psychoanalysis, "ambivalence" refers to a simultaneous attraction and repulsion from a person or an object, or a wanting of both a thing and its opposite. Applying the concept of ambivalence to the relations between colonizer and colonized, Bhabha shows how colonial discourse fluctuates between mimicry and menace (see Figure 2). Mimicry, a process forced on a colonial subject, "is the desire for a reformed recognizable Other, *as a subject of difference that is almost the same, but not quite*" (Bhabha 1994, p. 86). However, mimicry is charged with the danger of mockery. It threatens to undermine the prevailing norms and authorities—the 'normalized' knowledges and disciplinary powers of the dominant discourse. For instance, Bhabha discusses a literary character of an Indian man (Ralph Singh in V. S. Naipaul's *The Mimic Men*) who strives to become a perfect English gentleman. His mimicry, however, results in a mockery of Britishness. Thus mimicry turns into menace.

Discursive relationships between colonizer and colonized take a form of a Freudian *fort/da* game: a colonial subject is required to become "like" a colonizer and to correspond to the norms and models. However, when the subject mimics the colonizer and attempts to become "the same," the threat of mockery is so great that the colonizer's desire for the "same Other" is withdrawn, bringing forward remorse and anxiety. In Bhabha's words, "The ambivalence of colonial authority repeatedly turns from *mimicry*—difference that is almost nothing but not quite—to *menace*—a difference that is almost total but not quite" (1994, p. 91).

However, it is this ambivalence, pregnant with mockery, that gives hope for empowerment and liberation. Colonial relationships become a site of cultural production, which results in new hybrid identities that are "neither the one thing nor the other" (Bhabha 1994, p. 33). Bhabha calls such sites the 'third space'. Located on the borderline of cultures, the 'third space' enables other positions to emerge; it "displaces the histories that constitute it, and sets up new structures of authority, new political initiatives" (1990, p. 211). Such hybrid discursive constructions are constituted of voices, bearing the traces of different discourses. The hybrid constructions have no "pure" origin—they are indefinable. This indefinability gives them a transformative power. The third space, where polarities are blurred and different discourses are woven together, gives a chance for minority voices to be heard rather than silenced. Hybrid constructions "give narrative form to the minority positions they occupy; the outside of the inside: the part in the whole" (Bhabha 1996, p. 58).

Bhabha's theory of the colonial discourse offers insights into the ambivalent relationships between colonized and colonizer. What about the relationships between immigrants and their hosts?

Mutual Colonization

Despite the differences in historical and cultural contexts, the discursive practices of immigration are similar to that of colonization. In both cases, there is a binary relation between colonizer and colonized, between the dominant and subordinate voices, and in general, between hegemonic and marginalized discourses. In both cases, paraphrasing Fanon, the relationship vacillates between narcissism and inferiority.

In Israel, the dominant Zionist discourse plays a colonizing role in respect to the subordinate discourses of the cultural Others, including Palestinians,

Mizrahi Jews, and, recently, immigrants from Ethiopia and Russia. This argument is based on Ella Shohat's claim that a Jewish nationalism, Zionism—

> assumed that the 'national' is produced by eliminating the foreign, the contaminated, the impure, so that the nation can emerge in all its native glory. In the name of national unity, contradictions having to do with class, gender, ethnicity, race, region, sexuality, language, and so forth tend to be erased or glossed over. (Shohat 1999, p. 11)

However, in the case of the relationship between the veteran Israelis and the Soviet immigrants, both sides exhibit colonial attitudes, so that it is not clear who is the colonizer and who is colonized. The cultural attitudes of veteran Israelis and the Soviet immigrants reflect the colonial histories of Israel and Russia.

Russia emerged as a major colonizer during the nineteenth century. The Russian empire held sway over Central Asia, Siberia, the Caucasus, and the Far East. During the Soviet era, the colonization continued. In addition to the republics of the former Soviet Union, colonialism spread to other parts of Eastern Europe, and to countries as far away as Afghanistan and Cuba. All these territories were politically, economically, and, most importantly, culturally colonized.[2] The colonial attitudes are evident in the fact that in Russian slang the terms for dark-skinned people from the Caucasus and Central Asia are racial slurs (e.g., *chuchmek, churka*). These attitudes set the Soviet immigrants up to assume the position of colonizer.

Simultaneously, Russian culture was also colonized by Western European culture. In the nineteenth century "in sharp contrast to other politically strong imperializing modern states, Russia found itself in a culturally subordinate, one might even say colonized position" (Wachtel 1999, p. 49). This colonization found expression in the Europeanization of the Russian elites, which "laid the groundwork for the great Russian literary, musical, and artistic achievements of the nineteenth and twentieth centuries, but it also produced a strong case of culture shock and a nagging sense of inferiority" (Wachtel 1999, p. 50). The attitudes derived from this sense of inferiority set the Soviet immigrants up to assume the position of colonized.

The situation was even more complex for Russian Jews. They fully shared the Russian cultural attitudes explained above. But also, they were subject to humiliating anti-Semitism, which they internalized to some extent. The resulting self-hatred made the Russian Jews feel inferior vis-à-vis the Russian cultural majority. On the other hand, they developed a defensive reaction to anti-Semitism and took great pride in their ethnic heritage and traditional

2 For further discussion of Russian colonialism see Thompson (2000).

Jewish values of family, education, and orderly life. This defensive response allowed Russian Jews to feel superior to ethnic Russians who they saw as a nation of disorganized drunkards.[3] This attitude is evident in the fact that Russian Jews sometimes referred to ethnic Russians with such slurs as *goishe copf* (in Yiddish, literally–gentile head, figuratively–a moron). These conflicting attitudes set up the Soviet immigrants to simultaneously experience the ambivalent feelings of cultural inferiority and superiority in Israel.

Israeli cultural attitudes are ambivalent as well. Israeli history is rooted in Russian and Eastern European culture. The idea of a Jewish nation-state came as a response to the position of cultural inferiority to which Jews were confined in Eastern Europe in the nineteenth century. However, in the struggle for the establishment of their state, the Jewish settlers (future Israelis) took a colonizing position towards the native Palestinian population. This position was reinforced during the years of statehood, including not only the politics of expansion and conquest of the Palestinian territories, but also discrimination against the Palestinian Israelis. The colonizing position was extrapolated to include the fellow Jews: the Mizrahi immigrants in the 50s, then Ethiopian and Soviet immigrants in the 80s and 90s.[4]

What contributed to the emerging colonizing position of the veteran Israelis is a certain type of bureaucracy produced by the Israeli immigrant absorption apparatus (first the parties and the Jewish Agency, later the Ministry of Absorption). In the process of what Katz and Eisenstadt (1960/61) called "debureaucratization," a bureaucrat (a public officer) develops informal personal relations with immigrants, instead of impersonal and businesslike ones. What might look like a positive event, in fact, leads a bureaucrat to take a role of teacher along with (or, rather, at the expense of) other functions. This seemingly bureaucratic dysfunction leads to a condescending infantilizing attitude towards new immigrants, which allows any veteran Israeli to give lessons to a presumably incompetent immigrant. This attitude is not limited to the bureaucratic context. It spread out to other public and private spheres in Israel, including that of cultural production. This infantilizing attitude is ideologically rooted: even in pre-Israel Palestine Ashkenazi settlers enjoyed

---

3 For more detailed and nuanced discussion of the culture of the Russian Jews and their relationships with their neighbors, see Slezkine, 2004; Roi, 1995; Goluboff, 2003; Brym & Ryvkina, 1994.

4 An important distinction should be made between the discriminations against different cultural Others. The discrimination against Soviet immigrants lies mainly within the politics of recognition–social practices of representation, interpretation, and communication.

higher social status "simply by virtue of living in Palestine, and thereby fulfilling the Zionist ideal" (Gitelman 1982, p. 20).

Yet, simultaneously with the position of the colonizer, Israelis assume the position of colonized. For instance, within the cultural hierarchy of Israeli society, the Ashkenazi minority is placed above the Mizrahi majority who are forced to occupy an inferior position.[5] But even those Israelis who are on top of social pyramid express feelings of inferiority in respect to European, including Russian, cultures. Such an attitude toward Russian culture is predicated on a number of historical connections. The ideology of Zionism has roots in Russia. The forefathers of Zionism, whose shadows still hover over the Israeli social landscape, came from Russia and Eastern Europe. The great Russian literature, music, and theatre had high status in the nascent Israeli culture, and remain beyond reproach. These attitudes set Israelis up to assume the position of the colonized.

The ambivalent position of Israelis in respect to their identity is exemplified in the public debate about the cultural orientation of Israel: one camp envisions Israel as an essentially European (or in general, Western) country that just happens to be located in the Middle East; whereas another camp identifies Israel as a part of the Levant (the countries on the Eastern Mediterranean, from Egypt to Turkey).

The Soviet immigrants bring to the Israeli cultural hierarchy their own baggage, which fits into Israel's colonial ambivalence. On the one hand, the Soviet immigrants feel inferior to upper and upper-middle class Israelis (many of them Ashkenazi Jews). The immigrants admire them for their Western life style, their economic wealth, their heroic role in the founding of the state of Israel, and the country's military victories. However, the Soviet immigrants assume a position of superiority in respect to working or lower-middle class Israelis (many of them Mizrahi Jews). The immigrants bring into this relationship their colonizing baggage. They frame the Mizrahi Israelis (or Israelis who look Mizrahi) as the non-Russian ethnicities in the Former Soviet Union. They even describe such Israelis using the same racial slurs (*chuchmek, churka*) that referred to the dark-skinned people from the Caucasus and Central Asia. They consider Israel as a kind of non-Russian republic in the Soviet Union.

As a result of these ambivalent cultural attitudes, the vectors of colonization in the relationship between veteran Israelis and Soviet immigrants are not clear. Who is colonizer and who is colonized?

---

5 For further discussion of the hierarchy of Israeli society see Swirski (1989) and Shohat (1999).

In fact, these positions are not fixed, but fluid, switching places depending on context. Both sides, Soviet immigrants and veteran Israelis, simultaneously admire and condescend to each other, thereby letting mimicry and menace work double shifts. This process results in the mutual colonization (see Figure 3): Soviet immigrants take an inferior (colonized) position in respect to Israelis, admiring their Western and Jewish values, their economic prosperity, and more advanced technology. At the same time, these immigrants take a superior (colonizing) position in respect to Israelis, dismissing them as 'uncultured', 'primitive', dark-skinned people, like those from the Caucasus Mountains and Asian plains.

For their part, the veteran Israelis take an inferior (colonized) position in respect to Soviet immigrants, considering them high-cultured, sophisticated intellectuals. Yet they also put themselves into a superior (colonizing) position, questioning immigrants' Jewish and Zionist commitment, and dismissing them as technologically backward and morally loose. As an expression of such an attitude, the Russian immigrant women in Israel are stigmatized as prostitutes, and immigrant men as mafiosis or con-artists, corrupting Israeli society. We can see that the mutual attitudes of Soviet immigrants and native Israelis swing between demonizing and worshipping, replicating the double figures of colonization: narcissism and inferiority.

Internal Colonization

Discursive operation of colonization is not limited to the relations between subjects. Once internalized, colonization structures subject's relations with herself. As a result, along with the mutual colonization, an internal colonization contributes to the process of colonial subjugation.

Colonial discourse operates according to the same principle as hegemonic ideology. Drawing on the works of Antonio Gramsci (1991), and Louis Althusser (1971), I define hegemony as domination by consent, and ideology as a discursive practice producing subjects.[6] Consent is achieved by the interpellation of the colonized subject through the colonizing discourse. Apparently, such discourse takes into account the interests of the colonized (subordinate classes), but, in fact, it establishes the values, beliefs, and attitudes of the colonizer (the dominant classes) as the "natural" and common for all. As a result of interpellation, the colonized internalize their peripheral status, and assume the centrality of the values of the colonizer. Thus, colonization

6 For further discussion see Mouffe (1979) and Williams (1997).

interpellates subjects. Acting as the ideological state apparatus, colonizing discourse 'calls people forth', thereby providing conditions and context for obtaining colonial subjectivity. As a result, the mutual colonization is internalized, and the colonial process becomes self-generating: it can go on without any contribution from an external colonizer. A colonial subject forms a complete colonial system all by herself (see Figure 4). She is both a colonizer and a colonized. This phenomenon was described by Fanon, who wrote, "After having been the slave of the white man, he [the black man] enslaves himself" (1952, p. 192).

The effects of internal colonization on subjects are profound because the process causes a fundamental change in the individual, turning the subject's relations with herself colonial. Now the subject is locked into a permanent struggle between narcissism (inner colonizer) and inferiority (inner colonized). The mimicry and menace are internalized as well and are ever-present in the internal struggle of the split subject.

According to Gramsci (1991), the condition of hegemony is characterized by a dual consciousness of the subordinate classes, that is, by holding incompatible sets of beliefs, one set derived from hegemony, the other from their personal experience. In contrast, the dual consciousness that emerges as a characteristic of both Soviet immigrants and native Israelis reflects two colonial sets of beliefs, those of the colonized and those of the colonizers.

Mutual and Internal Colonization

When both of these mechanisms—internal and mutual colonization—are at work at once, the subject colonizes herself vis-à-vis another subject (see Figure 5). In the colonial discursive system, subjects vacillate between narcissism and inferiority; the narcissism of one subject comes at the expense of the inferiority of another. When the colonization turns inward, the subject splits into Inner Colonizer and Inner Colonized, but relationships remain the same—the narcissism of an inner colonizer is coupled up with the perceived inferiority of an inner colonized. The vectors of internal and mutual colonization, directed both inside and outside, make subjects shift positions between narcissism and inferiority. As a result, colonization creates a realm of antagonistic hierarchies, where one cannot be in peace—neither with herself, nor with the other.

How to break this vicious circle of colonization? The colonial discourse itself is endowed with the potential for resistance and liberation. Following Bhabha's argument about the transformative potential of hybridity, I would suggest that cultural hybridity provides the way out. Hybridity defies the set structures of authority and established categories of judgment. It negotiates contradictions and inconsistencies, and opens up new discursive possibilities.

This is the importance of Gesher within Israeli discourse, its cultural hybridity. Gesher occupies an in-between space. It is neither quite Israeli, nor quite Russian. This position has the potential to destabilize the dominant discourse, and thus get over what Shohat and Stam call "the monocentric system of values" with "normative culture of reference" (1998). A polycentric system would allow for multiple value systems, where subjects can be different but not better or worse than each other. This is the liberatory prospect.

• CHAPTER THREE •

In the Field and in the Archive

I collected data for this research during the summers of 1999, 2000, and 2001. I spent most of the time in Tel Aviv, in Gesher's homebase, Noga hall, and in its rehearsal hall on Nachmani Street. I also observed Gesher performances on tours in Israel (in Karmiel and Holon) and abroad (London, UK). During this fieldwork, I conducted participant observation of the professional and social life of the troupe, interviewed the troupe members, and constructed a media archive of Gesher. In the summer of 2003, I also conducted several follow-up interviews.

In the Field

By far the most fascinating and the most challenging source of data was my fieldwork. I took notes during rehearsals, breaks, performances, tours, troupe parties, and informal conversations. Whenever possible I wrote down entire conversations, word by word. When it was impossible, I jotted the key-words, and immediately afterwards reconstructed them as accurately as possible.

I also recorded and transcribed twenty-eight hours of formal interviews with the past and present professional and managerial staff of the theatre (See Interview Guide). All the interviewees were given the option of keeping their information confidential. I carefully recorded their requests and kept my promises, so that not all the information that I collected is included in this study. I also kept the anonymity of my interviewees in the cases in which revealing their identities could be potentially harmful to them.

The reason that my fieldwork was so challenging is that my access to the site was contingent upon my personal relationships with the participants and their willingness to volunteer. My own identity as a young female academic, who is a Russian-Israeli living in the US, played a huge role in my interactions with the participants. My identity eased my acceptance with some troupe members, and made it difficult with others. Thus, despite being a native Russian speaker, I was culturally removed from the older Russian-born actors, who perceived me as a "foreigner." They also disapproved of my research because they thought that I should focus exclusively on the analysis of Gesher's productions from a theatrical point of view. As a result, these actors were somewhat reluctant to participate. However, other actors and staff members (especially younger Israelis and Russian-Israelis) found more commonality in our cultural and academic background. They supported my research, were eager to participate, and sometimes even used the interviews as an opportunity for safe venting.

My archival work allowed me to overcome the limitations set by the interpersonal dynamics. The archival documents were indispensable for complementing the subjective perspectives that emerged from the personal narratives of the interviewees.

In the Archive

A media archive of Gesher Theatre constitutes my main body of data. It includes the previews and reviews of Gesher's productions as well as profiles and interviews with Gesher troupe members that were published in the Israeli printed media in the years 1990–1999. Most of these materials came from the files of Gesher's publicists. However, I discovered that this collection was incomplete, as the files were maintained by different publicists over the years. That is why in my reconstruction of the media archive I supplemented the original pool of data with the materials that I found at the Israeli theatrical archives of Tel Aviv University, the media collection of the Israeli National Library in Jerusalem, and on-line archives of the foreign newspapers.

I decided to focus primarily on the printed media as it is a traditional channel of theatre criticism. Two factors contributed to this decision. The instrumental factor was that focusing on printed media allowed me to compile a comprehensive archive of media materials about Gesher, because, unlike programs in the electronic media, these materials could be retrieved and documented.

The conceptual factor was the special status of national newspapers in Israel that makes it particularly relevant to this research. The Israeli printed media originated in "party journalism" in the pre-state era. Like other cultural venues, newspapers then were mobilized to serve the needs of society, and thus were important socialization and acculturation agents (Caspi and Limor 1999). Even though by the 1980s "party journalism" as an institution had died, the traces of its discourse are still pronounced in privately-owned media in contemporary Israel. Thus, the printed media most directly serves as a channel through which the Zionist ideology operates.

As for the choice of publications, I decided to focus on the most widely read (and thus presumably influential) media outlets, such as the national daily newspapers, local weekly newspapers in Tel Aviv and Jerusalem, and popular weekly magazines (see Table 7).

In order to contrast Gesher's media coverage in Israel and abroad, I included in my data the coverage of Gesher's tours in USA, UK, Switzerland, Germany, France, and Australia in the 90s.

I also included in my data several documentaries and television programs about Gesher Theatre, produced in Israel in the years 1990–1999. I decided to include them because of their wide circulation. These films and programs were broadcasted on Israeli television numerous times, and as a result had an established presence in the Israeli cultural scene.

Another component of my data is Gesher's promotional materials (posters, programs, and brochures) and internal documents, reports, and correspondence of the theatre. These materials helped me to trace self-representation of the theatre, to establish the organizational and financial structure of the theatre, and to document its history.

I analyzed all the media materials, fieldnotes, and interviews that were in Russian or in Hebrew in the language of the original. The quotes that I cite are my own translation. In these quotes, I use some Hebrew terms in transliteration. The media materials in German and French were translated for me.

Discourse analysis is the main tool used in this research. In each text I coded its subject matters and rhetorical strategies. Then I combined these results and found the recurring patterns in the media reception of each individual production, as well as in the coverage of the pivotal points in Gesher's history. Thus, I found overarching trends in Gesher's media reception, which helped me to organize my analysis. Thus, the current organization of this book reflects the trends and patterns in the history of Gesher Theatre and its media reception. All the following chapters have a similar structure: I start with telling the history of the Gesher troupe at a specific cultural and historical moment. Then, I describe Gesher's shows produced at that time, and proceed with a critical analysis of their media reception. Thus, the story is told twice—once through the voices of Gesher members, and the second time through the voices of the media. In both cases, I quote generously from interviews and media materials in order to recreate the discursive practices of my participants and let them "speak" to the reader directly.

In my analysis, I pay close attention to the specific language used by the critics, especially the Hebrew terms marked by ideological Zionist connotations (see Glossary). Such terms form an ideological sublanguage of contemporary Hebrew that identify the author's political orientation. The use of these terms dissociates between authors' Zionist and post-Zionist positions, thereby identifying a locus of controversy in the current Israeli public discourse.

• CHAPTER FOUR •

The First Steps

At the end of the 90s, Gesher Theatre presented its early history with a self-celebratory rhetoric, erasing all the traces of conflict that once surrounded it. Here is the version from the 1996 Gesher brochure:

> Gesher Theatre was founded in January 1991 with the support of the Ministry of Education and Culture, The Jewish Agency, Tel Aviv Municipality, The Tel Aviv Foundation and Zionist Forum. This very young theatre, the brainchild of new immigrants from the former Soviet Union led by Yevgeny Arye and Vyatcheslav Maltzev, has come to be regarded as "...the most professional theatre in Israel" (Yediot Ahronot, September '91). Two years after its debut, Gesher was recognized as an inseparable part of Israeli culture, and granted the status of public theatre. No mean achievement.

In the 1999 brochure, Gesher's co-founder and artistic director Yevgeny Arye recalls some of the ambivalence surrounding Gesher in its early stages, but only as a backdrop to a current triumphant picture:

> When Gesher was founded in 1991, it seemed like an impossible dream coming true. Serious people expressed doubts as to the necessity and validity of Russian-speaking theatre in Israel. Today we can proudly say that those doubts no longer exist. It appears that we have won the hearts of our spectators in our new homeland. Through deep and true integration in the life of the country that welcomed us with open arms, we have been able to create a new life for ourselves and a new kind of theatre for Israel, our own special brand.

Of course, these quotes are taken from the promotional materials, a genre inviting a certain degree of polish. They do not say much about a complex chain of events leading to the foundation of Gesher that took place back in 1990 and 1991 in Moscow, Tel Aviv, and New York.

Interviews with the Gesher members, documents from theatre archives, and media coverage of Gesher's foundation unravel a confusing and contradictory story. The foundation of Gesher is a story of survival and a story of sham. It is a story of organizational genius, financial miracles, political foresight, and ideological manipulation. The appearance of Gesher on the Israeli cultural scene was staged by Yevgeny Arye, the artistic director, and Slava Maltzev, the manager. Maybe, it was their most successful show.

Setting up a Stage

At the end of the 1980s Soviet Jews increasingly considered the possibility of emigration. In 1989 they started leaving what was still called the Soviet Union by the thousands. For many artists this time was a time of decision: to stay within the culture in which their art is grounded, or leap for new ground.

Yevgeny Arye and Slava Maltzev were among such artists. Arye, holding degrees in psychology and directing, was a disciple of the great Russian director Georgy Tovstonogov. By 1989 Arye had directed at such leading venues as Maly and Bolshoi Drama theatres in Leningrad, and Mayakovsky, Drama, and Ermolova theatres in Moscow. He worked as a film director (*The Dresser*, 1987) and as a theatre professor at the prestigious GITIS (State Academy of Theatre Arts). His theatre productions won several major directing awards in the Soviet Union and abroad.

Maltzev, with academic training both in theatre management and directing, was one of the most enterprising producers of Russian theatre at that time. In Moscow he founded the Creative Laboratories (*Vsesouznoe Ob'edinenie Tvorcheskie Masterskie*), a conglomerate of several theatre troupes, united under one managerial and financial roof. This project became famous throughout the USSR and Europe as the most innovative force in contemporary Russian theatre.

By the end of the 80s, responding to the grim social and cultural prospects of the disintegrating Soviet Union, both Arye and Maltzev started thinking about emigration. The prospect of leaving stirred for them, as well as for other theatre-makers, a lot of anxiety and raised many questions: Where to go? What to do there? Without language? Israel appeared as a possible destination:

> We started to think and to discuss, we wanted to work in our profession. Is it possible in Israel? A lot of people [Soviet emmigrants] are heading there, maybe it's possible to create a theatre there. Various organizations geared towards establishing cultural connections [between Russia and Israel] appeared then, Israelis started to visit Moscow, there was a festival of Jewish film, a day of Israeli culture, so we met some people, started networking. (Maltzev 2001)

Establishing a Russian theatre in Israel seemed to give a perfect answer to the questions of artistic careers abroad for Arye and Maltzev, but that was not what the Israeli organizations, such as Zionist Forum envisioned. Zionist

Forum, a non-profit organization that assisted Soviet immigrants, was interested in creating a cultural center for a Soviet Jewish community in Israel, and they offered this project to Maltzev and Arye. In October 1989, during a private visit to Israel, Arye met with Scharansky, the Forum's president. The verdict was unambiguous: "everyone wants a cultural center; theatre is out of a question" (Maltzev 2001). But neither Maltzev nor Arye gave up on the idea of establishing a Russian theatre in Israel.

Rumors spread quickly in the Moscow theatre circles: some actors were moving to Israel, others wanted to leave Russia, but were not sure where to go. Arye and Maltzev kept thinking about their idea: they were considering its chances to succeed, trying to define the best strategy and the best timing. However, this prospect was still tentative. Finally, in May 1990 Maltzev broke down:

> I said, let me call Scharansky and make a decision. I called him in Jerusalem and told him that while we waver to make *aliyah*, or not to make *aliyah*, we have thousands of questions. If you could provide me with the minimal conditions, travel and accommodations, I'd like to come for a month, or month and a half, and look around. I will try to understand what should be done and how, and whether [our idea] can be developed, whether a theatre is possible. (Maltzev 2001)

Indeed, Scharansky responded positively, and already in June 1990 Maltzev landed in Israel on a tourist visa. As promised, Zionist Forum provided him with accommodations, a workplace, and administrative support. In the two months of his stay in Jerusalem under the auspices of Zionist Forum, Maltzev accomplished an immense amount of groundwork. He started with exploring the Israeli cultural scene:

> I immediately understood two things: first, that it [a new theatre] has to be in Tel Aviv and not in Jerusalem. It's very simple, the creation of a new cultural entity is possible only in a developed cultural environment, because there they already have culture and audience with a habit of supporting the theatre. Second, after familiarizing myself with the situation in the Russian community, I understood that by no means can I count on them....I decided that I should forget about it, because of snobbery and the appalling attitude of the Russian old-timers towards newcoming artists....It was because they [Russian old-timers] thought, we've been here for a while, and we didn't succeed [in establishing our own cultural venues], so you will not succeed either. (Maltzev 2001)

At that point Maltzev made a choice that would define the whole concept of the future theatre, and that would predetermine the cultural debate around it later:

> I took another route. I went to Israeli public figures and intelligentsia. I was fully aware that I was appealing to their patriotic Zionist feelings. I was aware that as people

> with Russian roots (and many of the cultural producers here have Russian roots) they feel compelled to support this *aliyah*, which brought a lot of artists. They feel this responsibility—to help the newcomers. (Maltzev 2001)

As a result, the concept of a new theatre was formed under the influence of the Zionist ideological values, which place immigrant absorption high on the list of national priorities. It would be a theatre comprised of new immigrants, producing in Russian for the immigrant audiences. However, in the future, the theatre would transition into Hebrew, stage Israeli plays and co-productions with other Israeli theatres. Thus the theatre would fully correspond to its symbolic name—*Gishron*—a little bridge in Hebrew, gradually connecting immigrants to the new culture and language. The name Gishron later underwent a slight transformation and became *Gesher*—bridge, but its symbolism remained the same.[1]

With this idea—a Russian-language theatre cum immigrant absorption enterprise—Maltzev went to seek conceptual, organizational, and financial support. He met with Ben-Zion Tomer, an Israeli writer and dramaturge; Arye Harel, a former Israeli consul in Moscow; Hanoch Bartov, a writer and a director of the Tel Aviv Fund for Literature and Art; Avner Shalev, head of the Culture Administration at the Ministry of Education and Culture (for all practical purposes, a minister of culture), and with representatives of *Omanut le-Am*.[2]

Maltzev also tried to learn as much as possible about the functioning of the theatre industry in Israel. He visited Habima in Tel Aviv, the Chan Theatre in Jerusalem, and Haifa Municipal Theatre, and befriended their artistic and administrative management. Shmulik Omer, a head of Habima, proved an invaluable resource and shared his "know how" of structural and financial theatre management in Israel.

Equipped with this practical knowledge, Maltzev prepared a proposal, where he suggested a structure, prospective productions, financing and even a potential location of a future theatre. He found a dilapidated municipally owned building (4 Nachmani Street, in Tel Aviv) that once housed other Israeli theatres (the famous Cameri Theatre among others) but by 1990 was not in use. Financing was supposed to come from three sources equally: the Ministry of Education and Culture, Tel Aviv municipality, and Zionist Forum. The proposal was distributed to all the key figures, but Maltzev was not

---

1 Later, this symbolic name became a common object of journalistic puns and witticisms: "Where is this bridge [Gesher] leading to?", "Bridge [Gesher] and not Ghetto", "Bridge [Gesher] to nowhere", etc.

2 *Omanut le-Am* is a program supported by the Jewish Agency and the Ministry of Education and Culture that brought theatre to immigrants and other disadvantaged groups.

satisfied because "all that [discussion] had a somewhat abstract character, just a discussion...when it will all happen was unclear" (2001).

At that moment of uncertainty, Maltzev, with the help of Vladimir Gluzman (of Zionist Forum), came up with a truly revolutionary idea. In order to expedite the process of bureaucratic decision making, the theatre had to stake a claim and to pronounce its existence. Gesher had to be a fact of life, not just a proposal:

> We decided to put on a performance. We had to show what we are talking about....We assessed our expenses; it should not cost a lot, in the region of $50,000. And we discussed it with Scharansky and he agreed to provide us with $50,000 for the performance. When I left for Moscow, it was after this decision had been made. And I decided that the performance would take place in December. (Maltzev 2001)

In August 1990, when Maltzev came back to Moscow, Arye was already in the US (he moved there with his family fully prepared to relocate to Israel as soon as the opportunity arises). Maltzev and Arye made their decision to prepare a presentation of a future theatre in Israel over the phone. Maltzev also reached an agreement with the manager of a Moscow theatre, *Gruppa Grazhdan*, who would help logistically with the tour arrangement.

In the meanwhile, actors, who were prospective immigrants, were recruited to the new theatre. Arye, a charismatic teacher, had a following among his former students. If Maltzev was the energy and organizational genius of the project, Arye was its spiritual leader.

However, officially Gesher had not been established yet, so Maltzev and Arye could not promise employment. Therefore, they only offered actors a two-week tour in Israel with a concert program. Immigration was presented as an individual responsibility.

Even this meager prospect drew together a true collection of stars. Among potential immigrants were Gregory Lyampe, a Soviet movie star (over 100 roles) who acted once in the legendary Moscow Yiddish theatre of Solomon Michoels; Mikhail Kazakov, one of the leading film and theatre actors, Leonid Kanevsky, a Soviet TV star who made his name playing a detective in a nationally acclaimed serial; and Valentin Nikulin, a famous comic and drama actor. In addition to these celebrities, young and promising actors who were Arye's former students joined in: Alexander Demidov,[3] Natalya Voitulevich

3 Later, Alexander Demidov took a Hebrew name Israel. But most of Gesher's playbills refer to him as Israel (Sasha) Demidov. Regardless of Demidov's personal reasons for changing his name, in Israel changing one's name from diasporic to Hebrew is an act of compliance with the Zionist ideology. The fact that Demidov chose to maintain his Russian nickname next to his Hebrew name testifies to the hybrid cultural and ideological practices at Gesher.

with her husband Igor Voitulevich,[4] and Yevgenya Dodina. They all were planning to go to Israel on tourist visas. The troupe also included actors who had already immigrated to Israel: Roland Heilovsky[5] and Yevgeny Terletsky, a renowned puppet theatre actor. The troupe also included singer Maria Itkina, who, according to Maltzev, never intended to emigrate, but was invited to the troupe because of her repertoire of Yiddish and Hebrew songs, and, as Maltzev bluntly puts it, "her conspicuous Jewish looks" (2001).

The program included a hodge-podge of excerpts from famous theatre shows, such as *Don Juan* starring Mikhail Kazakov, a puppet show *Adventures of Gulliver* with Yevgeny Terletsky, and other Russian and European classics. Maria Itkina's songs completed the program.

The tour was planned for the end of December: two concerts in Tel Aviv, and three concerts in Jerusalem, Haifa, and Beer-Sheba. Maltzev and his wife Katya Sosonsky, a trained dramaturge and a natural-born publicist, arrived in Israel at the end of October 1990 to take care of the organization and promotion of the concerts and to arrange for ticket sales. Maltzev was at an interesting juncture: how was he going to promote these concerts? Gesher Theatre at that point existed only virtually—as a proposal that was under consideration at the Ministry of Education and Culture. The troupe members for the most part had not yet immigrated to Israel and were about to land there as tourists. Then Maltzev made an extremely risky decision:

> I chose a sham. You see, technically, we were a theatre troupe *Gruppa Grazhdan* which came to Israel on tour, but everywhere on the posters we put: "Opening of Gesher Theatre." We had no intention of letting others know how we came to Israel, that's our technical problem. (Maltzev 2001)

Logistical and financial issues were approached creatively as well. At that point Gesher-to-be could not afford to rent halls. Therefore, Maltzev contacted theatre directors in Tel Aviv, Jerusalem, Haifa, and Beer-Sheba and asked them to use their halls free of charge. They agreed. Shmulik Omer let Gesher use Habima's small stage *Be-Martef* not only for both nights of the concerts, but also for a week of rehearsal. This was a great help.

The choice of the halls and ticket price was strategic. Maltzev and Arye wanted to create a stir with these concerts in order to show Israeli culture bureaucrats the potential of the proposed theatre. Therefore, Maltzev chose small halls that were easy to fill (ranging from 200 seats in Tel Aviv to 400

---

4 After their divorce, Natalya remarried and changed her name to Voitulevich-Manor.

5 His wife, actor Lilian Heilovsky, joined Gesher in 1991 (*If Only*). Like Demidov, she also changed her diasporic name to the Hebrew name Ruth. After Roland passed away she married another Gesher actor, Klim Kamenko.

seats in Jerusalem) and a cheap ticket price—20 NIS (approximately $7). The choice was right: new immigrants were eager to spare a part of their scarce budget to see their long-loved TV and movie stars. The demand for tickets was enormous and all the shows sold out.

Along with the promotion of the concerts and ticket sales, Slava Maltzev and Katya Sosonsky prepared a press-conference. It took place at Beit-Sokolov, a journalist center in Tel Aviv, on December 13, 1990:

> It was an odd press-conference. It was titled "Opening of Gesher Theatre," but bureaucrats took part in it....It was a strange situation: a theatre as such didn't exist; on the other hand no one could deny it, since they are eye-witnessing the activity around it. But to say that it exists was also impossible....So that's what the bureaucrats said, "We are thinking, we are deciding." (Maltzev 2001)

And finally, the opening night came, and everything went as planned. The concerts proved to Israeli authorities that Gesher would become an important cultural venue. Maltzev's risk worked:

> Israeli TV crew that came to our first concert went crazy from so much agitation around our shows. Public figures, whom I invited, Harel, Bartov, Tomer, and others who were at the theatre, understood that the real superstars had arrived. In Jerusalem, people who couldn't get tickets were crying, and Scharansky begged them to step away from the doors. Finally, the director of the hall, despite the rules of fire safety, said: "I can't [bear it], I will let everyone in." And he let all the people in, to sit on the steps....They [representatives of the Ministry of Education and Culture] saw what was going on, and two days after these concerts I was invited to the Ministry and was told that the financing of the theatre was approved. Starting January 1, 1991, we received one million shekels under the guarantee of the Ministry of [Education and] Culture: 300,000 [NIS] from the Ministry, 300,000 from municipality, and 300,000 from Zionist Forum. (Maltzev 2001)

Maltzev was dealt a weak hand but he bluffed with confidence and gusto. And the Israeli authorities, whether they were partial or not, decided to buy into it. A new page opened in the history of Gesher—now a real theatre, not just a proposal.

What Maltzev does not mention in his story is that officially the new theatre had a status of a "project," i.e. a temporary action purported to assist in immigrant absorption. That way Gesher was defined in ideological and not artistic terms.

While working on the foundation of Gesher, Maltzev, Arye and others involved made several critical decisions. The most crucial was about the concept of the theatre as a cultural bridge for new immigrants. This concept enabled Maltzev to phrase his appeal in Zionist terms, and to turn to the Israeli public figures for social support and to the government agencies for funding. One way to interpret this choice is to claim that Maltzev, who correctly understood Zionist ethos with its commitment to support immigration (at least on the level of public discourse), decided to exploit it to his own ends. Essentially, he manipulated Israeli public figures and intelligentsia into establishing a Russian-language theatre—a highly questionable enterprise from the Zionist point of view. Avner Shalev, a top Israeli cultural official, makes this point in an interview in the documentary *Gesher Family*:

> Maybe it's a legacy of bolshevism, but sometimes I feel that when they [Gesher management] argue with me, deep down they think...let him talk. I understand that someone who had to adjust to this [Soviet] regime, had to come up with a mechanism of defense against authorities...[they think] we persevered under Stalin, Brezhnev, Chernenko, we'll persevere here too. (Mafzir 1993)

Another way to read Maltzev's decision is to see it as an example of hegemonic ideology at work. Indeed, Maltzev understood the requirements and constraints of Zionist ethos. However, he also understood that if he wants to survive under these conditions, he necessarily had to comply with them, i.e. present his idea of the theatre in the ideological terms that would appeal to those in power. His understanding is clear from his cynical comment, "Gesher was staged like a show" (2001). It is because of the requirements of the Zionist ideology that Maltzev had to emphasize the absorption of immigrant actors and to downplay the fact that they would perform in Russian. Given Maltzev's and Arye's Soviet background, with its dominant ideology and severe punishment for deviation from it, it was not that difficult for them to learn the rules of a new game. And they chose to play by them—a choice that ultimately led to the establishment of the theatre as "a project."

Thus, the Gesher founders became both the prey and the hunter. Yes, they were victims of hegemonic ideology, coerced into playing by its rules in order to survive. And yet, they successfully used this ideology to their own ends, thus tacitly resisting it and turning their "strategic weaknesses into tactical strengths" (Shohat and Stam 1998, p.31). As a result of this dual use, their actions not only subverted but also perpetuated Zionist ideology. Later, this ambiguous position made it impossible for Gesher to break free of ideological constraints.

However, neither Maltzev nor Arye realized the reflexive connection between ideology and their actions. When the theatre was up and running, the concept of "theatre of immigrants," became obsolete for them. By that time Arye and Maltzev wanted Gesher to be a "normal Israeli theatre." But when Gesher tried to re-position itself beyond politics, as just a theatre, an artistic venue, their attempts were in vain. Gesher never succeeded in shaking off the ideological interpretation which it received when it was first established. Thus, taking advantage of the ideological motivation for creating a new theatre, Gesher inadvertently dug itself into a hole. What began as a successful jumpstart to the new theatre grew into an eternal predicament.

These issues sparked an ongoing cultural debate surrounding Gesher in Israel. It first started on December 13, 1990, when Arye and Maltzev announced the establishment of the new theatre at their press-conference. At that time, the Ministry of Education and Culture was still deciding about the status of the new venture. *Haaretz* reported on the difficult decision process: "In the Theatre Division of the Culture Administration they still ponder the question, whether to found a Russian-language theatre, or to stay loyal to the classic tradition of *klitat aliyah* [immigrant absorption, see Glossary] in lieu of the slogan 'only Hebrew'" (Luzie 1990).

When, finally, the Ministry of Education and Culture came up with the "project" formula, an editorial in *Haaretz* reported that Gesher was established with the sole purpose of absorbing immigrants. Thus, the Ministry could support a non-kosher theatre without subverting national values:

> Emphasis on the term "project" is important, as is emphasis on temporality. The Ministry of Education and Culture does not want to be associated with the foundation of a non-Hebrew speaking theatrical enterprise (with permanent status). Support of Gesher...is justified by the urgent need of *klitat aliyah*. ("Laavor et hagesher" 1991)

This way it was safe: artists got their funding, and the public got their ideological security. The "project" formula implied that once actors were properly "absorbed," there would be no need for this strange foreign body in the healthy organism of national art.

Hanoch Bartov, one of the board members of the new theatre, offers another euphemism for Gesher—"workshop."

> In the past we had experiences with the waves of *aliyah*, but such a wave we haven't seen before. In every wave the same phenomenon took place: elite groups—scientists, writers, artists—emigrated to the other countries where they obtained key positions. Israel lost. Because of this we decided to found a theatrical workshop for the transitional stage, and the emphasis was on these words, transitional stage, a workshop that will turn *aliyah* into a creative endeavor. And this is exactly what happened: Gesher serves *olim* masses and they are proud of their theatre. (Ohed 1991)

It is interesting that Bartov does not even mention Arye or Maltzev, the founders of the theatre. Instead, he uses the royal "we," justifying Gesher's foundation by the national priorities: to make immigrants stay in the country.

Both the theatre producers and their work are reduced to the primordial ideological need—to increase the population of the state of Israel.

Another aspect of the public discussion about Gesher's foundation was the responsibility that the established Israeli theatres have with respect to the absorption of Soviet immigrants. The editorial in *Haaretz* makes the following argument:

> Logically speaking, there are enough theatres in the state of Israel, and a large part of the expenses could have been saved if the existing theatres produced shows in Russian in order to answer the needs of the *olim* who are theatre artists on their way to *klita*, and the needs of the audiences that require Russian-language culture until they learn Hebrew. This combination would have brought audiences closer to Hebrew theatre, providing means for productions and marketing in Russian; and also would have brought the Russian theatre artists closer to future work in Hebrew....But this has not happened: Hebrew theatre, with few exceptions, such as Chan [a theatre in Jerusalem] or Sifriya [a theatre in Ramat-Gan] theatres, did not mobilize to produce shows in Russian for the Russian audiences and theatre artists. ("Laavor et hagesher" 1991)

The editorial criticizes not only Gesher for cultural separatism, but also Israeli theatres for ideological mistakes, their failure to *mobilize* for immigrant absorption. The language use (*mobilization*) belongs to the domain of war, rather than art.

This ideological critique is closely connected to financial issues. According to the editorial, producing Russian-language shows in established Israeli theatres, instead of founding Gesher, would have saved precious public money. The value of frugality, an important part of Zionist ideology, legitimizes this argument. According to this value, dedicated Zionists should limit themselves in their own needs, and sacrifice their own desires for the sake of building a national home. The value of frugality explains why the journalists are critical of the Ministry's decision to allow the Soviet immigrants to have their own theatre. This decision violates the commitments to both the Hebrew language and Zionist frugality. According to the author of the *Haaretz* editorial, in desiring their own company, immigrants act as spoiled children. But the author would expect the Ministry to act as a wise parent, and to reject this idea "for the sake of their own good" because, "this is not a way to a good absorption" ("Laavor et hagesher" 1991).

The Ministry was under pressure from Soviet immigrants, who wanted to produce and to attend shows in Russian, and from journalists, who were afraid of a dissolution of linguistic hegemony. The officials had to decide what to do. By August 1991, the Ministry had defined a policy of absorbing immigrant actors, which approved productions in Russian as a temporary measure. Such productions would both provide income to the actors and answer the cultural needs of the Russian-speaking audiences. However, the ultimate purpose of the decision was to integrate immigrant actors in the Israeli theatre, and to assimilate them. A member of the steering committee reported in *Haaretz*:

> Despite disagreements on these topics among department members, everyone was convinced that a permanent Russian-language theatre should not be established. Conversely, we are confident that we need to encourage professional immigrant actors to mount special productions in Russian, and that we need to support every such production separately. (Michman 1991)

In accordance with this policy, several immigrants seized the opportunity to work in Russian.[6] However, none of these ventures survived; Gesher was the only exception.

Behind the Scenes

Gesher started its work in the increasingly difficult social and economic situation. The Israel of 1991 did not exactly offer them, as a Hebrew idiom goes, "milk and honey." New Soviet immigrants could not find affordable housing and suitable employment. They were treated with growing resentment. The Gulf War, which started in August of 1990, made it worse. Spending nights wearing gas masks and listening to the sound of sirens added to the immigrants' confusion and anxiety.

Finding employment was particularly hard for immigrants with professions deeply grounded in language and culture, such as theatre. Out of hundreds of actors who arrived in Israel in the early 90s, only a few integrated into the Israeli theatres. Immigrant directors, who were less limited by their accent than actors, could not find work either. Most immigrant theatre professionals were desperate for work.

The few allowed productions in Russian could not make it in the local theatre market, which at that time was not just well established, but rather ossified (Nagid 1993a). It was difficult for newcomers to break through. The major public theatres catered to the conservative tastes of their mass

---

6 Two plays in Russian were staged at the Sifriya theatre in Ramat-Gan, another one was produced at Beit-Zvi Drama School with the support of the Jewish Agency and the Ministry of Absorption. Chan theatre in Jerusalem let a group of immigrant actors stage a play in Russian. Dramaturge Semion Zlotnikov tried to establish a drama-reading theatre in Jerusalem, and even put together two drama readings at the Cultural Center of the Soviet Jewry. Later, the Ministry of Absorption subsidized a project at the Habima theatre, which consisted of staging a production about immigrant life written and directed by immigrants.

audiences. Their funding was established long ago, and it was virtually impossible for a new company to get on the list. The alternative theatre scene in Israel included independent productions; small and semi-professional theatres, army and kibbutz troupes. Their productions had shoe-string budgets and rarely survived to become permanent venues. They hardly ever covered expenses, let alone made a profit. As for the festival scene, the annual Israel Festival was a national showcase for the major public theatres. Most of the independent productions were presented at smaller venues: the Acre Festival of experimental theatre, the Teatranetto festival of solo-performances, the Haifa Festival of Children Theatre, and a Week of Original Theatre at the Simtah theatre in Tel Aviv.

This was the cultural landscape in which Gesher made its first steps. However, the new company members were enthusiastic: the theatre was under way. At the beginning of 1991, Gesher management registered the theatre as a non-profit organization, opened bank accounts, and rented an apartment on 109 Rothschild Street, used at first both as office and rehearsal space (a proper rehearsal space at 4 Nachmani Street was rented later). The first board of directors was formed. Chaired by Hanoch Bartov, the board included the same public figures who helped to establish Gesher: Ben-Zion Tomer, Arye Harel, Shmulik Omer (The Habima Theatre), Yosi Kioso (Tel Aviv municipality), Sara Lisovsky (the Ministry of Education and Culture), and Vladimir Gluzman (Zionist Forum).

With the meager budget of 1,222,851 NIS the salaries at Gesher were low (an actor's yearly income was 30,000 NIS, which was less than $10,000). According to the initial plan, Gesher had to receive public funding in the amount of 1,000,000 NIS. In actuality, Gesher's financial report showed that the public funding was lower—710,496 NIS. Ticket sales, though, contributed 512,355 NIS to the budget, helping the theatre to finish the year with a relatively small deficit of 299,069 NIS (See Table 1). Gesher's budget equaled approximately one tenth of the budget of a comparable Israeli troupe (Handelsaltz 1991a).

Gesher's first actors included Sasha Demidov, Yevgenya Dodina, Natalya and Igor Voitulevich, Lilian and Roland Heilovsky. In January 1991, Gesher held auditions for its first production—*Rosencrantz and Guildenstern Are Dead*. Hundreds of desperate actors showed up, but only four were hired: Yevgeny Terletsky, Vladimir Halemsky, Michael Asinovsky, and Mark Ivanir. Terletsky, an actor from the nationally acclaimed Magnitogorsk puppet theatre, participated in the concerts in 1990 and was admitted without auditions. Halemsky was a well-known Moscow comedian with brief experience of work at the Chan Theatre in Jerusalem. Asinovsky brought with him years of experience at *Lenkonzert*, an entertainment association in St.Petersburg. The youngest of the bunch was Ivanir, an Israeli-trained performer of Russian origin. Later, Yevgeny Gamburg and Boris Achanov, both from acclaimed theatres in Riga, and Avi Nedsevetsky,[7] the future in-house Gesher composer, joined the troupe as well. Israel-born Shaul Alias was an exceptional member of the troupe. He didn't know Russian and had no professional theatre training; he was hired mainly for his appearance—he was a midget. Later, Lena Kreindlina, who worked as a director's assistant with Arye in Moscow, also became a member. She came to Israel from the US, where she was on an exchange program at that time.

In January 1991 the original Gesher troupe was formed (see Table 6). The work started in high spirits. The actors and the director were full of hope for the great future: "At the beginning everything was easy and went incredibly well," recalls actor Israel (Sasha) Demidov (1999). The actors were happy to work hard in order to build their own theatre. In comparison with other recent immigrants, Gesher actors were really fortunate. Instead of cleaning streets and taking care of the elderly—the classic immigrants' occupations—they could follow their vocation of theatre work.

Tatiana Suchanova, who was on Gesher's staff from the start, remembers the selfless dedication of the first period:

> What motivated me to work was a pioneering spirit. We wanted to work—to establish a theatre, to justify its existence, not to lose face. Pioneering spirit, I can't find better words. It was like being in love with work. I made sets myself, we had these huge portals, I sewed all the curtains with my own hands. I made wigs for *Moliere*. I made mannequins from straw....I took on any mission, and it was without any additional pay. (Suchanova 2001)

Yevgenya Dodina recalls this period in the life of the theatre with nostalgia. She describes it romantically, recreating the intense emotional charge of that time:

> I really miss the state we were in for the first three years. It was very difficult on the one hand, but also there was a feeling of euphoria, because so many things happened at once, practically everything. Your life is split in half. Theatre is a very energetic, very emotional place. Especially when you are building a new theatre, and everything is new, new actors, new friends, new love. We [actors] were very irresponsible, maybe because we didn't understand. Arye and Maltzev felt responsibility, and we, we were young, and we didn't feel that it was a matter of life and death: "We have to succeed." We just were having fun with our work, enjoyed it, it was like flying. (Dodina 2001)

7 In Israel, Avi changed his diasporic last name Nedsevetsky to the Hebrew name Benjamin. Like Demidov, in some promotional materials he is referred to by his Hebrew name only, and in others by its hybridized form Benjamin (Nedsevetsky).

The atmosphere that Dodina describes can be explained by the troupe composition. There were a number of couples in the troupe, most of them young (Katya Sosonsky and Slava Maltzev, Lilian and Roland Heilovsky, Natalya and Igor Voitulevich, to name just a few). There were even entire families (for instance, the Suchanovs, including the wife, the husband and the grown son all worked at Gesher). Gesher members fell in love, and fell out of love, they married, divorced, and shared not only professional life but also private triumphs and agonies. Yevgenya Dodina and Avi Nedsevetsky (Benjamin) fell in love and got married. Natalya and Igor Voitulevich got divorced, and he left for Russia. The troupe suffered the loss of Gregory Lyampe (who was already in his 70s when he joined Gesher). Another blow, much later, was the death of Roland Heilovsky (in a tragic accident). The troupe went through it all together. They were more than just company members—they became like a family.

Even later, the troupe maintained the familial mode of life. In 1999, I witnessed a *kabbalat Shabbat* (welcoming of the Sabbath on Friday night) conducted by Demidov (who is religious) in his dressing room right before beginning of the show. The ceremony culminated in a communal moment when everyone sipped from the same glass of wine. *Kabbalat Shabbat* is normally celebrated with the family at home. Here, the troupe is a family, and the theatre is their home.

Another example that I witnessed involved a troupe member, who on her one day off baked a cabbage pie (*pirog s kapustoi*—a Russian delicacy). But she couldn't bring herself to eat her pie while her fellow troupe members were at work. So, she wrapped up her pie and drove to the theatre and shared the pie with her Gesher family. This type of relationships within the troupe dates back to the first years of Gesher, the time charged with an enormous emotional voltage. It is in this exhilarating atmosphere that Gesher's first play was produced.

The First Production: *Rosencrantz and Guildenstern Are Dead*

Rosencrantz and Guildenstern Are Dead by Tom Stoppard was an unusual choice of play for a Russian-language theatre of immigrants in Israel. Arye explained:

> When we discussed our future plans in Moscow, I said, of course, we can't stage such a play as *Rosencrantz and Guildenstern*. We need something more democratic, low-brow. But as a result of our tours, I understood that here [in Israel], there is a layer of intellectual audience, and then I thought that we should start with a performance of

> what we really intend to do here, [to show] what kind of theatre we are going to build. Not to count on financial success, but, first, to stake a claim for the future repertoire of the theatre, and second, to introduce the whole ensemble. And that's how I came to chose a play that I least expected to stage—*Rosencrantz and Guildenstern Are Dead*. We chose a play for people who know what *Hamlet* is. (Arye 2003)

Arye staged the play in the Russian translation by Joseph Brodsky, a Russian Jewish poet and also an immigrant (to the US). Back in Moscow, Arye directed the play at the Mayakovsky theatre in Moscow. It was a successful production that remained in the repertoire long after Arye moved to Israel.

In Stoppard's now classic play, the main heroes, Ros (Mark Ivanir) and Guil (Yevgeny Terletsky), are drawn from marginal characters in Shakespeare's *Hamlet*. Claudius, the new king of Denmark (Yevgeny Gamburg), sends them to follow Hamlet (Michael Asinovsky) to find out why he has been acting so strangely. Hamlet's mother, Gertrude, Queen of Denmark (Natalya Voitulevich), is worried about her son, and wants Ros and Guil to help him. They stumble along, but see no purpose or meaning in this mission. They pursue Hamlet with apprehension and confusion. The real plot is concealed from them.

The figure of the Player (Boris Achanov) poses questions of the relationship of art to life, and the nature of theatrical fiction. The characters of the Tragedians (Igor Voitulevich/Roland Heilovsky, Sasha Demidov) highlight the absurdity of the world and the theatricality of the staging. The deep sense of absurdity is reinforced by the sets: the action takes place on a narrow ramp stretched across the stage and the hall, a road leading to nowhere.

Some of the distinctive features of Gesher emerged already in its first production. One of these features was the use of metatheatre, i.e. theatre about theatre, a variation of the play-within-the-play form. [8] Metatheatre probes the distinction between the real and the fictional, allowing theatre-makers to explore role playing versus self, and truth versus illusion. Thus, Ros and Guil are not "real people," they are Shakespeare's characters. They have no identity outside of *Hamlet*. They are "always in character," and they understand their limits:

8 Metatheatre was introduced by Luigi Pirandello in 1921, in his play *Six Characters in Search of an Author*, and since then has become a part of contemporary theatrical language. For more background on metatheatre, see Abel (1963).

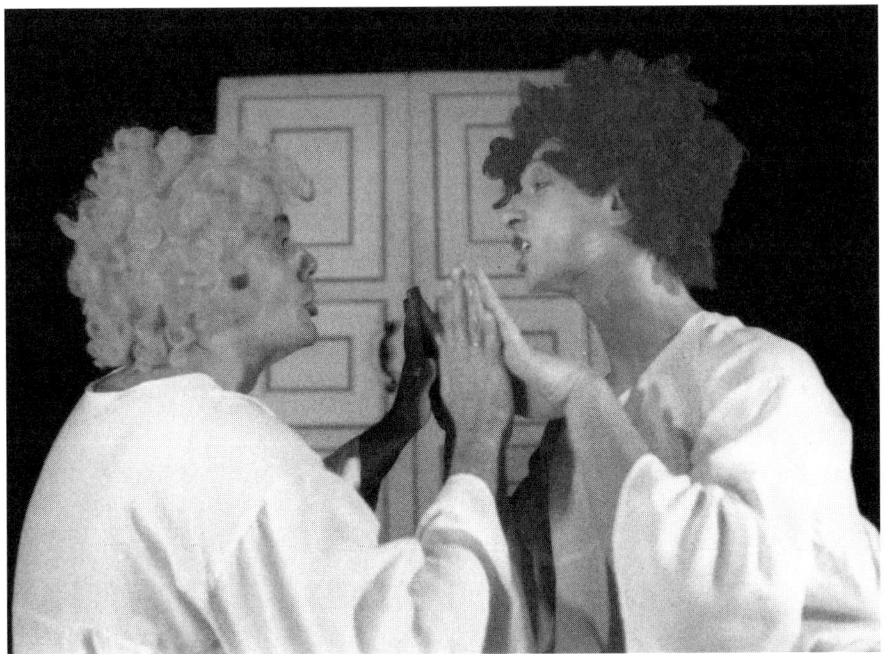

Figure 1: *Rosencrantz and Guildenstern Are Dead*
Roland Heilovsky (on the left) and Sasha Demidov as the Tragedians
(Courtesy of Gesher Theatre)

> GUIL:...We can do what we like and say what we like to whomever we like, without restrictions.
>
> ROS: Within limits, of course.
>
> GUIL: Certainly, within limits.

Using metatheatre, Gesher problematizes the theme of artistic creation. Like Ros and Guil, the Gesher actors are free to perform what they like "within limits." The limits are the limits of ideology.

Metatheatre also changes the interaction of the actors with the audience. It signals to the audience that the play is a fabricated theatrical reality. The actors are conscious of being part of a spectacle—an object of the audience's gaze. In Gesher's production, the Player becomes a mouthpiece of the theatre-makers. He tells Ros and Guil: "We're actors...we pledged our identities," hoping that an audience would be watching. Thus metatheatre creates a Brechtian "alienation effect" (1964/1957), distancing the audience from the characters of the show, and making the audience aware of the staged nature of the production. In Brecht's words, "...the narrator is no longer missing, along with the fourth wall" (1964/1957, p. 71). In this way, metatheatre allows for an exchange between audience and actor, rather than a broadcast from actor to audience.

The second distinctive feature of Gesher's artistic style was a carnivalesque aesthetic. For instance, in one of the play-within-the-play scenes, the Tragedians, dressed in oversized nightgowns and colorful wigs, engage in a whirlwind parody of shouting, copulating, and thrashing each other. It is not surprising that Gesher, the hybrid cross-cultural theatre, emerges as a carnival site. Mikhail Bakhtin defines the carnival idiom as "filled with pathos of change and renewal, with the sense of the gay relativity of prevailing truths and authorities" (1984/1965, p. 11). The carnival has its own logic "of the 'inside out' (*á l'envers*), of the 'turnabout', of a continual shifting from top to bottom, from front to rear" (1984/1965, p. 11). Thus, the carnivalesque aesthetic has a disruptive transgressive power: it destroys the boundaries between genres, reverses "up" and "down," and ultimately shatters the hierarchies of power.

As the premiere approached, the theatre prepared its first bilingual playbill. It was an opportunity for Gesher to make public their mission of creating a Russian-language theatre in Israel. A comparison between Russian and Hebrew versions of the mission statement reveals telling differences. The Russian text said:

> We intend to turn our theatre into a welcoming home. Home, where old culture is preserved and a new one is acquired. Home, where both Russian and Hebrew would sound. We would like to avoid big statements, but we do declare that our theatre will not be elitist. It will be open to all. Together with you, we will learn the culture, language, and customs of the country that accepted us into its family. We hope to help those for whom culture is a necessary part of life, help them not to get lost in the new circumstances and new language. It will be difficult, but only together we will be able to become full-fledged citizens of Israel and be useful to our newly-found motherland.

This text professes the intercultural mission of the theatre, commitment to popular audiences, and an outlook on art as ideologically and socially functional. It is interesting that the Hebrew version alters one sentence, but it radically changes the overall message. The Russian version reads: "...we do declare that our theatre will not be elitist." Instead, the Hebrew text states: "...we do declare that our theatre will not be only for *olim*." If elitism was a concern with the Russian audiences, in addressing Israeli audiences, Gesher tried to avoid the image of "theatre of immigrants" or even "cultural ghetto." Thus, as early as 1991, Gesher made an attempt to appeal to wide Israeli theatre audiences. Paradoxically, parallel with its ideological vocation ("to become full-fledged citizens of Israel and be useful to our newly-found motherland"), Gesher strove to be "just a theatre," without an ethnic or ideological agenda.

Gesher rehearsed *Rosencrantz and Guildenstern* under dramatic circumstances. Beginning of 1991 was the time of the Gulf war, and Tel Aviv was under attack from Iraqi missiles. The entire rehearsal process, including staging, lighting, sound, and movement, took place in a single room of a basement apartment (on Rothschild Street). Arye recalls that two days before the premiere, when Gesher moved to Habima's small stage, where the premiere was to take place, they found out that Gesher's computer was incompatible with Habima's equipment. The entire lighting design had to be reset from scratch. The Gesher staff was ready to work day and night, but they needed help from Habima's technical staff, who were unaccustomed to such urgency. Habima's staff was ready to walk away. Arye recalls, "We had to literally beg them on our knees to work overtime" (2003).

The premiere took place on April 20, 1991. The location was symbolic: the small stage of Habima, *Be-Martef* (in Hebrew—basement), dubbed in Israel "a national basement." The stakes were high. The performance could either make or break Gesher. As Arye recalled later: "We didn't have a right to make a mistake. This situation was particularly difficult for me, because a director should have a right to err. Our very existence was at stake" (Shohat 1994).

Miriam Yahil-Wax, an Israeli dramaturge and translator, who became a devoted friend of the theatre, recalls the night of the premiere:

> In 1991 there were a lot of *olim* actors' shows and we [theatre critics] had to go and look at them in order to give an expert opinion, whether to support them or not. And so, it was in 1991 that we came to yet another one of these *olim* productions. And I remember that one of the critics said: "Poor us." This show was *Rosencrantz and Guildenstern Are Dead.* Five minutes into the show I realized how excellent it was, and that it was a different level of theatre. And then I thought to myself, maybe it is they who should look at us with pity. (Yahil-Wax 1999b)

The show was reviewed in the major newspapers, which was exceptional for what was perceived then as an immigrants' production. The critics divided into two camps. The first camp included those who wholeheartedly admired the production and assigned Gesher a position of cultural superiority. Boaz Evron (*Yediot Ahronot*), Yoram Kanuk (*Tel Aviv*), and Michael Ohed (*Davar*) belonged to that camp. Critics from another camp, including Shosh Avigal (*Hadashot*), Michael Handelsaltz (*Haaretz*), and Haim Nagid (*Maariv*) also received the production favorably. However, instead of being enchanted by the Russian theatrical tradition and "the wonderful melodic language" (Ohed 1991) of the production, they posed questions about the ideological correctness of the show. They also decisively framed Gesher as "a theatre of immigrants," thus indicating the critics' ideological agenda.

An emotional review by Yoram Kanuk, a renowned Israeli writer, is an example of analysis written in deep awe of Gesher. He calls the show "one of the peaks of the Israeli theatre" (1991). Arguing with those who claim that Gesher works in "a cultural ghetto," Kanuk assigns value to the experience of foreignness that, according to him, is inherent in Israeli culture:

> The foreignness that they [Gesher] create is nothing else but a contribution [to Israeli culture]. What is the best of Israeli culture if not the culture of refugees and foreigners? There is no poet here who has not dreamt of a different city, of a different shore, and of a different language. When culture was here, and not only islands of it like today, it was a culture of immigrants. (Kanuk 1991)

In his review, Kanuk takes a colonized position, casting Israeli culture into an inferior role. He criticizes Israeli popular culture and romanticizes Russian culture to which he assigns a high status. For Kanuk, Russian culture is a culture where "it is still legitimate to quote Shakespeare." Along with this tendentious idealization, he also recognizes the hybrid character of Gesher's cultural production. Russian-speaking audiences of Gesher's performances "come to the theatre to pray in their own language, in the country that is both their own and foreign, and also new" (1991). Kanuk concludes his argument insisting on the inherent hybridity of Israeli culture: "All Israel is a painful foreignness."

Boaz Evron of *Yediot Ahronot* called his review "Surprise." He admitted that in contrast to his expectations he saw:

> ...a play by Tom Stoppard brilliantly directed by Yevgeny Arye; all the participants are excellent professionals who play along in a perfect synchrony, as if they have been acting in the same ensemble for years. They create a kind of electricity that flows between the stage and the Russian-speaking audiences. (Evron 1991a)

The attuned work of the ensemble and the symbolic location of the performance seduced critics to draw parallels between the newly formed Gesher and Habima:

> Since Gesher, like Habima, came from Moscow and performs at the *Be-Martef*, one wants to match it up to Habima, but the comparison is wrong. We all grew up hearing the wonderful story of a bunch of young amateurs who founded a studio in the midst of the Russian revolution that was adapted by the great Stanislavsky himself...they came out after 300 rehearsals with the show *Dibbuk* that conquered the world. Gesher also was founded in Moscow, but the rehearsals took place in Tel Aviv, in the days of the Gulf War. Vachtangov presented a fairy tale with songs and dances in his expressionistic style. Gesher's actors do not sing or dance, they act in a realistic manner, even though less restrained than is common here. Habima spoke Hebrew

> from the first days (in an Ashkenazic accent in Moscow, in a Sephardic accent here). In Gesher they speak Russian—a wonderful melodic language. Habima's name was known here even before its *aliyah* to *Eretz Israel*. The most important critics, Russians, Germans, Americans, English, praised Habima. Because of its celebrated past, they [the Israeli establishment] built a home for it, and nominated it to be a national theatre. Gesher had been discovered so far only by *olim* from the USSR and by Israeli critics. Vachtangov worked with the bunch of young amateurs—part of them ended up on stage by chance. Rovina and Maskin were a minority. Even today a gap between a few great actors and an average majority is characteristic of Israeli theatre. The Russians, who met in Tel Aviv only a few months ago, created a real ensemble. (Ohed 1991)

This description does not do justice to Habima, which in the pre-Israel Palestine struggled with the same problems Gesher would face years later. In actuality, some critics then thought that Habima was "too Russian," i.e. too distanced from the Jewish community of pre-Israel Palestine, while others claimed that it favored artistic values over ideological (Levy 1979a, pp. 97–102). Sixty years later, critics voiced similar complaints in regards to Gesher's production.

Some critics acknowledged the multiple cultural sources of Gesher's production, for instance:

> There is something surreal in this combination: a Russian-language theatre comprised of new *olim* presents a British play by Tom Stoppard which was considered to be avant-garde in the 60s, in the translation of the Russian-Jewish poet that migrated to the US, in the *Be-Martef* of Habima, our national theatre that was born in Moscow. (Avigal 1991)

But the critics did not know what to make of this cultural polyphony. Some of them insisted on an interpretation largely based on the status of actors as immigrants. Thus Handelsaltz from *Haaretz* sees an analogy between Ros and Guil, lost in the bureaucracy of Ellsinore, and immigrants, looking for identity in a new country, or perhaps facing a lot of difficulties in dealing with Israeli bureaucracy. According to him, the immigrant identity of both the artists and the audiences gives new interpretation to the play:

> The situation of the two court figures pulled out of their home for an unclear mission, and brought to the Ellsinore court, where they feel disconnected and no longer sure about their identity, is a reflection of the situation of these *olim*, both on stage and in the audience. They came to Israel for the sake of some mission and to find meaning, without which their life and death turn into something absurd, painful, and tragic. (Handelsaltz 1991b)

Another critic compares immigrants to the main characters of the show: "In essence, like Ros and Guil, they [immigrants] find themselves in the midst of a play that was written a long time ago. And now we can only wait to see if they will also learn the rules of the game quickly" (Nagid 1991).

Such an interpretation of Gesher's *Rosencrantz and Guildenstern Are Dead* reduces its meaning to the discussion of the problems of immigrant absorption. This reception favors an ideological reading of the show, since the immigrant identity of the producers is brought to the forefront, stamping out other possible interpretations. This reception indicates an emerging critical trend: in their judgment of Gesher, the critics rely on the politics of identity. Such criteria of judgment are different from the standards applied to other Israeli theatres.

Another trend in Gesher's critical reception is the fixation of the media on the politics of language. Despite their favorable response to the show, reviewers become critical of the use of Russian, pushing the theatre to perform in Hebrew. The subtitle of Avigal's article states: "Everyone involved in the production at Gesher Theatre deserves praise, and the talent is just pouring over the stage, but it is a shame that they insist on performing in Russian" (1991). Taking a position of a colonizer who knows what's good for a colonized, she advises the Gesher theatre-makers "to make a bit of an effort to try to approach us in Hebrew. As they [Gesher] themselves write in their program: 'Audiences determine the existence of a theatre, and it is a defining factor'. And this audience, dear sirs from Gesher, is Israeli and Hebrew" (Avigal 1991).

The issue of language, in particular a commitment to Hebrew, is extremely important in Israeli cultural production infused by Zionist ideology. Even the experience of watching a show in Russian with a simultaneous translation produces an uneasy reaction: "You are sitting in the headphones for simultaneous translation, like at the show of some visiting troupe at the Israel Festival, and feel a little strange among the mainly Russian-speaking audience" (Avigal 1991). This excerpt shows the clash of the critic's expectations. It is clear to her, that if a theatre claims to be Israeli, it has to perform in Hebrew. Conversely, if a theatre performs in a language other than Hebrew, it is foreign. As a result, the critic does not quite know what to make out of the new troupe.

Haim Nagid joins in: "If this theatre was brought here from the USSR to the Israel Festival, the local theatrical aristocracy would have defined it as a must-see innovative theatre" (1991). However, since the theatre is local, then the only possible reaction is to push the theatre towards ideologically correct language.

Some reviewers took such an extreme colonizing position towards Gesher, that their responses, sometimes written without even watching the show, gave expression to xenophobic self-righteousness. Thus, Israeli playwright Yosef Mundy confides that he "got mad" just after seeing a news report on Gesher on television. He denies Gesher's right for existence on the ground of its cultural inferiority:

> A Russian actor, like a Soviet person himself, was completely separated from what was happening in Western culture, and therefore, if someone has to learn something, it is them from us and not us from them. Of course, it is necessary to attract every Russian actor to our theatre and allow him (*sic*) creative work and fair income. But in the meanwhile, maybe it is better for them to first learn something. Although the Israeli theatre suffers from big problems, for me and for all those who live here, this is the only possiblity. And the Russian Gesher not only is alien to me, but also I see that it cannot bring me anywhere but backwards. (Mundy 1991)

The main debate centers around the question of symbolic capital. Who holds the ownership over it? Who should learn from whom? Mundy assumes the artistic superiority of Israeli theatre. His argument is based on the cultural and ethnic identity of Gesher members.

A similarly xenophobic attack came from the director Yosi Alphi: "This theatre will be swallowed, like other theatres that came from outside were swallowed....They are alien forces." He calls Israeli critics to search in the Israeli "projects" for authentic creative forces, "without technique and artistic tricks, without culture imported here from different countries." Even though his comments are quoted in a later documentary (*Gesher Family* from 1993), they vividly represent the kind of criticism Gesher had to face.

In sum, not all the reviews raved about the show, yet its reception definitely put Gesher on the map of the Israeli cultural landscape. With the production *Rosencrantz and Guildenstern Are Dead*, Gesher was invited to its first festivals. In the summer of 1991, *Rosencrantz and Guildenstern Are Dead* went to the Israel Festival, the most prestigious showcase of national and international arts in Jerusalem. This national premiere revealed a cross-cultural problem with the marketing of Gesher shows to Russian-language audiences. Maltzev explained to a journalist in an interview from 1991:

> We got stuck: despite the excellent reviews the production received, the festival did not succeed to sell even one ticket. We took the tickets out of the Jerusalem theatre and we sold them all up to the last one. What's the miracle solution? One has to deal with the Russian audiences in a different way. Russian audiences rely on the opinion of friends who saw a show. Good reviews won't bring them to the theatre. In the USSR they learned that even bad shows could receive good reviews....[For Gesher] it's not worth spending money on [traditional] public relations. Personal contact is better than advertising. When I succeed in establishing contact with a group of people who love theatre, I know that half of the people who listened to me will buy tickets. (Ohed 1991)

This cultural attitude of the Russian-language audience led to the establishment of marketing mechanisms relying largely on personal contacts and non-traditional public relations.

Rosencrantz and Guildenstern Are Dead also exposed Gesher to the international theatre community. The production was invited to the Festival of Israeli Culture at the Brooklyn Academy of Music [BAM] in January 1992. However, Gesher's shoe-string budget did not allow it to go on this tour. Nathan Scharansky came to help again. Maltzev tells the story:

> And then they [the organizers of the BAM festival] suggested organizing a fund-raising dinner in New York. When we started thinking about it, I decided to ask Scharansky. I called Scharansky and said: "I need you to go for one day to New York for dinner." He said: "You are insane." I said: "I really need it." He cursed me, but agreed to go. And the public there responded to the invitation: "Honorary director of Gesher Theatre'—that is how it was presented—'invites you to a dinner." And he collected money, and we went to New York to this festival. (Maltzev 2001)

The *Rosencrantz and Guildenstern Are Dead* performance at BAM received excellent reviews in *The New York Times* (Gussow 1992) and *The Village Voice* (Croyden 1992). In contrast to Israeli critics, the American reviewers mentioned the cultural identity of the producers, but it did not become a centerpiece of critique.

The audiences received the production warmly as well. This success abroad had raised Gesher's status at home. Arye explained:

> A lot of things changed with this tour. At that time Shlomo (Chich) Lahat was the mayor of Tel Aviv. We invited him probably ten times, but he never came to the theatre. But in New York, the last performance was a benefit (not for Gesher—for Tel Aviv), and all the well-to-do Jewish New Yorkers were there. And we were successful with them. Our friendship with Chich started then. This friendship lasts to this day, he's done a lot for the theatre. (Arye 2003)

Gesher became the first Israeli theatre to be invited to the Festival D'Avignon (France). In July 1993 *Rosencrantz and Guildenstern Are Dead* was successfully performed there, and in August 1993 at the *Welt in Basel* Festival (Switzerland).

The Jewish Play: *Dreyfus File*

Almost simultaneously with *Rosencrantz and Guildenstern Are Dead*, Gesher started working on their next production. *Dreyfus File* by Jean-Claude Grumberg premiered on July 5, 1991. By that time, several other immigrant actors joined the Gesher troupe, among them Leonid Kanevsky, Gregory Lyampe (both participated in the tour of 1990), and Nelly Gosheva.

A play within a play, *Dreyfus File* tells the story of a group of small-time amateur actors in 1930s Poland staging a play about the 1890s Dreyfus case in Paris. Moris, the director (Roland Heilovsky), has a political and educational agenda: the story of the Dreyfus trial should increase awareness of the "Jewish question" in Europe. His troupe consists of Motl, the tailor (Vladimir Halemsky); Arnold, the actor who always wants to play every part (Leonid Kanevsky); Zina, his wife (Natalya Voitulevich); and Michael, an awkward young man ill cast as Captain Dreyfus (Sasha Demidov), who falls in love with Arnold's and Zina's intelligent and pretty daughter Miriam (Yevgenya Dodina). Everyone in the troupe has advice for Michael to help him improve his acting, but no one recognizes the relevance of the plot to their own life. They all eventually perish in camps and ghettos.

The seemingly straightforward plot posed great challenges for the performers. *Dreyfus File* makes use of metatheatre, presenting not just a play-within-the-play, but a rehearsal-within-the-play. Gesher's actors had to play amateur actors without looking like amateurs themselves.

Their acting received high praises: "The acting is sparkling, vocal, and even schmaltzy" (Ohed 1991). "Grumberg's play is difficult because it requires professional actors to play amateurs. The success of the show is that it showcases professional actors" (Handelsaltz 1991c). However, critics questioned the choice of play: "The play is too simple, if not to say simplistic" (Handelsaltz 1991c).

Another concern was expressed by Boaz Evron, a critic generally sympathetic to Gesher. He asked question about the future of the company in lieu of its repertoire choices:

> The question is how the company will reach out to the wider theatre audiences in Israel, given that it definitely is able to meet all their high expectations. (In fact, there is no other company here of such high level of professionalism.) I am not sure, though, that the "Jewish plays" will lead to these audiences. (Evron 1991b)

In 1991, after the premiere of *Dreyfus File*, Gesher produced three other shows. The young theatre had to build its repertoire, but the budget was tight. Therefore, when the theatre festival in Acre invited Gesher to participate, Maltzev asked the organizers for a grant. With this money Gesher produced the show *If Only*. It was a compilation of excerpts from three classic Russian plays: *The Infant* by Denis Fonfizin, *The Marriage* by Nikolay Gogol, and *The Bedbug* by Vladimir Mayakovsky. The idea was to compare marriage in three different time periods. It was a colorful comical show. It premiered in September 1991, at the Acre Festival. Despite simultaneous translation into

Figure 2: *Dreyfus File*
Yevgenya Dodina as Miriam and Sasha Demidov as Michael
(Courtesy of Gesher Theatre)

Hebrew, the show failed to attract Israeli audiences even at the festival. The newspaper *Hair* reported that some performances had to be cancelled ("Teatron Gesher" 1991). However, *If Only* was received well by Russian-speaking audiences.

Despite the box-office failure at the festival, critic Boaz Evron wrote such an enthusiastic review of the performance that it was quoted in the Gesher press-kits for years afterwards. After giving high evaluation of acting, he arrived at the real apotheosis:

> This is the most professional theatre in Israel today. It establishes a new level [of performance]. One can feel an immense cultural tradition, demonstrating in contrast to our prejudiced views, that they [Gesher's actors] are much more proficient in Western theatre and culture than we are. (Evron 1991c)

This critical claim assigned Gesher a position of cultural superiority. Not surprisingly, it proved to be inflammatory for other critics. Thus, Eliakim Yaron responded with a review aligned with Zionist ideology. He took a colonizing position towards Gesher, making it look inferior. For Yaron, the theatre's professionalism leads to "detachment from the Israeli reality." Specifically, he claims: "Based on this particular show, their [Gesher theatre-makers'] creative process takes place inside a bubble completely separate from the reality. On their own free will, they are imprisoned inside the cultural ghetto, which they want to eternalize" (1991). The review ends with two recommendations: "to get in touch with the Israeli artists" and "to act in Hebrew." Both positions, that of Evron and that of Yaron, approach Gesher's work with ideological and hierarchical yardsticks. Therefore, whether the reviews are positive or negative, they remain within the discursive framework of mutual colonization, perpetuating the hierarchical view of culture.

In the summer of 1991, Gesher also produced a children's show, *Balaganchik* (Russian for circus or carnival). At that time, four actors were without parts in other shows and needed employment. Vladimir Portnov,[9] director of the *Na Maloi Bronnoi* theatre in Moscow, directed this show, while he was visiting Israel. Based on movement, sound effects, and physical comedy, the show was performed by four clowns (Michael Asinovsky, Mark Ivanir, Yevgeny Gamburg, and Yevgeny Terletsky). *Balaganchik* remained in the repertoire for about a year, toured locally, and brought income to the actors and to the theatre. A side project, *Balaganchik* did not leave a significant trace in the theatre's history.

Around the same time, the theatre worked on a production of *Small Demon* by Fyodor Dostoevsky. Igor Voitulevich directed the show. However,

---

9 Later, Vladimir Portnov immigrated to Israel and joined the troupe as an actor.

his direction was not successful and the production was closed even before it premiered. *Contract* by Slawomir Mrozek, directed in 1992 by Vladimir Portnov, had almost the same fate: it was performed just a few times before it was taken off Gesher's stage.

From Russian to Hebrew: *Molière*

In the fall of 1991, Gesher rehearsed their next production—*Molière Or A Cabal of Hypocrites* by Mikhail Bulgakov. Bulgakov's play was based on his biography of Molière, which written in 1932–33, was not published until 1962, twenty-two years after Bulgakov's death.

Bulgakov's play focused on Molière's relationship with Louis XIV, his patron, exploring the questions of coercive power and artistic freedom. Its plot is reminiscent of Bulgakov's own relationship with Stalin. The story revolves around the production of *Tartuffe*, a play in which Molière (Yevgeny Gamburg) ridicules the hypocrisy and corruption of religious institutions. *Tartuffe* enrages the archbishop of Paris (Leonid Kanevsky). The only obstacle to the archbishop's wish to destroy Molière is the patronage of King Louis XIV (Israel [Sasha] Demidov). But even the royal powers gradually give in, and Molière's play is banned (as were Bulgakov's plays in Soviet Russia).

Molière premiered on January 12, 1992. The reception was warm. Critics admired the play, the directorial concept and the work of actors. A review in *Haaretz* pronounced:

> The most important quality of the show is that it has enthusiasm and determination lacking from many other good theatrical productions. These people [Gesher] make good theatre, as if it is the most important thing for them. As if despite everything, the show must go on. And it is fascinating and beautiful. (Handelsaltz 1992a)

Another critic joined in: "They [Gesher] know how to create good eye-opening theatre. Bulgakov's play gives them a wonderful opportunity to demonstrate their great talent....Many moments in the show are unforgettable" (Yaron 1992).

However, an interesting phenomenon took place. The more critics liked the production, the more they condemned the troupe for performing it in Russian. The new round of culture wars about the legitimacy of a non-Hebrew theatre had started. The most glaring example of such critique is Handelsaltz's review in *Haaretz* (1992b). After praising "the magical ambiance of the theatre" building "a colorful and impressive vision," the critic brings up an old adage:

> All this causes me to wonder if Gesher is a bridge to nowhere. It answers the immediate needs of the theatre producers and audiences, but there is no doubt it costs a lot, and also slows the *klita* down. It slows down the *klita* of the artists. They linger and labor in a transitional stage, instead of making an effort to cross over and to be assimilated into Hebrew theatre, which is waiting to absorb talents. Gesher also slows down the *klita* of the audiences. Why should they make an effort and go to theatre in Hebrew, when they can attend theatre in Russian? (Handelsaltz 1992b)

This review infuriated theatre figure Miriam Yahil-Wax, one of Gesher's most ardent supporters. She wrote a passionate response, published in the same paper. The subtitle of her article states: "A confident society does not erase cultures, and Gesher really has a lot to offer to Israeli theatre" (1992). She connects Gesher's emergence to the recent changes in Israeli politics of immigrant absorption. She clearly welcomes the turn from the oppressive "melting pot" to a more liberal multiculturalism:

> Despite the fact that our parents learned and spoke Hebrew, they felt in young Israel like in a cultural desert. Israeli life and literature are full of stories of tragic pining for Polish theatre, Hungarian song, and German music. We do not have to doom the generation of parents and grandparents of the present wave of *aliyah* to the same destiny. It is necessary to avoid the mistakes of *mizug galuyot* [the melting pot policy, see Glossary], i.e. erasing culture. The Culture Administration deserves praise for supporting and financing these wonderful artists in spite of opinions like the one expressed by Handelsaltz. (Yahil-Wax 1992)

Yahil-Wax condemns the cultural politics of Israel criticism predicated on political correctness, and supports the governmental establishment that turned out to be more progressive than the critics:

> The call to absorb the whole artistic community in a mechanical way—by making them learn Hebrew and act in our theatres—indicates the distorted perception of arts in our society. Maybe it is because we are used to thinking that the existence of a theatre depends on its willingness to cooperate with the establishment, which funds a theatre according to its correspondence to the dominant culture. This time the establishment made an exception and acted as a representative of the society confident in itself and in its culture, and thus encouraged multiculturalism. (Yahil-Wax 1992)

But this article was the only one that argued for the legitimacy of performance in Russian. All other reviews insisted on an urgent transition into Hebrew.

Indeed, already in 1992, even before the actors could speak the language, Gesher transitioned two of its first performances from Russian into Hebrew. Two main factors influenced this decision: first, ideological pressure from Israeli theatre critics, who acting like watchdogs of Zionist ideology, insisted on Gesher's performance in Hebrew. And second, pressure from the wide Israeli audiences, who would not attend Gesher's performances in Russian, thus endangering the theatre's financial survival.

Critics' pressure was the first factor. One of the goals of Israeli cultural policy is the dissemination of Hebrew. Therefore, language became a pressing issue in the discussion of Gesher's foundation and in the critical reviews of Gesher's early shows. In his review of *If only*, Eliakim Yaron demands Gesher "to act in Hebrew" (1991). In a review of *Rosencrantz and Guildenstern are Dead*, Shosh Avigal advises Gesher "to make a bit of an effort to try to get to us in Hebrew." The critic even takes a condescending motherly tone, promising to be kind in her future reception of the theatre: "It would be possible to forgive them [Gesher's actors] all the mistakes in Hebrew, if they had tried to do an authentic original play...even if it was in the broken and stuttering Hebrew of new immigrants" (1991).

In the Israeli context, the choice of language is a political question because it determines the legitimacy of the theatre, and thus justifies public funding. Therefore, in Israel, discussions of the language of performance quickly transform into debates on cultural policy:

> Is there a place for a public theatre based on Russian in the state of Israel? Is there a place for a cultural ghetto that will eternalize the Diaspora, and will turn them [Soviet immigrants] into some sort of new *yekim*?[10] Gesher Theatre creates a precedent by its mere existence, because it receives public subsidies (from the same meager source from which all theatres are subsidized). (Avigal 1991)

In this review, Gesher is perceived as a cultural Other threatening familiar ideological and cultural frameworks. The comparison with the German wave of immigration is telling: the critic is threatened by the potential superiority of Russian culture, which Gesher represents. Thus, the newspaper pages become a cultural battlefield, establishing a pattern for the future reception of Gesher's work. This ideological pressure, applied by the critics, is intertwined with the pressure from the audiences, which magnifies questions of language, cultural identity, and culture policy in Israel.

At first, both Arye and Maltzev were oblivious to the pressure to perform in Hebrew. In his interview on Israeli television in 1991, Arye expressed a utopian outlook on the universality of theatrical language that crosses over cultural and linguistic divides:

---

10 The word *yekim* refers to German Jews who immigrated to Israel in the thirties and forties. *Yekim* were notorious for their high-cultured background and condescending attitude towards nascent Israeli culture.

> I saw recently in Moscow a German show, *Three Sisters* by Peter Stein. I absolutely didn't care what language they were performing in, because theatrical language is somewhat international. I understood what filled their life. I dream that when Israeli audiences come to our show, they will have a similar experience. (Ais 1991)

Later Maltzev and Arye realized that general Israeli theatre-goers would not attend unless Gesher performed in Hebrew. Simultaneous translation with the headphones was not an option with these audiences. Yet, without their attendance the theatre would never become part of Israeli culture.

Maltzev and Arye were afraid of cultural marginalization—the threat of Gesher being perceived as an 'ethnic venue' haunted them. When I interviewed him, Arye recalled his rationale: "I realized that three years [of performing in Russian] was impossible, we wouldn't survive. We would turn into a ghetto theatre, like *Romen* [the Roma theatre] in Moscow, like the Yiddish theatre here. I understood that if we wanted to be a theatre for all, we needed to perform in Hebrew" (2003). Maltzev, who was aware of the politics of theatre reception in Israel, makes his point even more poignantly: "We don't want to be hostages of the Russian audience" (Ben-Shaul 1992). Maltzev explained to me:

> It was very difficult to attract Israelis, they came, said that we were wonderful, but didn't stay. And then I understood that this is a critical question, a question of our future, that no one will advance us as a Russian theatre, no one needs us, we'll be pathetic losers, like Russian street,[11] like Russian deli stores. And we wanted to be part of them, their favorite thing. (Maltzev 2001)

Here, Maltzev referred to another important aspect of the cultural situation in Israel, namely the low social status of immigrant cultural and economic venues.

In addition to his fear of cultural marginalization, Maltzev had financial reasons for his assimilationist zeal. The government subsidies were modest and had to be complemented by ticket sales. That meant that attracting audiences was Gesher's first priority. The only way to do that was to speak to the audiences in their own language. And that is why Gesher made a historical decision—to perform in Hebrew.

The transition to Hebrew became a milestone in Gesher's history. The most interesting result of this transition was an unprecedented model of theatre production in a multilingual environment, which Gesher created by trial and error.

The decision was made to start the transition with two plays: *Dreyfus File* and *Molière*. The next stage was to implement this decision, and here the

11 "Russian street" refers to the Russian-language culture industry in Israel.

theatre encountered real problems: no one knew how to stage a play in a language that none of the actors spoke or even understood.

Arye and Maltzev decided to take advantage of the Hebrew proficiency of one of Gesher's actors, Mark Ivanir. Being bilingual and bicultural, he occupied a unique position. Born in the USSR, he was raised and trained as an actor in Israel. In 1992 Mark Ivanir became the resident linguistic and cultural expert at Gesher, or as the troupe put it, "a bridge within the bridge." To support him, the theatre turned to Miriam Yahil-Wax, who did not know Russian but had a lot of experience in translation and theatre training. Despite her enthusiastic attitude towards Gesher, she was initially very skeptical about its transition into Hebrew:

> At first when they had the idea to perform in Hebrew, they brought me as an expert, and I said: "That's impossible, totally impossible, cannot be done." And then they started in the usual Israeli way—from impossible. They said to me: "Mark knows Hebrew." "Yes, Mark knows Hebrew, but they don't know! How do you want them to speak?" "He will tell them how to speak and they will imitate." I said: "Ok, let them work with Mark." I was sure that nothing would happen. And Mark dictated texts to them and they wrote it down in Cyrillic letters. (Yahil-Wax and Ivanir 1999)

This work laid the foundation of the unique system of linguistic training practiced by Gesher. Mark Ivanir explained the details of the process:

> We are talking about people who don't speak Hebrew at all....And they had to start to play a role in Hebrew—by learning it by heart without understanding what they were saying, like singers in opera...and it was hell....And we are talking [about transcribing] every sentence, every word. The emphasis on every word and in every sentence, otherwise you wouldn't be able to say what you are trying to say. It means doing the entire thing word by word. (Yahil-Wax and Ivanir 1999)

The Gesher actors, together with Mark Ivanir, had to process the Hebrew texts in the following way: on one page of a lined school notebook they put Hebrew text transcribed in Cyrillic letters, on the adjacent page they put diagrams of sound waves, indicating intonation and pitch of the words. After a day of rehearsals in Russian, the actors had to learn the Hebrew texts by night, memorizing not only the text, but also every rise or fall of intonation, the pitch and the pace of every single word.

This process was painful, especially for the actors of the older generation. In the documentary, *Mishpahat Gesher* [Gesher Family] (Mafzir 1993), the actors described their experience of acting in a new language. Leonid Kanevsky: "It was horrifying—unrecognizable language. French—recognizable, German—recognizable, Hebrew—is unrecognizable, unfamiliar." Vladimir Halemsky used a brutal metaphor to render his experience of learning Hebrew texts: "We hit the texts into ourselves as if with a hammer." Gregory Lyampe, a veteran of Russian theatre, disagreed with the whole idea: "An actor should act in a language he thinks in." Later, Maltzev confirmed to me: "It was a tragic work" (2001).

How did the actors learn their parts without knowing the language? Actor Yevgenya Dodina had her own method; she tried out her Hebrew on cab drivers:

> I learned texts in Hebrew, I just learned them by heart without understanding, and I tried my Hebrew texts out on the cab drivers: "I am begging you, yield to your destiny, go through all the most horrifying challenges which you will face. What is the opinion of the crowd to you? You know how wavering it is." I checked to see what would happen, whether they understood me or not, and if he responded: "Why, honey?"—it meant that he understood. (Dodina 2001)

After the actors learned their parts well enough, they started the rehearsals, using Russian, Hebrew, and English. The rehearsal on stage was in Hebrew; Arye and the actors spoke Russian; and Arye and Yahil-Wax communicated in English. Both Yahil-Wax and Ivanir also served as the director's "ears"—they translated for Arye into Russian or into English what the actors were saying on stage, and enabled him to direct the rehearsals in Hebrew. In terms of vocal work, Arye had to rely on Yahil-Wax and Ivanir completely.

Gesher's three-language process was "patented" during the transition of the first two shows into Hebrew. For years to come the theatre followed the same scheme. First, the play was read or staged in Russian; then actors together with a linguistic coach learned the texts in Hebrew, and only then the Hebrew version was rehearsed on stage. Later on, when the Gesher troupe included actors who did not speak Russian, their rehearsal process became even more complex. The play was no longer first staged in Russian. The rehearsals were in Hebrew all along, and a translator was required to mediate communication between Arye and the Hebrew-speaking actors. And so Gesher's method was completed: laborious, but productive.

Gesher's multilingual model had unexpected consequences for its artistic production, including the acting and directing style of the theatre. First, differences in pace and intonation caused the actors to alter their style for performance in Hebrew; second, close work with the texts resulted in greater acting precision; third, prioritizing language over performance changed an established hierarchy within the troupe. Alongside the changes in artistic production, there was a revolutionary change in the media and audience reception of the theatre: the critics cheered and the audience arrived.

The linguistic shift greatly affected the acting style. One reason for that is a linguistic difference—Hebrew words are shorter than Russian, and the pace of speech is faster. Therefore, the same performance in Hebrew is 10–15 minutes shorter than in Russian. Since the early productions were rehearsed in Russian, and only later transitioned to Hebrew, that meant that the whole show, every gesture, every movement on stage had to speed up. The faster pace required a significant amount of acting skill.

Other differences stemmed from the social use of language. Hebrew intonation is dramatically different from Russian. Therefore, in order to project a certain feeling in another language actors need to employ different intonation and other expressive vocal strategies. In order to express a certain emotion in Hebrew, Russian-speaking actors could not use their affective memory to the same extent as they could in their mother tongue. In that case both the actors and director had to rely on Mark Ivanir, Miriam Yahil-Wax, and other linguistic coaches.

However, Gesher turned the potential recipe for disaster—a lack of Hebrew proficiency—to its benefit; due to the careful work with the text, the acting became precise and thoughtful. There was nothing random in Gesher's Hebrew performances, nothing artistically unexplained. Careful work with the texts and almost compulsive attention to detail paid off. Miriam Yahil-Wax reconstructs how a multilingual work led to great artistic achievements:

> The work that Mark was doing all these years, the work that I am doing, is bringing us to work on a text in such great detail that we never would have reached had we worked on it only [one] time. It reminds me that when Beckett was asked why did he write his plays in French, he said, because in French he had to think about every word. And it is the same for us—we have to think, we have to explain, have to prove: why is it that way? Why is it there? And we came up with fine results. (Yahil-Wax and Ivanir 1999)

The linguistic change also influenced the social hierarchy in the troupe. Traditionally, the older and more distinguished actors had enjoyed a higher status within the theatre. However, the linguistic transition made them the students of a much younger and inexperienced colleague. Mark Ivanir was 26 in 1992, but he knew the language, and the Russian actors had to take his word for it. They constantly challenged Mark, and put his knowledge to test. However, they also were thankful to him, and grew to depend on his support and appreciate it. If Mark Ivanir was not on stage, he was behind the scenes, ready to help, to whisper a forgotten word, and to give a cue. When he was on stage in his part, in addition to his acting, he also monitored other actors' performances for problems, and came to the rescue if needed:

> A few times I helped. And the audience was quite confused, because the text had to come from the other side, but it came from me....We had an old actor, he is not with

us anymore [passed away] who refused to go onstage for three years if I didn't stand behind the stage, he was so insecure. (Yahil-Wax and Ivanir 1999)

Despite all these difficulties, both *Dreyfus File* and *Molière* were transitioned into Hebrew and ready for performance. The stakes were high: both Yahil-Wax and Arye recall the very first performances as a nerve-racking experience.

However, later performances showed that as difficult as it was, the work of Gesher was generously appreciated by the audiences. In interviews, the actors Israel (Sasha) Demidov (1999), Natalya Voitulevich-Manor (1999), and Yevgenya Dodina (2001), explained to me that they had different experiences of performing in front of the Hebrew-speaking and Russian-speaking audiences. According to them, the Russian theatrical tradition has a long and influential history. Israeli theatre, dating back to the beginning of the twentieth century, is young. As a result, Russian-speaking audiences, socialized into the rich theatre tradition, are analytical and critical. In contrast, the Hebrew-speaking audiences have unreserved responses and intense emotional connection with the performers. As the Gesher actors say, the Israeli audiences are "naïve," they don't contextualize or historicize a particular performance. It is interesting that even in these seemingly innocuous comments, Gesher's actors place themselves and their Russian audiences into a position of cultural superiority with respect to the Israeli audiences.

The Hebrew version of *Molière* premiered at the 1992 Israel Festival in Jerusalem, the most prestigious theatrical venue in the country. Enthusiastic previews, such as Aviva Zaltzman's in *Davar*, emphasized the transition to Hebrew: "Gesher Theatre does not want to be locked in the ghetto of Russian culture and language" (1992a). However, both Omri Nitzan, artistic director of the festival, and Slava Maltzev, Gesher's manager, worried about the fate of the production and its appeal to Israeli audiences (Ben-Shaul 1992).

The first performance of *Molière* was met with standing ovations—the audience was applauding the actors for their incredible effort of acting in Hebrew. Critical reception followed suit. However, whether or not the reviewers liked or disliked certain aspects of production, their main focus was language. The critics mixed ideological reference with aesthetic analysis. Their decisive criterion of evaluation became the theatre's correspondence to the ideological norms of commitment to Hebrew and assimilation into Israeli culture.

In her review of *Molière*, Shosh Weitz (1992) calls it "a beautiful and impressive show." After praising the acting, directorial interpretation, and staging, Weitz comments on several problems of the production. Firstly, Gesher "is definitely not an Israeli theatre. More precisely, not yet." Second, the actors were not fluent in Hebrew, and therefore "the gap between beautiful directorial concept and the level of text delivery is very conspicuous." Third, the Russian acting style that Weitz dubbed "bombastic" looked to her "exaggerated and archaic" in the context of Israel of the nineties. And yet, Weitz is willing to forgive Gesher all these problems because of their effort to "absorb." She even reminds the readers not to forget that Gesher is "an ensemble of immigrants" (Weitz 1992). Essentially, she is saying that Gesher's problems—Hebrew enunciation, acting style, and cultural identification—would be resolved during the absorption process. As a result of this process, Gesher will become indistinguishable from any other Israeli theatre, which, according to the critic, is an ideal situation.

Michael Handelsaltz also gives high praise to the artistic aspects of Gesher's work for "an interesting aesthetic claim and sweeping enthusiasm" (1992c). But his strongest support and appreciation refers neither to the actors, nor to the director, but to their Hebrew coaches. His evaluation of acting is based on the actors' mastery of Hebrew. His focus on language substitutes for analysis.

The reception of the Hebrew version of *Dreyfus File* followed the same pattern. The critics expressed a deep satisfaction from the transition of the theatre to Hebrew, and took a forgiving tone towards the Hebrew proficiency of the Gesher actors:

> Despite the fact that the Hebrew text sometimes sounds awkward, and it is clear that they [the Gesher actors] do not always understand it, their trustworthy acting transcends the accent. It is far away from what is recognized here as the Russian pathos of early Habima. Within minutes one stops thinking of immigrant absorption and gets immersed into the play. (Avigal 1992)

This response, like other reviews, jumbled ideological references to immigrant absorption with the analysis of acting.

Following its 1992 premiere, *Moliere* toured in Zurich (Switzerland). The production remained in Gesher's repertoire for two years, during which it was performed 70 times (50 in Hebrew and 20 in Russian). *Dreyfus File* was Gesher's "staple" for many years. In March 2001, Gesher went on an extensive tour in North America where it was performed in Russian. Overall, *Dreyfus File* had been performed 188 times (91 in Hebrew, 97 in Russian)—the numbers indicate a resounding success. (In Israel, a production is considered a box-office success if it is performed 100 times.)

The initial years were formative for Gesher. During this time it grew from a proposal, to a touring troupe, to an established theatre project with public funding. Gesher's structure, policies, mode of artistic production, budget, and relationships with audiences and critics took shape during these two years.

Gesher's structure was distinct from most public theatres in Israel. Israeli theatres, such as the Cameri or the contemporary Habima, are led by a manager, rather than an artistic director. Managers invite directors and actors for specific productions. The rehearsal and production period is short, and several productions are in the works simultaneously. In contrast, Gesher is based on the work of a permanent ensemble. A sole director with strong artistic vision, both an aesthetic authority and a spiritual mentor, heads the troupe. Russian theatrical tradition permeates this concept of the theatre. Its cultural values: the dedication to the art and high status of the theatre, defined Gesher's work.

These values also shaped the family-like nature of the company's life (Gershenson 2003). The troupe members spent long and intense hours of work at the theatre; they often slept, ate, and showered there. They grew physically and verbally affectionate with each other. The social organization of the company, based on close-knit relationships, formed a "soft" kinship hierarchy: a father-like figure of the director on top, uncles and cousins underneath, and young sons, daughters, nephews, and nieces on the bottom. Interestingly, there was no one in the position of a mother, aunt or older sister; as one of the young actors explained: "It's the father who is a mother. It's a family with a lot of fathers" (Ben-Zur 1999). Up to this day Gesher is structured as a traditional patriarchal family, where leadership is reserved for males. Even though Katya Sosonsky and Lena Kreindlina were "matriarchs" and founders of the theatre, they never enjoyed the same status and power as Maltzev and Arye. This patriarchal character of social organization is also part of the cultural legacy of Russian theatre.

Alik Loevsky, a contemporary Russian theatre figure, gives a historic and cultural perspective on such social organization: "Theatre-home is an ideal of the Russian theatre—of the repertory theatre. This model, permanent troupe and father-God director, was established in the early Moscow Art Theatre,[12] and was a result of the Stanislavsky's theatre reform" (1999).

During this early period, the theatre also developed artistically. Gesher's professional perfectionism and traditional theatrical standards shaped it as an innovative but not avant-garde theatre. Gesher did not do experimental productions with political agendas, direct audience involvement, and other features of non-conventional theatre. Gesher's technically immaculate productions resulted from lengthy systematic rehearsals and the detail-oriented approach of the director, actors, and other creative and technical staff. Gesher

12 The Moscow Art Theatre, established by Stanislavsky in 1897, was based on new theatrical principles that contributed to the theatre-home model; among them the harmonious work of a permanent ensemble, a dedication to art, and lengthy systematic rehearsals.

was both a director's and an actors' theatre. Its productions were a combination of both the director's concept and the acting of a coordinated ensemble, where every cast member had a striking stage presence, engaging personality, and Stanislavsky-cum-Goncharov[13] professional training. The conceptual character of Gesher's productions did not result in a minimalist staging. From the outset, Gesher was a theatre of production values. It greatly invested into the visual aspects of the staging (lighting, sets, costumes, and movement). As for sound, Gesher's composer, Avi Benjamin created an impressive score for every major production.

The transition to Hebrew was an important step in the theatre's development that in many ways defined its future. In the Israeli cultural and social context, Gesher's transition to Hebrew proved to be a savvy survival strategy. Moreover, the transition that started as a conformist adherence to ideological and financial pressures led to fine artistic achievements. Careful work with the text allowed the actors and director to reach a higher level of concentration and precision. By crossing the bridge from Russian to Hebrew, Gesher situated itself between the Russian theatrical tradition and the Israeli cultural context, and was able to succeed artistically and financially, by forging significant connections with a wider Israeli audience.

In doing that, Gesher identified itself as an Israeli theatre. In the documentary *Gesher Family*, Maltzev affirms: "We are Israeli theatre from the first day of our existence. We obey Israeli laws, we work together with people who surround us. Every day we are involved in a thousand contacts" (Mafzir 1993). However, this naïve definition of Israeliness, as living and working in Israel, was not going to convince Israeli critics. Indeed, most critics and audiences continued to respond with a resound "no" to the question of the Israeliness of Gesher. For them, Gesher remained "a Russian theatre," or "a theatre of immigrants."

---

13 Andrey Goncharov, a student of Meyerhold, was a major public stage figure and an artistic director of the Mayakovsky theatre. His bright, emotional and non-realistic style greatly influenced Yevgeny Arye and the Gesher actors. Arye worked with Goncharov at the Mayakovsky theatre and taught with him at GITIS.

• CHAPTER FIVE •

On the Road to Fame

The First Triumph: *The Idiot*

In the fall of 1992 Gesher rehearsed their new production based on Fyodor Dostoevsky's novel *The Idiot*. This production marked the end of the theatre's initial period and the beginning of a new era—the era of official recognition and critical acclaim.

By that time, Gesher's housing situation was stabilized. The Tel Aviv municipality, headed by Gesher's new friend Shlomo (Chich) Lahat, rented the building at Nachmani Street from the Culture Administration. The building became Gesher's permanent rehearsal space. Simultaneously, the municipality provided some funding for renovations and air conditioning. However, the renovations were only partial, and the building was unfit for public performances. Therefore, Gesher still performed at other locations: big halls in Tel Aviv and Jerusalem, and small halls in various towns and kibbutzim. At that time Gesher gave only 15–20 performances per month, the rest of the time was dedicated to the rehearsals.

Gesher's financial situation was still tenuous, but its budget had almost doubled since 1991 and by the end of 1992 had reached 2 million NIS (See Table 1). The box-office revenues stagnated, but the public funding grew to 1.4 million NIS (almost twice the size of the 1991 subsidy). In addition, two new sources of income appeared, both still very modest: private donations and corporate sponsorships (in exchange for advertisement in the theatre's promotional materials).

The troupe grew to 35 members, and underwent structural changes. The work slowly became more specialized. Thus, during the initial stages Katya Sosonsky, a dramaturge by training, had to function as the theatre's publicist. Now, she finally distanced herself from public relations and started working more closely on dramaturgy (choice of dramatic material and its adaptations for Gesher's stage). In her place, Gesher took on board a professional publicist, Michal Scheflan. It was a wise step. Israeli-born, Michal was a seasoned professional with local experience and connections, and she could better represent Gesher as a typical Israeli theatre. Miriam Yahil-Wax also joined the theatre as a freelance consultant for questions of translation, Hebrew language, and Israeli dramaturgy. Katya Sosonsky headed the department of dramaturgy and public relations, and coordinated the work of Michal Scheflan, Miriam Yahil-Wax, and two editors who worked in Russian and Hebrew languages.

Another important addition to the theatre troupe was Igor Mirkurbanov, one of Arye's disciples. Like the rest of Gesher's nucleus, he had acted at the prestigious Mayakovsky Theatre in Moscow. He immediately established himself as one of the leading actors at Gesher, and together with Israel (Sasha) Demidov, Natalya Voitulevich, and Yevgenya Dodina, constituted the key cast of Gesher—young, beautiful, talented actors, completely dedicated to their company and deeply loyal to their director and mentor, Arye.

Igor Mirkurbanov arrived in Israel in the fall of 1992. He had only two months of rehearsal time before the premiere of *The Idiot*. He also was immediately cast in *Dreyfus File* and *Moliere*. Like the rest of the actors, he did not know Hebrew and had to learn his part phonetically. However, while other actors already had been trained for months to perform in Hebrew, Igor had to plunge into it right away. Unlike previous productions, *The Idiot* was rehearsed simultaneously in two versions, Russian and Hebrew. But language was not the only challenge during the production process. Arye recalls:

> The production process of this play was excruciating. We rehearsed in the Nachmani [building], where absolutely everything leaked. It was horribly cold, and everyone was sick. Sasha Demidov rehearsed with a fever of 39°–40° C [102.2°–104° F]. Moreover, during that time his father passed away in Tashkent [in Uzbekistan], and I thought, that's it, there will be no premiere. And Sasha did not leave. (Arye 2003)

Despite the heroic efforts of his actors, Arye hesitated to decide until the very last minute whether the production was ready. As time went by things got worse. Arye: "Yoram Kanuk came to the last run, and said, you can't release this, no way. It was an atrocious run. Everything was falling apart. And after it, I had this sleepless night when I had to decide whether to release the premiere or not" (2003). Arye went ahead. It was a huge gamble.

The Idiot premiered on time (on December 20, 1992, performed in Hebrew). The production became Gesher's first triumph. Slava Maltzev describes the success:

> January 1993—a big premiere, lots of promotion, the theatre started to perform in Hebrew. And we just glided. It was an explosion....Unimaginable. It was impossible to get a ticket. Buzz in every paper. Everything fell together. It was a different approach to the theatre. They [Israeli audiences] just paraded us around the town.

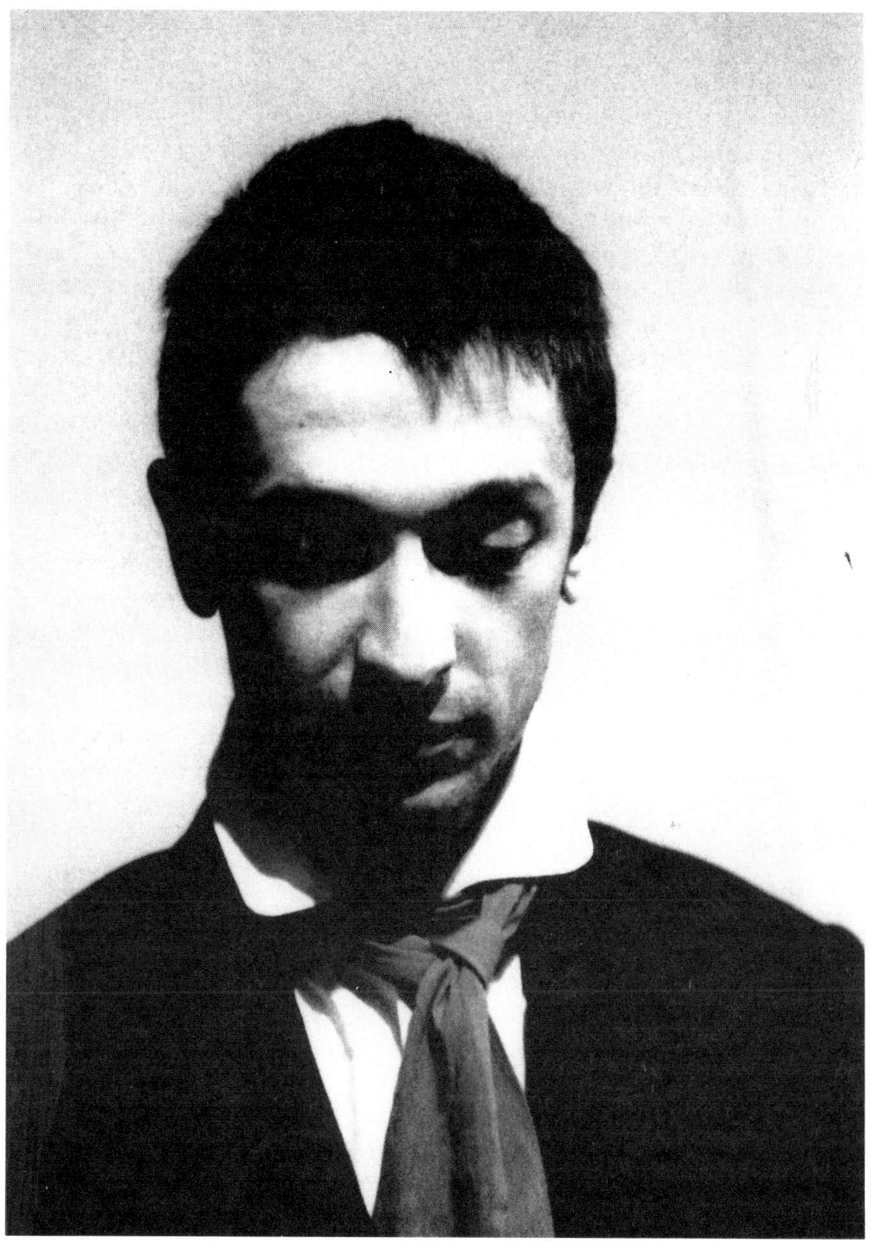

Figure 3: *The Idiot*
Israel (Sasha) Demidov as Prince Myshkin
(Courtesy of Gesher Theatre)

> They ran to the theatre, and there were no tickets. *Moliere* and *Dreyfus* were ordinary shows, uneventful. *The Idiot* was an event. (Maltzev 2001)

The Idiot received a number of awards both in Israel and abroad. A combination of carefully calculated and fortuitous factors led to this incredible popular and critical success.

One of the components of success was Gesher's adaptation of the novel. Yevgeny Arye and Katya Sosonsky turned the novel into a play, and Mark Ivanir translated it into Hebrew. They simplified the complex plot, but maintained Dostoevsky's emotional intensity and urgency of moral dilemmas. Prince Myshkin (Israel [Sasha] Demidov) and Rogozhin (Igor Mirkurbanov) meet on a train to St. Petersburg. There, both fall in love with beautiful Nastasya Philipovna (Natalya Voitulevich) and become rivals. Nastasya, portrayed as half-slut and half-saint, lived with a rich relative who made the orphaned girl his mistress. But now, in order to get rid of Nastasya, he makes a deal with Ganya (Mark Ivanir) who agreed to marry her in exchange for a lavish dowry. Prince Myshkin—the good-hearted idiot—interferes with everyone's plans. He wants to save Nastasya, so he breaks his engagement with another woman, Aglaya (Yevgenya Dodina), in order to marry her, but Nastasya runs away with Rogozhin. The tension escalates; the conflict is beyond resolution, and it comes to a tragic end with Nastasya's murder. Myshkin leaves again, this time for good. His good intentions, endless naiveté, and his loving soul does not bring happiness to anyone. In the context of a corrupted society, his trusting nature and his inability to recognize evil make him a pathetic fool.

Demidov's Myshkin, with a radiating smile and a childlike ability for joy, projected an aura of saintliness. Mirkurbanov's Rogozhin was his diabolic counterpart. Minimal sets (by Elena Stepanova, who was invited for this production from Moscow) could represent an immediate change of atmosphere with just a shift in lighting. Music by Avi Benjamin was charged with tension. The acting, sets, and music combined to create an overall sense of moral struggle between good and evil.

The critics unanimously hailed the show. Yosef Shiffman from *Davar* in his review titled "Miracle!" calls the production "a new peak." He continues: "They [Gesher's actors] allowed Israeli audiences to rediscover Dostoevsky: Dostoevsky as a source of grotesque, Dostoevsky as a spiritual father of Samuel Beckett, and above all, Dostoevsky as a source of excellent acting" (1993). Shosh Weitz raves: "*The Idiot* is one of the best and most interesting shows that was produced in Israel this season...one of the most important and pleasurable experiences" (1993a). She also admires the style of the production featuring "a fascinating combination of new and old: theatricality that reminds of early Habima and contemporary theatre codes" (1993a). Michael Handelsaltz writes: "Arye has a distinctive style. He makes the best use of the elements of sets (moving stages), music, and light in order to have a full control over atmosphere on stage and over audiences' emotions" (1993a). Eliakim Yaron hails Arye for his "realistic style that is about to turn into grotesque and stylized expression" (1993a). Shosh Avigal virtually orders her readers: "Run to see it!" She explains:

> ...there are no long and tiring monologues, instead of them—the body speaks, the stage speaks. With that, the director Yevgeny Arye does not slide into pointless movement theatre, general ambiance, and effects for their own sake. Everything is thought through, organized, and mobilized towards development of the story....This is theatre at its best. (Avigal 1993a)

The actors received high praise. Demidov was described to have "a rare ability to be funny and ridiculous, and then to switch to the moving moments that are touching in an exceptional way" (Handelsaltz 1993a). Yaron gave praise to the "cohesive ensemble" of Gesher, where "quality of acting and fascinating stage presence are real theatrical assets" (1993a). Fuks called Demidov's part "virtuoso acting" and added, "If we have a soul, then *The Idiot* touches it" (1993).

The critics were so unanimous in their rave receptions, that the later reviews started commenting on their favorable consensus (see, for instance, Kimchi 1993). However, besides the artistic reasons for the incredible success, there were other contributing factors.

The first factor was the choice of dramatic material. The Israeli critics and audiences had given Gesher approval to stage a Russian classic. Handelsaltz writes: "Gesher Theatre succeeds again: they mount a play, which they fit just right: it's entirely Russian culture and Russian soul" (1993a). Orion also emphasizes the choice of the stage material because it makes the theatre trustworthy: "Russian director and actors bring with them culture, and we believe them because they were born into it" (1993a).

The second factor for the success was the language of the production. As Yosi Shiffman put it: "They bring to us the pinnacle of Russian culture in Hebrew, in our language" (1993). The production was staged in Hebrew from the start (with a parallel Russian version). This unique combination—Russian repertoire and Hebrew language of production presented Gesher in a favorable light to critics and audiences. It was, as Maltzev put it, "a Russian culture in Hebrew" (2001). *The Idiot* exposed Israelis to a different sensibility in a non-threatening way: new immigrants, cultural Others, were domesticated, neutered. Their otherness was mitigated by their great assimilation-driven desire to perform in Hebrew and to be part of Israel. Yet, they did not claim to be "real Israelis" and to misplace Israeli cultural producers from their position of cultural competence—they did not dispute the ownership of symbolic capital. Gesher confined itself to the content of Russian classics. It was a win-win situation and everyone loved it.

In this context, even the cast's imperfect Hebrew accent was received indulgently: "Everyone speaks good Hebrew, in a distinctive Russian accent. While staging Dostoevsky, there is even a certain charm to it, not to mention a linguistic consistency," writes Eliakim Yaron (1993a). Amir Orion agrees: "The effort that they [the actors] make while speaking [Hebrew] is a positive component in the dramatic effect that *The Idiot* can create" (1993a). Shosh Avigal is of the same opinion: "On stage their Hebrew sounds with a pleasant Russian intonation, that does not take from trustworthiness of the production, just the opposite" (1993a).

Like all the other reviewers, Yitzhak Laor is ecstatic about the production, calling it "a wonderful theatrical event" (1993). However, he is the only reviewer who candidly acknowledges the language politics in Israel privileging Hebrew. He even admits feeling self-conscious while complementing Gesher's actors for their Hebrew: Laor does not know how to do it "without joining forces of 'Speak only Hebrew!' police" (1993).

In all these responses, Arye and the Gesher actors are inevitably essentialized as "Russians." Paradoxically, it is at this juncture that the Israeli critics were ready to accept Gesher as "simply a good theatre" (Avigal 1993a) or "an Israeli theatre in every respect" (Kimchi 1993). For Gesher, presenting Russian culture in Hebrew proved to produce just the right amount of mimicry, without becoming menacing.

Giora Manor announced: "Theatre of immigrants turned into theatre of new citizens in the state of Israel. A special and excellent theatre that can cope with the rest" (1993). Shosh Avigal encouraged: "Gesher Theatre is not an '*olim* theatre' that needs a forgiving attitude and encouragement, but simply a good theatre, and their *Idiot* is wonderful" (1993a). Alona Kimchi asserted: "Their *Idiot* that is performed alternately in Russian and in Hebrew, is going to turn them into Israeli theatre in every respect and will expose them to the audiences that cannot be bothered with the simultaneous translation" (1993).

The only voice of dissent regarding the Hebrew-only language policy is heard in Miri Litvik's review. Litvik, who is bilingual, saw the production in both Hebrew and Russian, and preferred the Russian version! She acknowledges that the attempt to work in a new language is interesting all by itself, but she feels that the translation does not do justice to the complexity of Dostoevsky's language; that the characters in Hebrew become stereotypical Russians "drinking vodka out of a samovar," and that the vocal work of the actors in Russian language is much more skillful (Litvik 1993a). However, her opinion was in the minority.

The third factor that contributed to the great success of Gesher with *The Idiot*, stemmed from the political changes in Israel at that time. In 1992, a new government was elected, and Yitzhak Rabin became Prime Minister. After 15 years of the right-wing Likud party in power, the left-wing Avoda [Labor] party won the elections. The vote of Soviet immigrants contributed to the longed-for victory of Labor. Even though they identified with the Israeli political right on territorial interests, they had a left-wing liberal orientation with respect to social issues, such as social security, civil rights, and separation of religion from state. Also, the Soviet immigrants were disappointed with the Likud government's failure to address their social and economic problems. This situation, and the Labor campaign geared towards Soviet immigrants, defined their voting pattern: nearly 60% of the immigrant vote went to the Labor or other left-wing parties (Jones 1996, p. 204).

However, the immigrants opposed one of the major political initiatives of the new government—a peace process with the Palestinian authority. Therefore, it was necessary for the political establishment to gain support of the Soviet immigrant community on that issue. Gesher, as a public representative of this community, became a political card in this game. The success of *The Idiot* coincided with the necessity of the new regime to adopt a "Russian theatre" as a metonymic stand-in for all other immigrants' endeavors, and to showcase its support for the immigrant community.

Leah Rabin, the first lady, held a special event at the Prime Minister's residence in honor of the Gesher troupe. This event publicly established the Rabins as eager supporters of Soviet immigrants. Ada Cohen from *Maariv* quotes the words of Leah Rabin, infused with ideological references:

> This theatre enriched [us] and made a special contribution to our country. After *The Idiot* performance I said to Yitzhak [Rabin] that once more an exceptional thing happened to us, when the gates of the USSR opened and enriched our lives in so many ways. This small group made an effort to learn Hebrew and to bring us the best of the theatre and the best of the stage. For years we said: "Let my people go." And now, when it happened, we didn't know that they would bring us also such benefits and raise our cultural level in all senses. (Cohen 1993)

Rabins' sponsorship granted Gesher an enviable (and thus potentially dangerous) status as the "spoiled child of the establishment" (Fuks 1995a). Shulamit Aloni, Minister of Education and Culture; Shlomo (Chich) Lahat, mayor of Tel Aviv; and Shimon Peres, Minister of Foreign Affairs, made a point to attend Gesher's performances. Later, in 1994, Arye was even invited to accompany Yitzhak Rabin to Oslo for the reception of the Nobel Peace Prize.

This revolutionary change of government also necessitated reconsideration of existing cultural policies. Shulamit Aloni, a left-wing liberal, was now in charge of culture.[1] She appointed a committee, chaired by renowned entrepreneur Hezi Shelach, in order to evaluate cultural policy regarding theatres. The Shelach committee issued a report that listed such deficiencies as poor financial management, ineffective public boards, ill-defined funding policy, and the Ministry's focus on bureaucratic details instead of issues vital to the theatre life. Among other recommendations, the committee recommended to establish public funding of theatres at the level of 55–65% of their budgets and to support fringe independent theatre as well as locally-written Israeli plays (Katz and Sella 1999). Even though the Ministry adopted the Shelach committee's recommendations only partially, the report was a seminal policy statement on theatre funding in Israel. Most importantly, the Shelach report facilitated the opening of funding opportunities for new theatres, including Gesher.

The success of *The Idiot* and the support of the political establishment finally sealed Gesher's status. On March 28, 1993, Maltzev and Arye held a press-conference where they announced that Gesher has been granted the status of public theatre (Shapiro 1993c), a step that can be hardly overestimated. Public theatres in Israel are supported from national and municipal funds on a permanent basis. Therefore, the new status meant, first and foremost, financial security for the still-starving Gesher actors and staff. The budget of the theatre in 1993 grew to 4.5 million NIS, 2.9 million was a public subsidy (see Table 1).

The board of directors also grew; in 1993 it consisted of nine members, among them such public figures as Ziva Lahat, Oded Feldman, and Hanan Ben-Yehuda. But even more importantly, through this official recognition, Gesher gained a permanent status: it was not a "project" or a "workshop" any more. It was a theatre. For Maltzev and Arye this was a very positive affirmation that they had made it.

Finally, the last factor that defined *The Idiot*'s success with the audiences was Gesher's clever repertoire policy. As mentioned before, *The Idiot* was the first performance that premiered in Hebrew; however, it was not the only production. By 1993, the theatre already had performed *Moliere* and *Dreyfus File* in Hebrew. During the rehearsal period for *The Idiot* the theatre toured

1 In Rabin's government, Aloni served as Minister of Education and Culture in 1992–1994, and as Minister of Communication, Science, and the Arts in 1995–1996. Arts and culture were included in both portfolios.

with their Hebrew repertoire around the country and "polished" their Hebrew performance. Therefore, after the big hit of *The Idiot*, there was repertoire continuity that was important for sustaining the audiences. Maltzev explains: "When we produced *Idiot*, we already had two ready shows in Hebrew. It wasn't like we performed one show and that's it. We didn't find ourselves in a vacuum: *The Idiot*, so what's next?" (2001).

Gesher's box office success is especially impressive because Gesher's management chose not to use a subscription system like the rest of the public theatres. Most of their tickets were sold through individual sales at the box-office.

Paradoxically, the positive reviews of *The Idiot* gave birth to a critical trend in Gesher's reception that was detrimental for the theatre's future relationship with the other Israeli theatre figures. In their reviews, some critics emphasized cultural and artistic inferiority of Israeli theatre as compared to Gesher. Yosi Shiffman claims: "This production establishes new standards according to which we'll judge every theatrical production from now on. There is nothing we can do about it—the Hebrew [Israeli] theatre can take classes from this company" (1993). Amir Orion is even more explicit: "...stage movement of Russian actors, their Hebrew still sounding like Russian, can cause jealousy in Israeli actors, who work on the borderline of Western culture and *haltura* [Hebrew slang for 'doing the minimum']" (1993). Such commentary provoked a great deal of anger and jealousy among Israeli cultural producers. Representations of Gesher as an emissary of 'high culture' became a crucial feature of the developing negative stereotype surrounding "the Russian theatre."

On May 17, 1993, *The Idiot* was granted a Meir Margalit Award [Israeli theatre Oscar]. The committee called *The Idiot* "an excellent show of an excellent theatre" (Yaron et al. 1993, p. 75). The committee members declared:

> Gesher Theatre has conquered, step by step, its place in the Israeli cultural scene. But it looks like in the production of *The Idiot* they reached a major peak, a peak not only in terms of art, as they had demonstrated their potential in other shows as well. They presented *The Idiot* in Hebrew, and on their part it's much more than just an announcement of the intention to be here and "to want to be part of Israeli culture." A decision to perform in Hebrew is an expression of recognition that a theatre that performs here in a different language is a cultural ghetto. And now [we] are saying to Gesher company: you are not ghetto, but flesh from our flesh, you are our brothers. (Yaron et al. 1993, p. 75)

This account sums up perfectly the reasons for *The Idiot*'s compelling success: artistic achievement accompanied by the ideologically correct choice of language and clever repertoire policy.

The Idiot succeeded abroad as well. In the fall of 1994, the international *City of Drama* Festival in Manchester, UK, sponsored by the British Arts Council featured a season dedicated to the Israeli theatre. Six productions, among them the story of a Bedouin woman (*Nomi* by Cameri Theatre), a play in Yiddish (*Stars without a Sky* by Leah Koenig), and *The Idiot* (marketed as "Russian"), successfully represented Israeli theatre as multicultural and diverse. *The Idiot* was a smash hit. Reviews in the major newspapers raved. "It is a powerful production....There are isolated scenes from the novel which are quite transfixing....No mean achievement," wrote *The Daily Telegraph* (Gore-Langton 1994). Venerable Irving Wardle stated in *The Independent*: "A transcendent piece of acting" (1994). *The Guardian* added: "Arye's production of *The Idiot* is stunning" (Billington 1994). Admiring Demidov's acting, *The Times* wrote: "For images such as this, and the dream-like chiaroscuro of the settings, Arye's vision of the novel will linger in the mind" (Kingston 1994). The newspaper *Manchester Evening News* nominated *The Idiot* as the Best International Production and Israel (Sasha) Demidov as the Best Actor at the Festival. These awards came to symbolize true success. The theatre's victory in Manchester received extensive coverage in Israel as well: every major newspaper proudly reported it.

Gesher's first hit, the production of *The Idiot* was a significant step in the development of the theatre. Its success is reflected in the triumphant number of performances. Since the premiere in 1992, Gesher has performed *The Idiot* 202 times (180 in Hebrew and 22 in Russian)—an inordinate number for Israeli stage. This production proved that Gesher is able to produce shows in Hebrew and helped Gesher to obtain the status of public theatre. The combination of these two factors established Gesher in the national arena. The awards at the festival in Manchester also allowed Gesher to claim a respectable place in the international theatre community.

Stardom in Immigration

As journalists and critics embraced Gesher, they published more and more profiles and interviews with the actors Israel (Sasha) Demidov, Igor Mirkurbanov, Yevgenya Dodina, and Natalya Voitulevich. The journalists represented these actors in a limited and stereotyped way, focusing mainly on immigration, absorption, and language acquisition. Yet, the mere presence of the immigrant actors in the mainstream media granted them a status of celebrity. It is an unusual status for immigrants. A penniless, incompetent, stuttering newcomer is hardly sexy, and does not make a good pop culture hero.

This is especially true in the Israel of the early 90s. In addition to all the minuses of immigrants' image, Soviet immigrants were seen in a particularly unfavorable light. Their Judaism constantly doubted, they were suspected in association with Russian mafia and prostitution.[2] The profiles of Gesher's stars reflect a struggle with these stereotypes and feed into them. The profiles put a defensive or apologetic emphasis on Judaism, and fixate on cultural or ethnic identity.

For instance, Alona Kimchi's article about Demidov and Mirkurbanov focuses on "the feeling of belonging" and "immigrant absorption" (1993). Aviva Zaltzman's (1992b) profile of Demidov privileges a story of his immigration over his work or other aspects of his life.

Some profiles attempt to present the "stars" in the ideologically correct light. Ruth Shapiro from *Maariv* writes: "In the cruel cold, in almost *halutzim* [pioneering, see Glossary] conditions, Gesher Theatre works on the rehearsals of *The Idiot* by Dostoevsky" (1993a). By comparing Gesher to *halutzim* Shapiro presents the theatre in a favorable light from the vantage point of Zionist ideology.

Probing the stereotype, Shapiro asks Yevgenya Dodina about her Judaism. Dodina says: "I don't look like it, but I am indeed a kosher Jew. My grandfather was a rabbi" (Shapiro 1993a). This response is complicit with the Israeli ideology of "the Jewish State." Both Shapiro's question and Dodina's answer aim to dispel doubts in the Judaism of Soviet immigrants.

Aeelet Shachar from *Hair* asks Igor Mirkurbanov the same question. Mirkurbanov responds: "I always felt genes of my grandfather, my mother's farther. I feel Jewish in a cultural sense, not religious." Shachar also emphasizes Mirkurbanov's desire to assimilate: "He does not have connection with a new Russian community in Israel...he wants to work for everyone, and especially for Israeli audiences" (1993). She uses other rhetorical devices as well, in order to improve Mirkurbanov's image. She titles her article: "Handsome Like Kevin Costner, Star Like Whitney Houston." This title gives Mirkurbanov the status and glamour of Hollywood stars, compensating for his position as an immigrant.

---

2 Indeed, at that time, some prostitutes were imported from Russia using fake documents. But the scope of this illegal activity was blown out of proportion by Israeli media.

In another interview, Igor Mirkurbanov gives a playful and indirect refusal to discuss his Judaism. A journalist reports: "In response to my not-so-discreet but unavoidable question, whether he is Jewish, he answers diplomatically that it seems to him that everyone is Jewish in the whole world, but not everyone is bold enough to admit it" (Shapiro 1993b). This response is ideologically resistant because Mirkurbanov refuses to answer the question in terms reflecting the mainstream Jewish-Israeli sensibility; and it is complicit because his reframing pays tribute to it.

In contrast, Natalya Voitulevich's portrayal focuses not on her ethnicity or religion, but on her sex-appeal. Emanuel Bar-Kedma's article in *Yediot Ahronot* is titled "Lolita and the Idiot" (1993). In the photographs, Natalya Voitulevich looks like an advertisement for Victoria Secret underwear: she is half-naked, in a seductive pose, with her lips promisingly opened. This representation feeds into a stereotype of a female Russian immigrant–blonde, beautiful, and sexually available.

The success of *The Idiot* made Gesher's actors into stars and exposed them to Israeli audiences. Israeli critics felt an existential need to categorize Gesher as either Israeli-Zionist or Russian-immigrant theatre. They either pronounced Gesher "an Israeli theatre in a full sense of the word" (Shohat 1994a). Or, alternatively, called it "a ghetto" (Shohat 1994b), "made-in-Russia theatre" (Milshtein 1993), and "an ensemble of new immigrants" (Weitz 1992). This trend continued throughout Gesher's history.

Yevgeny Arye was also represented in ethnic terms. For example, Sarit Fuks wrote about Arye:

> It's difficult not to describe Arye as a passionate Slavic man, a description that probably will annoy him. He is disgusted by an ethnic perspective on Gesher. He wants to be defined only by his art. Arye is an alien, almost an exile, in a non-idealistic and non-systematic theatre world in Israel and in the West. (Fuks 1995a)

Fuks was right–Arye, indeed, got annoyed with her "ethnic perspective." He rejected this representation and emphasized the universal value of his art. Ironically, in doing so he revealed his own ethnocentrism:

> I don't like when they say about us: those are immigrants. Our being *olim* does not define our work. We are not an ethnic dance group of Eskimos, when everything that is interesting about it is the fact that the dance is Eskimo. This is a very humiliating point of view. From the first day of founding Gesher we are trying to fight against it. (Fuks 1995a)

In Arye's argument, the Eskimo dance is at the bottom of cultural hierarchy. As such, it has an anthropological rather than artistic value. In contrast, Gesher's productions are at the top; they exemplify universal (read

European) art, and therefore Gesher's ethnic identity is not relevant to its artistic production. The journalists approached Gesher with yardsticks of Zionist ideology and ethnic stereotypes. In turn, Arye reciprocated with equal ethnocentrism.

According to cultural theorist Raymond Williams, culture can be defined as, first, "a general process of intellectual, spiritual, and aesthetic development"; second, as "a particular way of life, whether of a people, a period, a group, or humanity"; and third, as "the works and practices of intellectual and especially artistic activity" (1985, p. 90). In his statements, Arye relies mainly on definition of culture as a 'process of development', which allows for the colonial hierarchy to kick in.

Mimicry Turns into Menace: *Adam Resurrected*

After the incredible success with the Hebrew version of *The Idiot*, Gesher decided to push further in the direction of becoming a full-fledged "Israeli theatre." Katya Sosonsky explained that the theatre was responding to "an expectation that one day it will approach Israeli-Jewish material" (Litvik 1993b). Staging local plays was always a national priority in Israel. The theatres are even criticized for not mounting enough original Israeli drama (see, for instance, Tzipi Shohat's (1993a) review titled "Lots of Recycling and Few Original Plays").

What Gesher needed was a contemporary play by an Israeli playwright that deals with one of the major national topics, such as the foundation of Israel, national wars and conflicts, search for Israeli identity, issues of immigration, and the Holocaust. Gesher's theatre-makers were savvy enough to realize that as recent immigrants, they should limit their scope to topics that corresponded to their cultural background. This limitation ruled out the topics of Israeli history, wars, and identity. The topic of immigration was also out of the question since a production about immigration would only reinforce Gesher's stereotypical perception as "a theatre of immigrants." These limitations settled it: a new production had to be about the Holocaust.

By 1992, Gesher had an established relationship with the Israeli writer Yoram Kanuk, who became one of its most avid supporters ever since he saw *Rosencrantz and Guildenstern Are Dead.* He romanticized Gesher as "a theatre from the different world" (as quoted in Shohat 1993b). Yet, Kanuk also saw Gesher as a Zionist endeavor, a theatre which "contributes to the true definition of Zionism" (Kanuk 1991). Therefore, when Yevgeny Arye approached him in 1992 with an offer to dramatize his 1968 novel *Adam Ben Kelev* [Adam, Son of Dog], Kanuk was delighted.

This novel had been staged in Israel once before. An American-Israeli director Nola Chilton, famous for her docu-drama productions, staged a chapter of *Adam Resurrected* with the actors of Neve-Tzedek Theatre in 1983. Kanuk, though, felt that she freely changed the content of the novel and personalized it to an extent which made it difficult for the author to accept it (Shohat 1993b). But with Arye it was a different story. Because of Kanuk's admiration for Gesher's work, he trusted Arye with the novel.

The adaptation of the novel involved several linguistic transformations. A renowned Soviet playwright, Alexander Chervinsky, a fellow Russian-Jewish immigrant (to the US) and Arye's former collaborator, adapted the novel for the stage. He read Kanuk's novel in English, and wrote his adaptation in Russian. Further, Mark Ivanir, (who knew Russian) together with Yoram Kanuk and Miriam Yahil-Wax, translated the play into Hebrew.

The main character of the play, Adam Stein (Igor Mirkurbanov), is a former circus owner and a clown, whose routine was impersonating a dog. Under the Nazi regime, he, as Jew, is prohibited to own the circus. But when he ends up at the concentration camp, a "humane" Commandant Klein (Israel [Sasha] Demidov) lets Adam work as a dog-clown, entertaining the Jews (including Adam's own family) on their way to the gas chambers. Adam also lives like a dog, sharing his meals and lodging with Klein's German shepherd. Due to this arrangement Adam survives. Years later, in Israel, unable to forgive himself for letting his family die, Adam is going mad. He is committed to an asylum, founded by an eccentric American Jew Mrs. Seizling (Vladimir Halemsky). She donated a symbolic sum of six million dollars to build it, because she believes that God will appear to the mentally ill Holocaust survivors.

The audience pieces Adam Stein's story together from glimpses of memories going through his feverish mind. The play's narrative moves in leaps from the reality of the circus, to entertainment in a death camp, to the hospital ward. The associative non-linear plot and surreal imagery blurs borders between reality and nightmare, between God and an SS officer, between Nazi Germany in the 30s and Israel in the 60s. The show is based on these paradoxical metaphors. The overlap of the realities is illustrated by the casting. Demidov plays multiple roles: Commandant Klein, psychiatrist Dr. Gross, and God. Dodina plays the roles of Gretchen, Adam's wife, whom he entertained on her way to a gas chamber as well as Jenny, a cruel nurse at the hospital. The orderlies are simultaneously Nazi soldiers and cabaret performers. They wear surreal uniforms with the elements of sadomasochism and drag. The visual effects range from the spine-chilling scene of a naked woman who disappears into a wall of gas chamber smoke, to a poetic image of a cloud of blue balloons that float into a sky through a sudden opening in a roof. Intense colors dominate both sets and costumes: red curtains, black shining coats of Nazis, and white medical garb. Avi Benjamin's original score complements this visual imagery. Performed live by a group of musicians in striped uniforms, the music incorporates original German cabaret songs from the 30s and the 40s. As in the films *Cabaret* (1972) and *The Night Porter* (1974), the visual and music aesthetics of the production are imbued with the motifs of borderline sexual fantasy and erotic fascination with the aggressor.

The play is staged in a circus tent. The elements of the sets are mobile, everything and everybody is constantly in motion. The rail tracks cross the arena, letting a cabaret stage, a hospital bed, or a platform to roll in and out. The action takes place not only on these stages, but also on the trapeze, ropes, and a small stage high above the arena. The actors double as singers, acrobats, and circus performers.

The production *Adam Resurrected* echoed the renowned play *Ghetto* by Yehoshua Sobol about a Jewish theatre in the Vilna ghetto. Like *Ghetto*, Gesher's production used the device of metatheatre, creating theatre within the theatre (or, to be precise, within the circus). In this way, Arye developed the theme of the relationship between an artist and a coercive power (even if embodied in a charming patron) that he first posed in *Molière*.

The artistic approach to the Holocaust in the context of an absurd and cynical show allowed the theatre to face the genocide of Jewish people and disparage it. However, such approach also challenged the orthodox Israeli discourse of the Holocaust. In Israel, the Holocaust is singled out from the history of the Second World War and other genocides. Despite the passive political and military role pre-Israel Palestine played during the Holocaust, and a controversial attitude towards survivors in the early state of Israel,[3] today the Holocaust is framed as a central chapter in a national history and is an essential part of Israeli Jewish identity. The topic of the Holocaust is a permanent fixture of educational programs in schools, in youth movements, and in the media. It is perceived as a universal tragedy of the Jewish people and the epitome of persecution, which reaffirms an ultimate legitimacy of the state of Israel. Holocaust Remembrance Day (27th of the Hebrew month Nissan) is an Israeli national holiday.

---

3 Even though *yishuv* [Jewish settlement] activists helped to rescue the survivors after the war, and facilitated their illegal immigration to pre-Israel Palestine, the attitudes toward them ranged from sympathy and admiration to contempt and insult (Porat 1991).

There is an unspoken consensus in Israel that the society as a whole has not only a first-hand knowledge of the Holocaust, but also has ownership of the topic. Two factors contributed to this sentiment. First, after the war, over 150,000 survivors arrived in pre-Israel Palestine, constituting a considerable part of the population. Second, the six million Jews that perished in the Holocaust were endowed with a commemorative Israeli citizenship. Thus, Israel assumed the right to speak on their behalf and represent the dead in reparation agreements and other trials.

This ownership of the Holocaust set the standards for its representation. The figure of the survivor entered Israeli films, theatre productions, literature, and visual art, familiarizing the popular audiences with survivors' sensibility. Over time, the survivors' representation underwent a transformation. In the 40s and 50s, survivors were portrayed stereotypically as either passive figures led like 'sheep to the slaughter', or as heroic rebels.[4] Later, especially in the 80s and 90s, their representation gained complexity, and lost its clear moral judgment. But even then, the tendency was to associate the Holocaust with "heroism," or to structure the narrative as "a modern morality play" (Feingold 1992), preferring a realistic style as the appropriate means for describing violence and devastation.[5]

The Israeli assumed monopoly over the topic of the Holocaust delegitimizes the attempts of cultural Others to deal with the topic. This situation presented a problem for Gesher. When Arye staged *The Idiot,* Israeli critics presumed his knowledge of Russian culture and literature, and accepted his stage interpretation as trustworthy. Gesher's Russian cultural identity worked in their favor. In contrast, the Holocaust was not perceived as a part of Gesher's cultural capital. The theatre's choice to stage *Adam Resurrected* raised questions about its cultural identity in conjunction with its right to represent the Holocaust. The critics asked: as newcomers to Israel and as Soviet immigrants, are they competent enough to deal with the topic that is at the roots of Israeli national identity?

As I mentioned before, the earlier reviews (such as Avigal 1991) expressed an expectation that Gesher would stage local Israeli plays and thereby perform an act of mimicry. Yet, when Gesher actually responded to this expectation and staged a local play on local topic, the mimicry turned menacing.

---

4 For more background on representation of Holocaust survivors in Israeli art see Feingold 1992; Manor 1999; Gertz 1999.

5 Productions of Dudi Ma'ayan's theatre group are noticeable exceptions from this convention. Both *Abeit Macht Frei in Teutland Europa* (1992) and *Second Generation's Memories in The Old City* (1988) deal with the Holocaust offering new and daring theatrical language.

The topic of the Holocaust was not new for Gesher theatre-makers. In the former Soviet Union, the Second World War and its atrocities were also an important part of cultural and historical heritage. Yet, given the Israeli monopoly over the subject, it was safer for Gesher to have on their side a more experienced partner with long-term Israeli tenure. Therefore, originally, Gesher planned to co-produce the play with the Cameri, a well established public theatre in Tel Aviv. Israeli critics greeted this news enthusiastically, as they felt that Gesher would make a smooth transition to the Israeli topic: "Gesher and Cameri theatres will mount a co-production based on *Adam Resurrected* by Yoram Kanuk. They hope that this is a way to integrate into Israeli theatre" (Shohat 1992). The co-production meant that Gesher would not claim a mandate on local sensitivities, but rather would rely on Cameri for finding the right approach. However, the plans changed, and Gesher, sponsored by the Vienna Theatre Festival, started rehearsing the production on its own.

Arye's decision to stage the play as a circus performance posed several challenges. First, none of the Gesher actors had any experience as circus performers. They had to learn to walk on a rope, to swing on a trapeze, to act as clowns and cabaret singers, while learning their parts in Russian, German (the lyrics of cabaret songs), and later, Hebrew. Luckily, a Russian circus was on tour in Israel at that time, and its troupe members helped Gesher with the training. Second, Gesher had to find and purchase a circus tent—an unusual commodity. The tent was ordered from South Africa. It was delivered to Israel later than expected, which put Gesher into a crisis. Later, Arye recalls:

> The tent was two weeks late—a terrible story—and we had to finish everything in a week. We put it in the Hayarkon Park [in Northern Tel Aviv], in an open space. The heat was atrocious, just atrocious. And we worked on the production in order to finish it for Vienna. And we had to take a tent with us too (later this tent traveled around half the globe with us). We had to calculate everything precisely, with the trapeze [movement], otherwise an actor could not move from scene to scene. (Arye 2003)

Adam Resurrected premiered in Vienna on June 9, 1993 (performed in Russian). The premiere was accompanied by numerous organizational and technical problems:

> The opening in Vienna was horrific. In general, the fate of this production at the beginning was terrible. We came to Vienna, and they put our tent in a spot where two major highways intersect. The noise was awful. In the whole city there was not a single poster [advertising Gesher]. During the rehearsals there, Igor [Mirkurbanov] broke his toe walking on a rope. (Arye 2003)

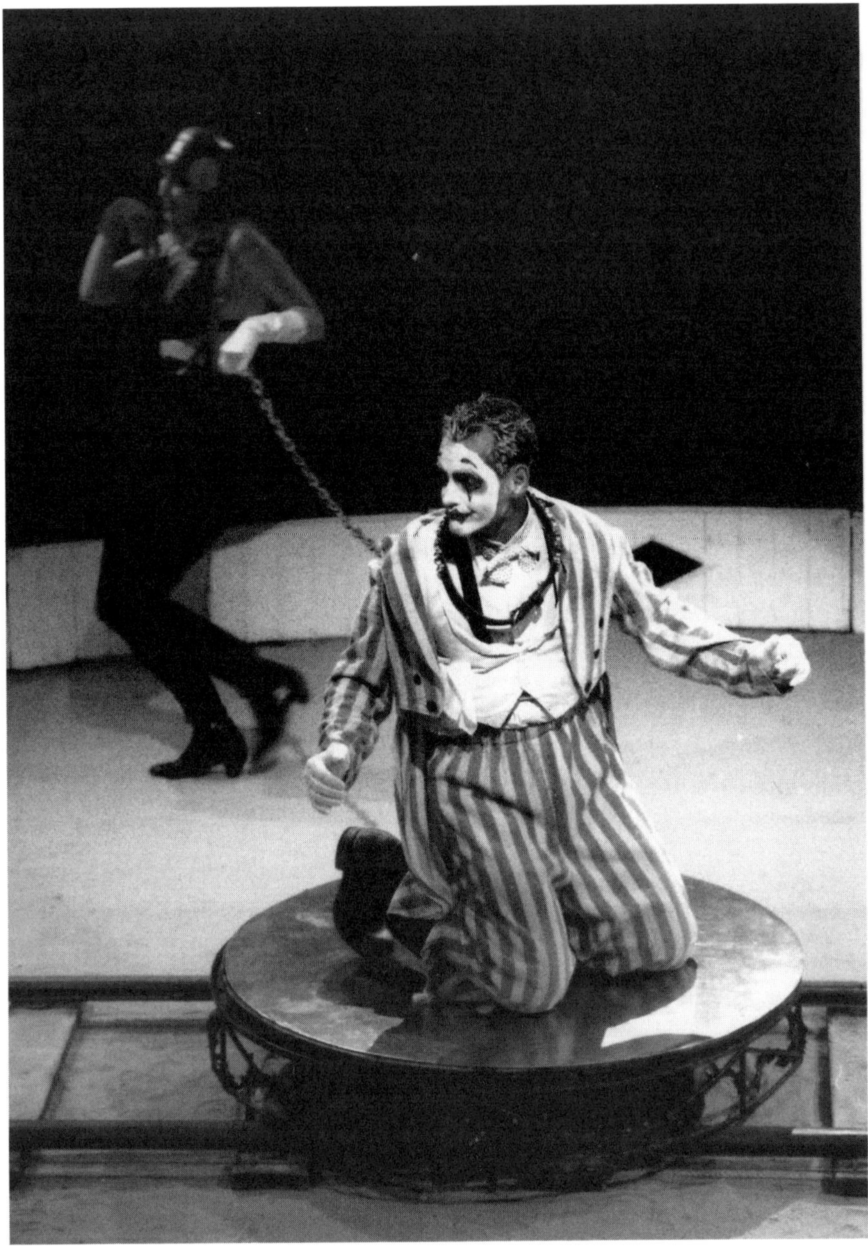

Figure 4: *Adam Resurrected.* Igor Mirkurbanov as Adam Stein and Ruth (Lilian) Heilovsky as SS soldier/cabaret singer *(Courtesy of Gesher Theatre)*

The festival failed to promote Gesher to the audiences, and even those who came reacted to the show uneasily: "The first night there were 20 people in the audience, maybe less (the tent sits 350). Half of them, when Sasha [Demidov] came out in his SS uniform, got up and left" (Arye 2003). Due to Mirkurbanov's injury and box-office failure the number of performances was cut. The only positive aspect of this ordeal was that representatives of the *Welt in Basel* festival attended the performance in Vienna. They liked it and immediately invited Gesher to take part in their festival in September 1993.

In Basel, the production was finally appreciated. Critics admired every aspect of the performance: "*Adam Resurrected* is a theatrical super-achievement in *Welt in Basel*...an impressive string of scenes. The Holocaust: to remember and to overcome" (Richard 1993).

After such a conflicted reception abroad, in Vienna and Basel, the Israeli critics and audiences were holding their breath for the Hebrew premiere. Meanwhile, Gesher continued to hone the production. The purpose was to tailor the Hebrew version for Tel Aviv audiences. Originally, the performance lasted five hours. After the Vienna premiere, it was shortened. After Basel, it was shortened even more to run three-and-a-half hours. Arye had to give up some of his favorite scenes, but Gesher continued working.

Numerous previews preceded the Hebrew premiere. For the critics the most significant factor was that *Adam Resurrected* was Gesher's first meeting with original Israeli material. Already in the previews, critics expressed concern with Gesher's interpretation of the topic of the Holocaust: "There is something in the way in which Gesher is dealing with this material, that causes the feeling that the theatre professionals who grew up in Israel, would not dare to touch upon the Holocaust in this way" (Lubits 1993). Singling out the Gesher theatre-makers for their cultural identity, critics simultaneously cheered Gesher's choice of topic and questioned the means of their artistic expression.

A different kind of preview was the documentary *Mishpahat Gesher* [Gesher Family] directed by Boris Mafzir, a Russian-born Israeli filmmaker. *Gesher Family* premiered in June 1993 in Tel Aviv (simultaneously with the Vienna premiere of *Adam Resurrected*) and later was broadcasted on Israeli television. The film documents the rehearsals of *Adam Resurrected*, interviews with Gesher company members, as well as with several Israeli officials, critics, and directors. The film celebrates Gesher members' work and their successful absorption as new immigrants. Both the voices of opposition to Gesher, and support for it, reaffirm traditional Zionist values. An Israeli theatre director Yosi Alphi, antagonistic to Gesher, insists on the necessity of assimilation: "This theatre will be swallowed, like other theatres that came from outside were swallowed." Whereas sympathetic Yoram Kanuk compares Gesher to the Zionist pioneers: "They work like crazy, they are obsessed with an idea... it is their essence and part of their history, and it is good, I like it. Sixty years ago kibbutzim were created like that [with the same dedication]."

The hegemonic Zionist position of the film is also realized through its cinematic language. For example, in one scene the Gesher actors go on tour to a kibbutz. After the performance they walk on the green rolling hills, covered with blooming poppies. The hills fill almost the entire screen, creating the illusion that they stretch out to the horizon. This effect is a visual metaphor representing the Gesher actors as new Israelis proudly "walking through the fields"[6] in their own land. This "optimistic geography" is loaded with ideological meanings. As Nurith Gertz explains in her analysis of the theme of earth in Israeli cinema: "Many elements in Zionist ideology are associated with space–the transition from Diaspora to the Land of Israel, from ghetto to open space, from 'ethereal existence' to a life rooted in the soil" (1999, p. 182). The scene embodies the transformation of passive Jews into active Hebrews acquiring, in Gertz's terms, "the identity of people who can circulate in their landscape fearlessly and dominate it with their legs and eyes" (1999, p. 183).

In the next scene, a group of actors encounter bushes of cactus, in Hebrew–*sabra*, a plant of considerable cultural weight. According to Israeli cliché, native Israelis are like *sabra* in being prickly on the outside and sweet on the inside. In this scene Shaul Alias, an Israeli troupe member, is picking and peeling cactus fruit for the Gesher actors, who devour it with surplus enjoyment. This ritualized eating reaffirms their induction into a new society. The antiquated ideological imagery of the film shows how deeply Zionist cultural myths are engrained in the pop cultural texts.

This was a setup for the premiere of *Adam Resurrected* in Israel. The Hebrew premiere took place on October 26, 1993. Gesher's circus tent was put on the parking lot of the Susan Dalal cultural center in Tel Aviv. As usual with Gesher, this location happened to be symbolic. The center occupies the same building where Nola Chilton staged the previous theatrical version of *Adam Resurrected.*

Once again, the establishment jumped on the opportunity to showcase its support for Soviet immigrants and their theatre. Politicians and public figures: Ezer and Rauma Veitzman, Leah Rabin, Yair and Shulamit Tzaban, Roni and Elisheva Milo, came to the premiere, reported *Yediot Ahronot* ("Shlomo lahat" 1993). The local royal couple, Shlomo (Chich) Lahat, the mayor of Tel Aviv,

6 My allusion here refers to an Israeli cult play by Moshe Shamir *Hu halah besadot* [He walked through the fields] staged by Cameri theatre (1948) and made into a film by Yossef Millo (1967). Its plot deals with the foundation of Israel.

and his wife Ziva, both supporters and fans of the theatre, hosted a post-premiere dinner for Gesher's actors at the Hilton Hotel. *Maariv* reported: "Our social elites know the Russian actors by their first names, follow up on them, take a personal care of them. There was a Zionist loving feeling [during the dinner], absorbing and encouraging *aliyah*" ("Festival chich veziva..." 1993). It is interesting that even this seemingly innocuous social event received an ideological framing. As we see, in addition to reportage of menu and outfits, the gossip columns in Israel put a Zionist spin to the high-society glamour.

All major newspapers reviewed the premiere of *Adam Resurrected*. The critics paid tribute to the significance of the material choice. Some announced Gesher's complete integration: "With its production *Adam Resurrected* Gesher finally crossed the bridge between its Russian origins and its announced goal—integration into Israeli theatre" (Nagid 1993b). Other reviewers were conflicted. They simultaneously welcomed Gesher's turn to the original Israeli material, and expressed doubts about Gesher's ability to cope with it. A review in *Hadashot* was ironic: "After they established their status and name, members of the Russian theatre Gesher seem to think that they are ready to cope with the original Israeli material" (Habim 1993). A review in the magazine *Haulam Hazeh* seconded this doubled message (Litvik 1993b).

The critics assumed that the Holocaust was a totally new topic for Gesher company members; as if by having their roots in the Soviet Union, the immigrants did not have any exposure to this chapter of history, and that only in Israel did they learn about it for the first time. For that reason, the reviews made a point of emphasizing Gesher's preparation for the production, i.e., attending museums, reading literature and watching films on the Holocaust (see, for instance, Lavi 1993; Raisman 1993).

The critics' conflicted position in respect to Gesher's choice of material is evident in their questions to the Gesher actors and their director. Critics ask Arye about his Jewish identity, his exposure to the Holocaust, and his knowledge of it. Forced to demonstrate the appropriate credentials, Arye sounds defensive: "We are Jews to the same extent" (Fuks 1995a). Referring to family losses during the Holocaust, Arye insists: "I know this topic not only from books and films" (Lubits 1993). He feels that "it is important to explain to *sabras* that they don't have a monopoly over the topic of the Holocaust" (Lubits 1993).

Adam Resurrected got mixed responses. The main reason for mixed responses was the 'not quite' Israeli cultural identity of the theatre-makers. Both the public and critics felt conflicted about the right of Gesher to represent the Holocaust. But the critics also were confused by its unorthodox theatrical language. Built on grotesque, macabre humor, and cabaret aesthetics, the theatrical language of *Adam Resurrected* was transgressive, and as such posed a challenge to the Israeli discourse on the Holocaust.

Critics fell into two camps: the minority who accepted the production, and the majority who opposed it. In the first camp only one critic, Eliakim Yaron from *Maariv* fully accepted the directorial concept, the visual imagery, and the work of the ensemble: "The show, staged at the circus tent, is an all-encompassing stage experience...original, wonderful, and spine-chilling" (Yaron 1993b).

Critic Amir Orion from the local newspaper *Hair* also loved the production. However, he gave an alternative interpretation to the show: "It is a mistake to think that they [Gesher's actors] processed Yoram Kanuk's book and produced a show about the Holocaust. They used Kanuk in order to give expression to the personal intimate Holocaust of an artist, who turns into a dog-man in the totalitarian regime" (Orion 1993b). According to Orion, this interpretation of the play stemmed from the cultural reality familiar to the Gesher actors. He presents this interpretation in the context of a supportive review of Gesher's work. And yet, in the disguise of cultural sensitivity, Orion's reading of the production denies Gesher's right to represent the Holocaust. The critic refuses to accept that Gesher's show is about the Jewish Catastrophe, since according to him it is too remote from the actors' experience. Instead, Orion reads *Adam Resurrected* as a story of an artist under the Soviet dictatorship.

All sixteen reviews by critics in the second camp praised the production values of the performance (to varying degrees), especially the superb acting and the coordinated work of the ensemble, but disapproved of the treatment of the Holocaust topic. Gesher's representation of the Holocaust as an absurd and macabre show was deeply disturbing for them.[7]

According to Haim Nagid from *Davar*, the production is unsuccessful because the play violates the dramatic conventions of a linear conflict-based plot. However, what he really objects to is the representation of the Holocaust in a circus: "[Gesher's actors] carry on talking about conflicts, characters, actions, and plots, but what we see in front of us is not realization of these conflicts, but a circus show accompanied by screaming music" (1993b). Nagid reduces description of the visual aspects of the production to "stage pyrotechnics." Even though he admires the acting of Mirkurbanov, Demidov, and Dodina, he claims that Adam's story gets lost in the effects.

---

7 Similar critique addressed Roberto Benigni's film *Life is Beautiful* (1997) that gives an unusual playful portrayal of the Holocaust.

Shosh Weitz has a similar critique. Even though she recognizes the high production values of the show, she also critiques it as "a weak, trivial, and confused play that leaves the taste of failure" (1993b). Weitz realizes that the theatrical metaphor allowed Arye to "move freely between tragic and grotesque, and to insert the wonderfully performed scenes of circus and cabaret into images that hit a nerve" (1993b). And yet, her conclusion is that "there is feeling of lack of clarity in respect to the message of the production, which gets lost in the broad theatrical grandeur" (1993b).

Like Weitz, Michael Handelsaltz gives Gesher credit for high production values, (staging, acting, design, choreography) but refuses to accept the show. His critique refers mostly to the Holocaust representation, which defies the customary norms of "good taste." Handelsaltz writes: "...the concentration camp is represented boldly, by exploiting nakedness and smoke to an extent that reflects an audacious attempt to turn death into colorful kitsch" (1993b). He further accuses the theatre-makers of failure to deal with the topic of the Holocaust with sensitivity:

> In the most cases the painful human experience [of coping with the Holocaust] is reduced to demonstration of cold, loud, and superficial virtuosity, which voids the human pain, makes it empty of subjectivity, discounts it to cheap bold symbols, used without much sensitivity....The pain turns into screaming, the suffering into circus, raping audiences to be impressed and astonished, but without ability to be moved and to experience pain. Maybe it's an impressive theatre, but it is exactly because of the topic that this show is so infuriating. It aims to cope with one of the most difficult and painful topics in history—the Holocaust—in a way, which arouses respect to the theatrical work, but not to the sensitivity of the theatre-makers to the greatness of the topic and its pain. (Handelsaltz 1993b)

According to Handelsaltz, the professionalism of the actors and producers worked against them. Gesher's theatre-makers do not have the understanding of the topic presumably possessed by local audiences. Therefore, the only alternative they have is demonstrating their artistic virtuosity. In his later article, Handelsaltz directly attributes the perceived flaws of the production to cultural background: Gesher's staging of "non-Russian material" revealed their problematic "attitude to the Holocaust, which for them is a foreign, new, and interesting topic" (1994a). Handelsaltz sounds like a school principal telling off the misbehaved pupils for their "attitude."

Shosh Raisman from *Tel Aviv* also writes her review from the position of the privilege to define the "right" approach to the Holocaust and its representation. Using a collective pronoun "we," she speaks not just for herself, but rather for all Israelis—copyright-holders on the topic:

> ...we would not be able to mount such a show on stage. The feeling of guilt wouldn't allow us. They [Gesher's theatre-makers] produced a show, a circus, a cabaret, [with] gas ovens and striped pajamas. And it was almost pleasant to me to feel their hand free from all sorts of limitations, feelings, and taboos... Later I read that in preparation for this production they visited *Yad-Va-Shem* [the Holocaust museum in Jerusalem], read books, and saw movies on the subject. How naïve it looks from this [Israeli] side. How innocent, devoid of pain and guilt. (Raisman 1993)

Raisman is condescending to Gesher's theatre-makers, whose knowledge comes from "books and movies," and is not innate, like hers. Their representation of the Holocaust also lacks the "right" assortment of feelings, which she expects from anyone coping with the topic, and which for her devalues their work. Her denigrating tone portrays Gesher's theatre-makers as clueless novices to the topic. This attitude is colonial, as the writer sees Gesher as "embodying an earlier stage of individual human or broad cultural development" (Shohat and Stam 1998, p. 28), and thus placed low in her cultural hierarchy.

Shosh Avigal announced that, "something basic is damaged," in the production, which is no more than "the march of effects" (1993b). Like Nagid and Weitz, Avigal claims that the novel in its stage adaptation does not correspond to the dramatic conventions. Like Handelsaltz, Avigal aims her main argument at the unorthodox representation of the Holocaust by cultural Others: "The images [on stage] stem from virtuosity of the performers instead of pain...the circus of the nightmares turns mainly into an impressive demonstration of effects and several images imprinted in the memory" (1993c). Both audio and visual effects are kitsch that "cross the borders of good taste, or function as effects for the sake of effects."

In her conclusion, Avigal uses the same reprimanding tone of a school principal that Handelsaltz favors: "It's worth it for the ensemble itself to do some serious homework towards their next coping with the material that did not come together with them from Russia" (1993c). Avigal reveals a true source of her (and probably other critics') discontent with the production. The Gesher theatre-makers do not have permission from the Israeli critics to represent the Holocaust. They are not Israeli enough to hold stocks in the Holocaust cultural capital. Yet, Avigal softens her tone towards the end: "And maybe time will just do its work. The time and the *yam-tichoniut* [mediterranianism]" (1993c). Her term *mediterranianism* refers to distinct geo-cultural Israeli sensibility, which is somehow more authentic in representation of the Holocaust than diasporic (Russian in this case) sensibility. In her review, Avigal expresses hope that the healing influence of the Levant, with time will force the ideologically questionable Russianness out of Gesher. A xenophobic grimace was hiding behind the reproving scowl.

In a later article, an Israeli theatre researcher Shimon Levy explains that the critical response to *Adam Resurrected* was negative because of "the 'Russian' perspective, which is alien to the sense of the Holocaust that prevails among Israelis" (Levy 1998, p. 89). However, he does not find disturbing the fact that Gesher's interpretation of the topic was rejected essentially because of "foreign" cultural identity of its creators. In this situation, Israeli critics, and even a theatre researcher, reject a different artistic approach to the topic of the Holocaust and judge it as incompetent and even unethical.

Arye was aware of both the sensitivity of the topic and the controversy of his artistic approach. He explained to a journalist: "It is so horrible to see again people in Germany or Russia with swastikas on their sleeves. When I see it today, after everything what happened, I have to laugh. This is a farce. But for people who were involved in what happened, it's a tragedy. And this is...a complexity of life itself" (Milshtein 1993). Arye was also concerned with the reaction of the Holocaust survivors to his interpretation of the topic:

> I was afraid. When the Holocaust survivors came to the show, what would they say? I was really tense. But they accepted [the production] really well. Almost without exception. What I mean is that they accepted the strange rules of the game [that we offered them in *Adam Resurrected*]. (Arye 2003)

In October 1994, Gesher went on an extensive tour to Germany with *Adam Resurrected*. It was an unconditional success: all the shows were sold out, and reviews appeared in the major newspapers and on several channels of German television. *Frankfurter Rundshau* wrote: "This is a production of highest voltage. Stylistically sharp, it grates on our ears and pierces the minds. The strongly visual and brilliantly directed scenes make the audience shudder" (Reinecke 1994). *Berliner Morgenpost* pronounced: "Heart-rending nightmare, with its tragic and poetic moments....Thanks to superb acting of the whole company and Arye's mise en scène, the performance makes an exceptionally strong impression" (Merten 1994).[8] However, the German Jewish community, like Israeli critics, reacted to the show "with mixed feelings" and decided not to include it into an upcoming week of Israeli culture (Schlosser 1994). In contrast, the Russian-Jewish immigrants in Germany received the production warmly.

---

8 In this context it is reasonable to ask whether this reaction is political as well. Ilene Winkler, a Jewish-American theatre director who worked in Germany for 29 years argues that it is feasible for a Jewish-Israeli production dealing with the topic of the Holocaust to receive a negative response in Germany because German critics usually focus their criticism on artistic aspects of the production regardless of topic (I. Winckler, personal communication, October 21, 2002). Based on her judgment, Gesher was received well due to artistic and not political reasons.

Arye could not help being disappointed with the reaction of the Israeli critics, especially in comparison to German, Austrian, and Swiss reviewers who fully accepted the production and appreciated its unorthodox approach to the Holocaust. Arye realized that *Adam Resurrected* was poorly received in Israel because of the cultural identity of the theatre-makers. In an interview, he bitterly summed up the Israeli critical response to *Adam*: "One of the critics wrote that Gesher are people who came from outside, they are not capable of having the same feelings about the Holocaust that we—the Israelis—have, and that is why the show does not succeed to touch us" (Fuks 1995a). He also objected to the patronizing position of the critics "like a teacher towards the student" (Fuks 1995a). The disparate critical reception of *Adam Resurrected* in Israel and abroad, especially in Germany, became the first instance of Arye's increasing disillusionment with Israeli theatre criticism. In an interview with a critic, Arye complained that the lack of serious analysis of his work makes him feel that he "lives in a vacuum" (Fuks 1995a).

Despite the mixed critical reception, the Culture Administration of the Tel Aviv municipality awarded Arye with a Gotlib and Hana Rosenblum Prize in the areas of art, theatre, and performance for "unique theatrical creation." *Adam Resurrected* also did extremely well with audiences: by 2001 it was performed 188 times (145 in Hebrew, 43 in Russian). It is mounted in Tel Aviv every year around the Holocaust Day. In July 1998, the production was performed both in Russian and in Hebrew at the Lincoln Center Festival in New York,[9] where it got excellent critical and audience reception (Robinson 1998; Barnes 1998b).

Adam Resurrected has had an unusual reception trajectory. It is, as Arye defined it, "a steadily increasing success" (2003). Off to a shaky start, the production has been growing more and more successful with each year. As of this writing, it is still part of the theatre's repertoire, and is still invited to festivals around the world.

After the Israeli premiere of *Adam Resurrected*, Gesher attracted the attention of another Israeli filmmaker Lihi Hanoch. She directed a semi-feature semi-documentary film about Gesher titled *Adam Circus* (1993). The film consists of a series of impressionistic scenes based on the Gesher actors' life and work. The actors "play" themselves, and the plots are based on the real events, but are clearly staged and highly stylized. Each scene is filmed in a

9 Gesher performed in New York in both Russian and Hebrew for two reasons. First, Gesher used its bilingualism as a marketing tool to advertise its uniqueness. Second, New York has large Russian-speaking and Hebrew-speaking communities. Gesher's performances in both Russian and Hebrew gave these audiences an opportunity to see the production in their preferred language.

single dominant color: Nelly Gosheva's drama over relatives left behind in Moscow is in green, Ruth (Lilian) Heilovsky's conflict with a teenage son is in orange. Israel (Sasha) Demidov's conversation with a *yeshiva* [an orthodox religious school] student is in black and white. The film presents a beatific refined picture of the immigrant actors, romanticizing dramas and events in their lives. Unlike *Gesher Family*, *Adam Circus* deviates from the hegemonic Zionist narrative. Proselytizing rhetoric of 'successful absorption', 'integration into new society', or 'becoming proud Israelis', is not part of the film. Like *Gesher Family*, *Adam Circus* was broadcasted on Israeli television, and still remains the only film about Gesher that does not speak in the language of the Zionist ideology. In 1998, it was screened at the theatre festival at Lincoln Center in New York, where Gesher performed *Adam Resurrected*.

Overall, few Israeli reviewers accepted *Adam Resurrected*. Even if their reviews praised the high production values of the show, they actively disapproved of Gesher's treatment of the Holocaust. What was at stake in this reception was Gesher's right to represent the topic. The critics could not let Gesher represent the Holocaust in a way that challenges local conventions. Reacting to this challenge, critics became gatekeepers.

It is in the reception of *Adam Resurrected* that the desired mimicry turns to menace for the first time. In staging Israeli play dealing with the core national topic, Gesher performed an act of mimicry and became 'almost' Israeli. But it is in this situation when the colonial subject mimics the colonizer, and becomes 'almost the same', that the mimicry turns menacing. The threat of mockery is so great that desire for the 'same Other' is withdrawn, and the colonial order needs to be restored immediately. The negative reception of *Adam Resurrected* by Israeli critics was activated by the defensive mechanisms of colonial dominance.

Rosencrantz and Guildenstern Are Dead Again

Despite the mixed reception of *Adam Resurrected*, the year 1994 started well for Gesher (see Table 1). Its budget grew to almost 7 million NIS, of which over 5 million came from public subsidies (still much lower than budgets of other public theatres). And the housing problem that Gesher faced for so long was resolved. Gesher acquired its own performance space, a converted warehouse in the old Arab port of Jaffa, at 15 Luis Paster Street. Gesher's theatre members nicknamed it *hangar* (Hebrew for warehouse). The lease was signed at the end of February 1994, and already by the end of March Gesher had renovated the building. At that time, Gesher's budget did not allow them to hire a professional construction crew; therefore, the Gesher staff accomplished the entire project themselves. They worked day and night, hurrying to finish before the next premiere. The renovation was completed with minimal cost 600,000 NIS (Shohat 1994a). The great effort paid off. As Maltzev described, the hall fit the theatre like a glove, "It was a wonderful hall...a unique combination of audience hall and stage: the hall was intimate, only 400 seats, with the feeling of proportion, with the sense that you are alone in the audience" (2001).

This location was planned as a temporary one, until a renovation of the building at 4 Nachmani Street would be completed. However, the hall at Nachmani was never fully renovated, and the theatre inhabited the *hangar* for four long years. This space, as Maltzev described, was a perfect fit for Gesher's performances; yet, it was not big enough to house offices and rehearsal space. The hall also had technical limitations, it had no stage tower, and no space behind the stage for set assemblage. Therefore, Gesher continued to use the old building on Nachmani Street as an office and a rehearsal space.

The move to Jaffa coincided with the three-year anniversary of Gesher. To celebrate both events, Gesher produced a Hebrew version of *Rosencrantz and Guildenstern Are Dead*, the production that once served as its calling card. Miriam Yahil-Wax translated the play. Symbolically, the premiere took place on April 20, the same day as three years before.

The celebration became a showcase of the establishment's support for Gesher. Politicians and public figures delivered celebratory speeches. The Prime Minister Yitzhak Rabin said that the enthusiasm of the Gesher company reminded him of the days of the founding of the state of Israel (Weitz 1994a). The Minister of Education and Culture Shulamit Aloni not only nominated Gesher as the best theatre in Israel, but also called upon the rest of the Israeli theatres to "set Gesher as an example" of collective spirit and ensemble work (Handelsaltz 1994a).

The company grew, and by 1994 included 50 members: 9 people in administration and management, 20 actors, and 21 in technical support (Riskin 2001). The changes were not only quantitative, but also qualitative. Yevgeny Terletsky temporarily left the theatre (he returned later), and the part of Guildenstern became vacant. Dror Keren, an Israeli actor, was hired to fill in the void. Officially, it was the first time that an Israeli actor became part of the troupe. Technically, Dror Keren was not the first Israeli actor in Gesher. In 1991–93 Shaul Alias was part of the troupe. But he was not an exemplary *sabra*, and Gesher never advertised his membership in the troupe. Dror Keren was a promising young actor, who played one of the main parts.

Conventionally attractive and successful, he was also a perfect candidate for the role of "first Israeli actor at Gesher."

Indeed, Keren's hire provoked a great deal of media interest. Haim Nagid wrote: "Keren's successful integration into the company proves that creating an ensemble is not a monopoly of the Russian immigrants, but a result of professional work" (1994a). Arye was quoted as saying: "We are not an encapsulated Russian enterprise. We are happy to welcome Israeli talents to the company, and Dror Keren is a real talent" (Ohed 1994). Around the same time, Arye announced that in the next season Israeli director Hanan Shnir would join Gesher as a visiting director (Shohat 1994a). This promise (never to be delivered, as it turned out later) reinforced the message that "Gesher's hermetic walls came down" (Shohat 1994a).

With the introduction of Israeli actors, first Dror Keren, and later others, the accent played an important role in casting decisions. Thus, in the Hebrew version of *Rosencrantz and Guildenstern Are Dead*, the roles of Ros and Guil were performed by Keren Dror and Mark Ivanir, the only two actors who spoke Hebrew without a Russian accent. Since these two characters are set aside from the rest, their different accents played into the plot. The casting took their accents into account.

The reception of the Hebrew version of *Rosencrantz and Guildenstern Are Dead* was overwhelmingly positive. Most reviewers admired the show as much as its previous incarnation, and nominated it "one of the best shows today on a Hebrew stage" (Nagid 1994a). Critics interpreted Gesher's remake of their first show in Hebrew as reaching a certain finish line—"closing the circle" (Ohed 1994; Yaron 1994a). As usual, the reviewers praised the acting and ensemble work (Nagid 1994b), especially "the chemistry" between Ivanir and Keren (Sofer 1994; Yaron 1994a). Critics also noted the acting of Igor Mirkurbanov and Boris Achanov, who took turns performing the part of the Player. Arye's directorial concept and his work with the ensemble were also highly regarded (Nagid 1994a). Critics emphasized that Gesher is a non-commercial venue: "It is the only Israeli theatre now that has a permanent ensemble and works as a company, and not as a privately-owned show-business" (Weitz 1994a). Despite this rave reception of the Hebrew version, the Russian version of *Rosencrantz and Guildenstern Are Dead* was more successful with the audiences. Out of 139 performances, 80 were in Russian and 59 in Hebrew.

Not surprisingly, Gesher's cultural identity came into play even in this overall positive reception. Shosh Weitz (1994a) interpreted subtle allusions to the Israeli reality found in the productions as pointless "gimmick." Such allusions would be perfectly acceptable in a production by any other Israeli theatre except Gesher. According to Weitz, the contemporary translation as well as the Israeli identities of Keren and Ivanir, gave the production an "Israeli-modern" taste, which was inappropriate for Gesher.

Other Israeli critics started to get upset with the newly established high status of Gesher. The defensive reaction, which emerged for the first time in the reception of *Adam Resurrected*, came to the full expression in the reviews by Michael Handelsaltz and Sarit Fuks. The notorious statement that Shulamit Aloni made at the premiere (inviting Israeli theatres to set Gesher as an example) turned out to be a major faux pas. It offended the majority of theatre-makers in Israel, who deemed a Soviet immigrants' theatre unworthy to be their ideal. As Handelsaltz puts it: "[Aloni] preferred to insult all of Israeli theatre by pouring praises over the heads of Gesher Theatre" (1994a).

Handelsaltz's review of the premiere, filled with obscure warnings, bore xenophobic overtones: "If there was somebody at the Gesher company, whose head wasn't spinning from vodka [pouring] at the three-year anniversary celebration, I hope that he would know that it's time to start worrying" (1994a). The reason for worry is that Gesher had turned into "the apple of the eye of the cultural establishment," and because, according to Handelsaltz's logic, "from this peak, they can only go down, if they are not careful." As Handelsaltz frowns at Gesher's laurels, his warning turns into a threat.

Handelsaltz found problems in the production as well. He criticized the actors' language proficiency as well as casting of Keren and Ivanir as Ros and Guil. This casting did not fit Handelsaltz's interpretation of these characters as new immigrants in Israel. Curiously, instead of reconsidering his reading of a show, Handelsaltz chose to disapprove of casting decisions.

But Handelsaltz's main point is that Gesher is not equipped to stage non-Russian drama in Hebrew: "It's difficult to believe that Gesher's actors are able to (or want to) to render all the complexity of this play, and it does not really interest the director Yevgeny Arye either" (1994a). He is essentially saying that Gesher's theatre-makers have an inferior understanding of the play. In this statement Handelsaltz's xenophobic attitudes come to full realization. He concludes: "[Gesher's actors] made a brave and important step when they all went to act in Hebrew, and it gives them stylistic unity, and saves them from complaints about accent and "music of language"—but they did not invent the theatre" (1994a). Handelsaltz wants Gesher Theatre to know its place. He states that Gesher's most important characteristic is its transition into Hebrew. This statement reduces the theatre to an ideological agent. Time and again, an Israeli critic asserts himself as a gatekeeper, siding with the hegemonic ideology.

Handelsaltz's article was so malicious that it provoked a response from an audience member, who wrote in his letter to the newspaper, "The article exudes fumes of envy and even xenophobia" (Avrahams 1994).

Alongside with Handelsaltz, Sarit Fuks from *Maariv* expresses concern with Gesher's success. The double figures of mimicry and menace are lurking in the lines of Fuks's article. She asks: "Did we bring them [Gesher's theatre-makers] too close to our hearts?" Her question projects fear of being displaced from a comfortable position of a colonizer. Now it is time to push the unruly subjects away, and to restore the order of colonial subjugation. Fuks dubs Gesher "the darling of the nation, a light beam in the Levant," mocking its enthusiastic reception presenting Gesher as heirs to European cultural tradition. To instantiate Gesher's difference, she insists that Gesher's production demonstrates "a severance of the Russian company" (1994) presumably from its Israeli environment.

Like Handelsaltz, she thinks that the previous version of *Rosencrantz and Guildenstern Are Dead* was a response to the Gesher actors' immigration, their foreignness, and their "horrible misery" (Fuks 1994). Now, that the theatre turned out to be successful, Fuks is visibly dismayed. Gesher's success, according to her, stands in the way of its artistic production: the Gesher actors strive to "recreate the lost spontaneity" and "try to fit the local rhythm." She suggests, "Maybe this land of *hamsin* [a hot wind from the desert—quintessentially 'Israeli' weather] and Israeli democracy harm Gesher" (1994). Once she has effectively demonstrated Gesher's difference, Fuks arrives to her final trumpet: "We need Gesher, a wonderful theatre, for the sake of beauty, grace, and culture. But it is its [Gesher's] responsibility not to go astray." Fuks promises that the local public, spoken for in collective "we," is ready to accept Gesher if it takes the designated route, and does not deviate from it. Like Handelsaltz, Fuks takes the position of an ideological gatekeeper, calling the theatre to order.

The Mockery in Mimicry: *The Lower Depths*

After its anniversary celebration was over, Gesher planned to start working on a new production. Arye had been writing the adaptation of a cult novel *The Master and Margarita* by Mikhail Bulgakov. Arye worked on it for months, alone and with Yahil-Wax, but he still was not pleased with the results. "And then one day," he recalls, "I was talking with the guys [Gesher's actors] and we dreamed up how one could stage *The Lower Depths*" (2003). And that was it—he abandoned *The Master and Margarita* and decided to stage *The Lower Depths* instead. To say that this decision came as a surprise to Gesher's actors would be an understatement. Arye: "When I announced the casting decision, no one believed me, the actors just decided that it's a joke. Everyone knew that I was working on *The Master and Margarita*, and then all of a sudden—*The Lower Depths*, Gorky, god knows what" (2003).

The reason for such disbelief was the dramatically different places that Gorky's play and Bulgakov's novel occupied in Russian-Soviet culture. Maxim Gorky was a Soviet classic, a Socialist realist, and a worshipper of the Bolshevik Revolution. His oeuvre (including *The Lower Depths*) was a much dreaded part of every school curriculum. For a Soviet director to stage Gorky was to hail the Communist regime, a position, incongruous with what the Gesher actors knew about Arye. In contrast, Bulgakov was an underdog of Soviet literature. Persecuted and unrecognized for decades he was known to his readership mainly through *samizdat* (underground literature). To stage Bulgakov, especially the verboten *The Master and Margarita* popular with Soviet intelligentsia, was a natural choice for someone like Arye. Therefore, when Arye decided to stage *The Lower Depths*, he had to explain his vision to the actors and convince them to cooperate: "After I read the play to them, and explained how I imagined it, they were inspired as well" (2003). And so, the troupe embarked on the rehearsals.

Gorky's play, situated in Russia at the dawn of the century, presents a gallery of juicy types from a boarding house and their environment: a thief Vaska Pepel (Igor Mirkurbanov), a prostitute Nastasya (Natalya Voitulevich-Manor), an alcoholic actor (Dror Keren), a fallen aristocrat Baron (Israel [Sasha] Demidov), impoverished laborers (Nelly Gosheva, Yevgeny Gamburg, Svetlana Demidov[10]), a drunk policeman (Vladimir Halemsky) and a vagabond Luka, half-saint, half-insane (Vladimir Vorobyov, a recent addition to Gesher). The play depicts the minutia of their everyday life, their intrigues, celebrations, finding and losing friends and lovers. Seemingly, the characters have passions and dreams, they strive to survive even as some of them die. Yet, they fail to be aware of their agency. The action takes place inside the boarding house—a mansion, once lavish but now decrepit and vandalized, like its tenants. Unaware of their humiliating condition, these are content with it. Their life goes on.

At the dawn of the century, Gorky, the realist, wrote this play to call attention to social injustice. The boarding house was a metaphor for a society that allows people to live in the humiliating conditions. Gorky's implied solution was a revolution that will restructure the society and put an end to

10 Svetlana Demidov, Israel (Sasha) Demidov's wife, joined the Gesher troupe in 1994.

human suffering. In Arye's production, the realism turns grotesque—social injustice is substituted with existential suffering. Gorky's accusative yet hopeful message of social revolution is challenged. Arye's interpretation poses daunting questions about awareness, responsibility, and individual agency in a society.

With *The Lower Depths* Gesher went back to Russian classics, but both the playbill and the press-kit presented the theatre as a bearer of both Russian and Israeli theatrical pedigree. The playbill traced the history of the play in Russia and in Israel. In Russia, Konstantin Stanislavsky directed *The Lower Depths* at the Moscow Art Theatre (1902) with such stars as Vasily Kachalov, Olga Knipper, and himself. Gesher's playbill features the black-and-while snapshots of that production. The previews (based on Gesher's press-kit) also emphasized the connection between Stanislavsky's and Arye's versions by comparing and contrasting them (for instance, Zaltzman 1994; Shohat 1994b). One preview (Elkariv 1994) is structured as a montage documenting the histories of Stanislavsky's and Arye's productions.

Gorky's play had a history in Israel. Gorky was one of the most popular Russian writers in pre-Israel Palestine and later in socialist Israel. His play *The Lower Depths* was translated by Avraham Shlonsky, a Russian-born patriarch of Hebrew literature. In 1933, Ohel, one of the first Jewish Palestinian theatres, produced the play starring the legendary Israeli actors Yehuda Gabai, Leah Dganit, Zeev Bervan, and Shoshana Barnea. Gesher's playbill features their black-and-white photos alongside Stanislavsky's actors. Gesher also chose to stage the play in the same translation as Ohel, which continued Israeli theatrical legacy.

Gesher publicized not only the history of *The Lower Depths* in Russia and in Israel, but also the fact that it was the first play to be produced directly in Hebrew, without an intermediate Russian version (see Scheflan 1994). No doubt, Gesher's theatre-makers understood that critics would see that as a step towards becoming "normal" (i.e. culturally unmarked) Israeli theatre (see, for instance, Zaltzman 1994, Elkariv 1994). Gesher also added to its press-kit: "Yevgeny Arye...is the only representative of the Israeli theatre who was invited to join Rabin at the Nobel Prize ceremony" (Scheflan 1994). This statement emphasized Gesher's relationship with the Israeli establishment and affirmed Arye's distinguished position among other Israeli theatre figures. It signaled to critics what was the distribution of power and political hierarchy in Israeli theatre at the moment.

The Lower Depths premiered on December 28, 1994. The production was an artistic success. Yet, as usual with Gesher, it is not the artistic success that counts with the Israeli critics, but rather the political and ideological alignment of the theatre-makers. In this case, their efforts to position the production paid off: *The Lower Depths* was given a glorifying reception. Critics raved about every aspect of the production, especially the ensemble work. Haim Nagid writes: "In *The Lower Depths*, Gesher claims another artistic victory. Coordinated ensemble, with a creative and exceptionally talented director, wonderful actors, and theatrical culture....Unbelievable" (1994c). Eliakim Yaron joins him: "[Gesher's actors] are truly touching, and their stage presence, their talents, their evident ability, and their togetherness are fascinating." He also noted "a mesmerizing set design, great musicality of the direction, breath-taking organization of space, and Fellini-style mise en scènes" (1994b). Michael Handelsaltz especially praised the choice of the dramatic material and its directorial interpretation, cleverly calling the production "the peak of the lower depths" (1994b). In her review titled "Better Than Superb," Weitz has to restrain herself: "I can go on and on with the praise, but there is no need. Run to see it" (1994b).

Critics also admired the cultural positioning of the production as: "Parody on Gorky's utopia," when "Gesher Theatre mounts *The Lower Depths* in Hebrew, but actually leads a dialog with the spiritual world of Russia at the end of the century" (Nagid 1994c). Another critic highly regarded "excellent direction by Yevgeny Arye, with a very 'Russian' performance in Hebrew" (Avishi 1995). Like *The Idiot*, *The Lower Depths* was perceived as "Russian culture in Hebrew" (in Maltzev's words), and thus was both fascinating and unthreatening to Israeli audience and critics.

Among these ecstatic critical responses the only negative review stands out. Eitan Bar-Yosef saw the production as an artistic failure: "Yevgeny Arye tries to turn human howl into an opera aria...or even into a musical—*La Miserables* by Gorky. It does not work" (1995). The claim, charging Arye with turning tragic scene into "a colorful carnival" is familiar from the reception of *Adam Resurrected*. But it is not the carnivalesque aesthetics that is at stake in this review.

What Bar-Yosef sees as the main problem of the production is that the language on stage "doesn't sound like Hebrew." He explains: "It is not that the Gesher actors don't try. They try too hard, and their efforts are considerable. [But] Hebrew should not be sweated out. It has to flow, to stream." For him, Hebrew on Gesher's stage sounds artificial, reproduced mechanically "like chicks in an incubator." In contrast to Gesher's actors, Bar-Yosef assumes the position of a bearer of authentic "natural" Hebrew.

Mastering Hebrew is one of the imperatives of the Zionist ideology with respect to new immigrants. Gesher seemingly corresponds to this imperative—the actors perform in Hebrew, and given their training with linguistic coaches, they imitate the Israeli accent better than other recent immigrants. Yet, as Bar-Yosef realized, it is just an imitation. Other journalists mentioned that the Gesher actors and director didn't speak Hebrew to each other (Shohat 1994a), and that the rehearsals were in Russian (Elkariv 1994). However, the critics conventionally portrayed the actors as complicit new immigrants, who are diligently and earnestly learning Hebrew. Their earnestness compensated for insufficient language proficiency.

It dawned on Bar-Yosef that, maybe, they are not so earnest. Hebrew for Gesher's actors, he writes, "is just another technical aspect of their work, like lights, costumes, or music." This realization is unsettling for the critic. Seemingly, Gesher's actors perform in Hebrew. But, in fact, the critic realized, instead of speaking the language, the actors just imitate it phonetically. The Hebrew words, stripped of their meaning, reduced to a technical issue, turn the performance into a mocking parody. Their mimicry becomes menacing. No wonder Bar-Yosef thinks that "the best actor in *The Lower Depths* is Dror Keren, a native Israeli...with the breathing Hebrew" (1995).

This horrifying revelation sent Bar-Yosef into a defensive frenzy. He suspects that "Arye despises Hebrew," and his interpretation of *The Lower Depths* is "a critical statement about life in the shadow of the Levant." The review concludes with the paternalistic advice: "Yevgeny Arye and his actors have to understand that in order to turn into a real Israeli theatre...they have to invest the majority of their efforts into language and to completely adopt Hebrew as a legal child" (1995). It is not clear what exactly this advice requires Gesher to do, but it is clear that it lies within the domain of ideology.

Bar-Yosef's review sets new standards for Gesher's reception. From now on it was not enough that Gesher performed in Hebrew, because it was just "a technical aspect," an imitation. Now, the actors had to completely submerge into the dominant idiom, to forsake speaking in ideologically subversive Russian language once and for all. Bar-Yosef intuited in Gesher's multilingual work an element of resistance, of disconcerting hybridity, and insisted that it had to stop.

Except for Bar-Yosef's attack, the overall critical reception was excellent. The audiences also received the production well. Arye remembers that "the first twenty performances were impossible to get in to." But then, something strange happened: "After that, the excitement subsided, but the shows still sold out. And after that—it was as if something was cut off" (Arye 2003). In just a few months, the production stopped selling. By June 1997, after only 42 performances, Gesher had to take *The Lower Depths* off its repertoire. Apparently, Gesher had all the components of the formula right—*The Lower*

Depths was "Russian culture in Hebrew," and the troupe maintained excellent cast and great production values. Yet, it was a failure. Why?

The failure of *The Lower Depths* had nothing to do with the artistic qualities of the show, nor with its critical reception. It was a marketing failure. Gesher was still a young theatre in a new cultural environment, and it was still learning its lessons. Arye: "Now, it is clear to us that if a show does not tour in other cities [in Israel], it is doomed. In Tel Aviv we can perform a new production four to five times a month at the most" (2003). Gesher learned from this experience the specificity of the Israeli theatre market. Tel Aviv audiences alone cannot sustain the show. If the theatre wants to reach out to the larger audiences, it needs to bring its productions close to audiences' home. The question then is, why it is only at this juncture that Gesher faced this marketing problem? *The Lower Depths* was not Gesher's first production. What was different about it?

The main difference was that by the time *The Lower Depths* premiered (1994), Gesher had its own building–the *hangar*. Before then, Gesher was a traveling troupe, and all its productions were mobile. But in 1994, the Gesher management assumed that since it had the performance space, and such a good one too, there was no need for extensive touring. And *The Lower Depths* was produced with that in mind–it was a stationary production with heavy complicated sets that could not be mounted on a small stage and could not travel easily. And so, the writing was on the wall: if the theatre was to survive financially, it needed to put more effort into marketing, to develop a sales strategy, and tour across the country.

• CHAPTER SIX •

The First Pitfall

The Crisis at Gesher

In 1995, in addition to the sliding sales of *The Lower Depths*, Gesher faced other difficulties. After four years of productive work and harmonious relationships, the theatre stagnated. The main reason was a conflict between Arye and Maltzev, who disagreed about the scope of their responsibilities and the future of their theatre. Maltzev envisioned a theatre with a structure similar to other Israeli public theatres, where a manager invites different directors for numerous productions. The financially savvy Maltzev realized that it is difficult for the theatre to survive in such a small country as Israel with just one or two new productions per year. He wanted Gesher to grow and to secure its place in the local theatre scene.

In contrast to Maltzev's vision, Arye saw himself as the artistic leader of the troupe and did not intend to let other directors into his domain. He was loyal to the Stanislavsky-inspired model of theatrical work with the long production period, systematic rehearsals, and intimate relationship with the actors. But like in any complex organizational and interpersonal conflict, other factors were involved, including Maltzev's reluctance to accommodate Arye's work outside of Gesher, both in Israel and abroad. In 1992–1996, Arye was a visiting professor at the Institute European de L'Acteur, France. In 1994, he received an offer to be the artistic director of Habima Theatre in Tel Aviv, which he turned down himself. But when in the winter 1994–95, Arye decided to direct a production at the Tisch School of Performing Arts at New York University, Maltzev said no. Nevertheless, Arye left for New York.

The disagreement over conceptual approaches had been brewing in the theatre for some time, but in the winter of 1995, the conflict surfaced. With the director absent, the troupe was paralyzed; there were no rehearsals, no work in progress, and no definite plans. When Arye came back, it was clear that the conflict needed to be resolved.

In April 1995, the crisis erupted. The theatre was not keen to advertise this news, but some critics who had access to the information jumped on the opportunity to exhibit Gesher in the least favorable light. Thus, Tzipi Shohat (1995a) mocked Shulamit Aloni's call for Israeli theatres "to set Gesher as an example" as premature. The crisis gave Shohat an excellent chance to attack the theatre: "Up until now [Gesher] worked in an artistic bubble, and now it's turned out that it picked up the same disease as other theatres." But her real question was, "Whether Gesher should be allowed to continue to separate itself from its environment, or to change this approach, and to bring to the theatre new actors and directors, and mainly to allow Arye to work at other theatres" (1995b).

Shohat's attack provoked Michael Handelsaltz (1995a) to defend Gesher. Even though he agreed that Aloni's call was a "considerable exaggeration," he disagreed with Shohat about her interpretation of the conflict as a "disease." In fact, Handelsaltz argued that a conflict over responsibilities and over future directions is a part of natural process of growth for a new artistic venue. He explained that such conflicts often result in the expulsion of a founder from a theatre. He gives examples of Nahum Zemah, who was forced out of Habima, Yosef Milo, forced out of Cameri, and Laurence Olivier forced out of the National Theatre in the UK. This historical evidence, coming from both Israeli and European context, gave legitimacy to Gesher's conflict.

The conflict between Arye and Maltzev was so serious that it required involvement of the board of directors, which gathered for an urgent meeting on April 11. Already by April 17, 1995, the board made the decision and announced it to the company: Arye will remain the artistic director, and will assume the responsibilities of a manager; whereas Maltzev will leave the company. Arye became the sole "owner" of the troupe. To help Arye, the board would hire a new administrative manager, accountable to Arye. This decision deviated from the Shelach committee's recommendation to appoint a manager (and not an artistic director) as a head of a theatre, but that didn't stop the board.

Handelsaltz not only supported the decision, but also called it "the only one possible" (1995a). He explained that a good manager could be substituted, but the unique vision and style of an artistic director were indispensable. Interestingly, he also expressed hope that a new administrative manager "will not necessarily be from among the Russian immigrants" (1995a). Thus, the "Russians" will take care of art, and the locals of management. According to Handelsaltz, such an ethnic divide will prevent future conflicts.

The decision to put Arye at the head of Gesher over Maltzev led not only to structural changes in the troupe, but also to a crisis of confidence and factions among the staff. When Maltzev left, ten other staff members followed him, among them dramaturge Katya Sosonsky and assistant director Lena Kreindlina. But most of the actors stayed, as they were unconditionally loyal to their mentor and director.

Already in mid-May of 1995, a new administrative manager was hired—former actor Ori Levy. Levy graduated from the Mikve-Israel School of Agriculture, was a member of kibbutz Izrael, acted in the Ohel and Cameri theatres, and later worked in administrative positions in Cameri. A *sabra* and a holder of an immaculate Israeli-Zionist record, Levy saw his appointment as "both a theatrical and Zionist challenge" (Shohat 1995c). And so the new period in the life of Gesher Theatre began.

The Marketing Breakthrough: *Tartuffe*

It took the theatre several months to recuperate. The financial consequences of the crisis were devastating. The budget deficit reached 3.5 million NIS, leaving Gesher unable to pay neither salaries, nor bills (Shohat 1995d). Ori Levy had to start his appointment by bringing the budget to balance, which would allow the theatre to function—to maintain the existing repertoire and to stage new productions.

Gesher's first production in its new incarnation was *Tartuffe* by Jean-Baptiste Molière. Arye had just staged *Tartuffe* at the Tisch School of Performing arts in New York. The production was successful; therefore, after the crisis was over, remaking *Tartuffe* was a natural choice for Arye. However, the play had only 12 parts, and in the wake of the crisis, Arye wanted to cast all the actors and boost their morale. Therefore, Arye decided to produce two versions of *Tartuffe* with two different casts. The show was rehearsed in Hebrew. By that time, another Israeli actor, Dorit Lev-Ari, had joined the troupe.[1] Another interesting addition to the troupe was Klim Kamenko, a Russian-born actor, who worked for several years as a stage worker at Gesher, after failure to obtain professional work. In *Tartuffe* he was given an almost silent part of a servant, succeeded with it, and since then was cast in every Gesher production.

The plot of the classic comedy revolves around Tartuffe (Israel [Sasha] Demidov/Igor Mirkurbanov), a religious hypocrite, who finds a way to be adopted into the genial family of Orgon (Boris Achanov/Leonid Kanevsky).

1 Dorit Lev-Ari entered Gesher as an understudy in *The Lower Depths* during Svetlana Demidov's pregnancy.

Figure 5: *Tartuffe*. Left to right: Yevgenya Dodina, Dror Keren, Nelly Gosheva, Vladimir Halemsky, Natalya Voitulevich-Manor, and Dorit Lev-Ari *(Courtesy of Gesher Theatre)*

Tartuffe seduces Orgon's wife (Natalya Voitulevich-Manor/Ruth [Lilian] Heilovsky), brainwashes his mother (Nelly Gosheva), tries to marry his daughter (Dorit Lev-Ari), and takes a complete sway over Orgon himself. The play ends with the divine intervention of the King Louis XIV himself who sets things straight by arresting Tartuffe.

Arye's interpretation put a contemporary spin to the classic plot, using the metatheatre device. In Arye's production, the dramatic characters on stage are aware of their participation in a theatrical action: they turn the music on and off with a move of a hand, they set up a stage. They are both characters in a play and actors themselves. This duplicity comes to full expression towards the end, when Tartuffe fails to believe that the King has ordered to arrest him, and demands to see the text of the play. Once he sees it, he gives in to the King's will. At that point the actors on stage quit their dramatic personae and read their lines from the text looking suggestively towards the audience as if pleading for approval. Thus, *Tartuffe* continued the topic of artistic creation and coercive power developed in Gesher's previous shows *Molière* and *Adam Resurrected*.

The conflict in *Molière* revolves around the clerical resistance to Molière's play *Tartuffe*, banned despite the King's patronage. *Adam Resurrected* problematized artistic creation under oppression and its role in the physical and spiritual survival of an artist. It is not by chance that the topic of artistic creation and coercive power emerged as a central topic for Gesher. Like the characters of *Molière* or *Adam Resurrected*, the Gesher theatre-makers had an ambivalent relationship with the Israeli establishment. Gesher was "a beloved of the establishment" (Fuks 1995a); it enjoyed both the financial and political support of the authorities. Yet, Gesher's theatre-makers paid dearly for this support: they had to be accountable to the ruling ideological norms. Gesher had to answer for its choice of language, repertoire, and public relations strategies.

Alongside a contemporary interpretation, Arye's production creates visual imagery in the spirit of Molière's era. The characters wear elaborate dandified costumes—long fancy coats with huge, decorated cuffs, lavish dresses, and curly powdered wigs. All the action takes place in hall surrounded by five richly decorated tall doors, through which the characters constantly go in and out. The music by Avi Benjamin incorporates elements of rap into the stylized baroque tunes.

Tartuffe's premier took place on July 29, 1995. Even though most of newspaper reviews were positive (6 out of 9), the overall critical reception was far from unconditional praise. Two patterns characterized *Tartuffe*'s reception: the critics disagreed over Gesher's theatrical style, and evaluated the production based on its ideological merits.

As for Gesher's style, the critics agreed about professionalism and production values of the new show. They acknowledged that Arye and his ensemble created a bright emotional theatre, using the aesthetics of the grotesque. This style not only marked Gesher as a Russian theatre, following the traditions of directors Meyerhold, Vachtangov, and Goncharov, but also signaled to critics the transgressive carnivalesque style of Gesher's production. Like in the reception of *Adam Resurrected*, this style became the sticking point.

Some critics appreciated Arye's directorial interpretation. Shosh Weitz: "The production is directed well, [it is] full of imagination and stage ideas, and is performed perfectly" (1995). Michael Ohed: "Lively and theatrical...Molière, crazy, burlesque, and yet authentic" (1995).

Other critics were relentless in their critique. Sarit Fuks announced that Gesher did not succeed. She blamed this failure on Arye's grotesque and emotional interpretation:

> [*Tartuffe* is] a comedy that is not wild enough, with the messages that are too general. Yevgeny Arye directed it with such heaviness, as if he had stones in his kidneys. Stage

energy runs around the stage without focus. The actors open and close the swinging doors for no good reason. The deafening music is streaming from the speakers....Yes, again a somewhat circus atmosphere. (Fuks 1995b)

Michael Handelsaltz also critiques *Tartuffe* for "tiring and vulgar screaming and running around" (1995b). Moreover, he argues that "Yevgeny Arye is so in love with his qualities as a director, that he wastes the good qualities of his production by overusing directorial gimmicks" (1995b). Eliakim Yaron thinks that Arye's "loud grotesque" lacks a human dimension, and does not let the audience identify with the characters on stage (1995). Yet, he arrives at a positive conclusion: "Even if we can argue about the approach, this is a moving and fascinating show that presents a different but wonderful Molière" (1995).

The acting also got mixed responses. Eliakim Yaron (1995) and Shosh Weitz (1995) praised the cast, especially Dodina and Kanevsky. Yet, Michael Handelsaltz disapproved of the acting style, and even called Dodina's acting "a ruined part" (1995b).

The second familiar pattern that occurs in the reception of *Tartuffe* is critical evaluation of the production based on its ideological merits. Weitz writes: "*Tartuffe* is not only a very beautiful production, it is also a Hebrew production. Yevgeny Arye and his actors crossed the bridge. Their *Tartuffe* speaks excellent Hebrew, and has contemporary messages" (1995). Her praise refers to fulfillment of the ideological imperatives: commitment to learning Hebrew language and absorption into Israeli culture. The same phenomenon takes place in Yehudit Orian's review. She situates Gesher within a context of immigrant absorption rather than artistic production:

I don't know how the Russian *aliyah* will adjust, and what will be its contribution to the Israeli society–to its music, literature, and culture–besides mafia, prostitution, and violence. But Gesher Theatre...is one of the most successful achievements of return from the Diaspora. (Orian 1995)

In her account, infused with the xenophobic stereotypes, Orian presents Gesher's production in terms of a "contribution of the Russian *aliyah*." Her description used the language of sexism and ethnocentrism, bordering on racial slur:

We usually imagine an Israeli macho standing in a warrior's pose as an ultimate man. Hairy, sunburned, he is on a tractor or in a tank. And it turns out, that among the immigrants, who, no doubt, come from mixed marriages, who are not kosher Jews in their customs of marriage and divorce, who are not even Jewish by *Halacha* [Jewish religious law], with Tatar faces, or African physique[2]–there are some hot and

2 This comment refers to immigrants from Ethiopia also mentioned in Orian's article.

> handsome guys like you wouldn't believe. In the *Tartuffe* production at Gesher, I discovered the most attractive and sexy man that I have ever seen on stage. (Orian 1995)

This account, despite its tongue-in-cheek tone, reveals a commitment not only to ideological norms, but also to ethnic stereotypes. The critic is sincerely surprised that someone who violates her ideologically infused expectations of gender and ethnicity can be sexually attractive.

After the Hebrew premiere of *Tartuffe*, Gesher prepared its Russian version, which premiered on October 26, 1995. In this version, the Hebrew-speaking actors, Keren and Lev-Ari, acted in Russian. However, the Hebrew version was far more popular. By September 1998, *Tartuffe* had performed 143 times in Hebrew, and only 35 times in Russian (total 178). Only then it was taken off the Gesher repertoire.

In 1995, Gesher received an Award of the Chairman of the Knesset. The same year, *Tartuffe* won the Israeli Theatre Award [Israeli Tony] in the categories of Best Director, Best Costume Designer, and Best Lighting Designer categories. Yet, *Tartuffe*'s main significance for the development of the theatre was neither its artistic achievement, nor its critical reception, but its marketing success.

In 1995, Zvia Binder, a seasoned marketing pro, whom Ori Levy recruited, became Gesher's marketing director. As we know from the sad history of *The Lower Depths*, before 1995 the theatre had not used its full marketing potential. Binder introduced a marketing strategy similar to that of other Israeli theatres—collective subscription and mass sales to the trade unions. In addition to traditional marketing through posters and ads in the media, she created an infrastructure with Israeli audiences in mind. First, she offered Gesher shows to trade unions, professional organizations, and other potential collective buyers. Second, she improved so called "external sales," when a performance was sold to a different venue (e.g., a concert hall outside of Tel Aviv) whose management was responsible for selling individual tickets. Third, she reinforced the so-called "sponsorships" of large companies, such as Visa or Mif'al HaPais [Israeli lottery], which subsidized theatre tickets for their customers in exchange for advertisement in Gesher's playbills.

These strategies exposed a general theatre-going Israeli public to Gesher. Beforehand, this public did not attend Gesher's productions because of the passive pattern of theatre attendance in Israel; as Binder puts it: "No subscription—no attendance" (2000). Israeli audiences are socialized to purchase subscriptions to theatres in an organized manner, once a year, through their workplaces or other institutional frameworks. Starting 1995, these audiences could buy tickets to Gesher in a similar way.

However, Binder had to adjust these standard strategies to Gesher's specificity. Thus, Gesher's artistic credo did not allow her to market the productions as "entertainment," rather she had to go with the line of "quality theatre." This definition resulted in class segregation. The "high-culture" profile intimidated working class audiences. The target audiences of Gesher's collective sales became educated, middle- and upper-middle classes. With the collective sales, Binder approached high-tech companies, universities, teachers unions, and other high-brow industries. Another challenge was the accent of Gesher's actors. Binder admits that the Russian accent was always a stumbling block for marketing; she had better chances of promoting it to the more educated audiences.

Binder's strategy also addressed the needs of the Russian-speaking audiences. As mentioned before, traditional promotion methods do not always work with Russian audiences for cultural reasons. In the Soviet Union, newspaper reviews were not trustworthy as they reflected artists' compliance with the regime rather than the artistic qualities of the show (not unlike in Israel). Therefore, the best marketing channel for Russian-born audiences remained personal communication. In order to answer these audiences' demands, Gesher established *babushka* marketing. *Babushka* (Russian for grandma) marketing consists of a number of independent agents, usually elderly women (hence the nickname *babushka*) who sell theatre tickets to their friends and neighbors. A *babushka* receives commission, and her clients receive not only tickets, but also personable reliable source of information about a production.

After Gesher started performing in Hebrew, it had only limited number of productions in Russian. Thus, if the Russian-speaking spectators wanted to see Gesher's productions, they had to attend Hebrew performances. In order to reach out to the Russian-speaking audience, Binder offered collective sales to Hebrew language courses and community centers in the neighborhoods with a high concentration of new immigrants.

Despite the inclusion of some elements of marketing techniques common in other Israeli theatres (such as collective sales), Gesher was still opposed to the full-fledged subscription system. According to the Gesher management, such system has the potential to take over the theatre, turning it into a production factory catering to the conservative tastes of the subscribers. Besides these aesthetic reservations, there were financial ones: the subscription system requires a monstrous marketing department (e.g., both Habima and Cameri employ about 40 people in their marketing departments). Gesher, whose marketing department consisted of Binder herself, a box-office manager, and a part-time cashier could not afford such increase of personnel.

Around the same time, in addition to the new marketing strategy, Gesher established *Amitei Gesher* [Gesher Friends]. Gesher Friends was a club of private donors who gained access to special performances of Gesher's productions in return for their financial support.

Both the new marketing strategies and the private donations supplied new sources of income: collective ticket sales earned over 1.6 million NIS, and Gesher Friends donated over 50,000 NIS. Gesher's budget in 1995 reached over eight million NIS, of which five million NIS came from public subsidies, and 686,773 NIS from the individual ticket sales (see Table 1).

Gesher's marketing mechanism not only reflected its aesthetic principles, but also shaped the ensemble's attitude to work. Without tickets sold in advance to subscribers, the financial future of a show was unpredictable. And since Gesher produced only one, at most two, productions per year, the stakes were extraordinarily high. Unlike a theatre with numerous productions and a subscription system, Gesher could not afford a flop. Therefore, the Gesher ensemble put considerable work and effort into each production, honing it even years after its premiere. However, with the marketing breakthrough, Gesher's artistic excellence started to backfire.

The incredible popularity of *Tartuffe* (nearly 200 shows in three years) posed unforeseen challenges. Arye explained:

> The actors came to hate *Tartuffe*, because they had to perform it every day...they started acting mechanically. They got tired. It was very difficult to keep the production alive. I argued with them, I rehearsed with them, trying to do something. But objectively, I understood them. (Arye 2003)

This is a difficult situation. If a production is a commercial failure, the theatre verges on financial breakdown. But if a production is successful, Gesher has to perform it ad nauseum potentially compromising its artistic standards. With limited governmental funding and a slow, expensive production process, Gesher apparently could not win. It had to choose between the lesser of the two evils.

• CHAPTER SEVEN •

The Peak of Fame: From *Village* to *City*

A Perfect Israeliana: *Village*

One day during the rehearsals of *Tartuffe*, Arye sat down in his office for a casual conversation with Yehoshua Sobol. Sobol, a famous Israeli playwright, was a friend and colleague. He translated *Dreyfus File* and *Tartuffe* into Hebrew. At some point Arye said that he'd like to stage a play like *Our Town* by Thornton Wilder, only grounded in Israeli soil. Sobol mentioned that, incidentally, he'd like to write about the place where he was born—a small village in Palestine. The collaboration began. Sobol finished translating *Tartuffe* and went to Germany to direct a play. From there, he started sending Arye fragments of the future play. Arye responded with feedback and his own ideas. And that is how *Village* was written.

Village was a critical and popular hit in Israel and abroad. It became the most popular Gesher production. By 2000, 240,000 spectators attended the show (Savel 2001). Performed 430 times by 2001, *Village* remains in the repertoire as of this writing. In Israel, *Village* was nominated as the best production in 1997. On tours, in the United Kingdom, Germany, the United States, Italy, Australia, and Ireland, it was enthusiastically received by both critics and public. What were the reasons for such unprecedented success?

As with *The Idiot* in the past, a unique combination of artistic and ideological factors brought about the smash hit. The historical topic of the play, Gesher's nostalgic and original interpretation of it, casting sensitive to accents, and the participation of Israeli actors, were among such factors. Unlike *Adam Resurrected*, *Village* paid tribute to the mainstream Israeli mythology, without posing a threat to a single sacred cow. Both the audiences and the critics loved it. But even in this raving reception, the Israeli theatre criticism was still ideology- and identity-driven.

On October 18 of 1995, Gesher conducted a press-conference, which gave the theatre a chance to give a public address after the crisis of 1995 and reaffirm its artistic program: "It is important for me to note that Gesher has been and still remains the same theatre and there is no change in our artistic policy," said Arye (Zaltzman 1995a). Arye also announced Gesher's plans for the future. He presented a new production in an agreeable ideological light. Newspapers quoted Arye:

> It is not just another production....It is important to me and to the actors to attach us to the Israeli reality and history. Our childhood memories are different, our dead fell in the different wars, our illusions stem from different realities, and we have to try to turn the Israeli experience into our own, with the help of the Israeli playwright. ("Mahazeh Hadash" 1995)

After such introduction, the previews in all major papers raved: "*Village* will speed the process of Gesher's integration into the Israeli life" ("Mahazeh Hadash" 1995); "Gesher signals another stage of its involvement in the life of the theatres in Israel" (Shohat 1995e); "Gesher is becoming more and more Israeli" (Zaltzman 1995a); "Big step towards Israeliness" (Zaltzman 1995b). Everything in *Village*—the choice of the play, casting, and language—signaled to critics that Gesher chose to assimilate. Critics welcomed this choice.

The historical topic of the play was a major component in its success. In *Village*, Sobol takes off his hat as 'a rebel of Israeli theatre', and turns his misty gaze towards his childhood. Reminiscent of *Our Town* by Thornton Wilder and *Under Milk Wood* by Dylan Thomas, his play is a poetic account of growing up in pre-Israel Palestine. The play starts with a Nazi threat at El-Alamein in 1942 and ends with the War for Independence in 1947. But these historical events appear only as a background for the unfolding of intimate events in the characters' lives.

The plot is not held by a major dramatic tension, instead it consists of a series of loosely connected vignettes from the life of villagers, seen through the eyes of Yossi (Israel [Sasha] Demidov). He is a Candide-like figure, a naïve and confused simpleton, who admits that "the longer he lives the less he understands." The impressionist narrative of the play draws together characters coming from different cultures and political backgrounds, before the War for Independence and the Israeli-Palestinian conflict made their coexistence impossible. Frau Dankeschoen, an ex-opera singer from Berlin, complains about her career as a peddler in Palestine (Adi Etzion-Zak); Sayid, an Arab merchant (Vladimir Halemsky) haggles with Yossi's farmer-father (Leonid Kanevsky) over the quality of manure. Yossi's communist

Figure 6: *Village*. Left to right: Nelly Gosheva, Efrat Ben-Zur, Israel (Sasha) Demidov, Adi Etzion-Zak, Svetlana Demidov, and Levana Finkelstein *(Courtesy of Gesher Theatre)*

grandmother (Nelly Gosheva) argues with Italian prisoners-of-war about politics (Vladimir Portnov and Michael Asinovsky).

But for Yossi (as well as for the nascent Israeli nation), it is a time of lost innocence. For the first time in his life, Yossi faces love and death. His brother Ami (Mark Ivanir) and village belle Dassi (Efrat Ben-Zur) fall in love. Dassi's mother Clara (Ruth [Lilian] Heilovsky) has a soaring affair with a British officer, Captain Drury (Igor Mirkurbanov). Then, comes death. First, Yossi loses his beloved pets, goat Dizza (Dorit Lev-Ari) and turkey Indik (Klim Kamenko); then he meets Sonya who lost her entire family in the Holocaust (Svetlana Demidov), and then his brother Ami falls in the War for Independence.

But Yossi refuses to grow up, and to face the fact that this reality is gone. A gravedigger by trade, he is surrounded by death. On stage, he is alone in the cemetery, digging his own grave. But even then, Yossi radiates unreserved loyalty and disarming charm. Thus, despite death and loss, the spirit of the play is life-affirming.

Gesher's interpretation of the play was instrumental in the success of the production. In *Village*, Gesher succeeded in presenting the history of the founding of the country, a familiar and revered topic in Israeli, not as a heroic epic, but rather as a nostalgic and warm personal testimony. Also, it was produced by an all-star ensemble. Yehoshua Sobol's play, Yevgeny Arye's direction, Israel (Sasha) Demidov's acting, Alexander Lisiyansky's sets, and Avi Benjamin's music were a winning combination.

The play's action takes place on the round catwalk that rotates between the bulrushes covering the stage. Reflecting the fusion of fantasy and reality, the sets and costumes are both realistic and symbolic. Bits of furniture are scattered in different locations on stage: a dresser with a mirror for Dassi's house, a table and a bed for Yossi's parents. The costumes of the characters and props are historically accurate: khaki shorts for Ami, who is working out using an iron as a dumbbell; a flowery dress for unfaithful and glamorous Clara; a British Army uniform for Captain Drury who cruises on a souped-up motorcycle. Yet, along with these realistic details, the farm animals Dizza and Indik are represented by the actors with giant puppets,[1] fully participating in the show, even after the animals' deaths.

The poetic fictional world of the production is breached with the real-life chronicles: the radio broadcast of the United Nations vote defining the future of the state of Israel, documentary cinematic images of the Jewish settlement in Palestine, and the atrocities of the war. The music incorporates Zionist marches and popular songs from the 40s into an original score by Avi Benjamin. The medley of languages also adds to the charm of the production. Besides Hebrew, the characters on stage speak English, Russian, Yiddish, Italian, and Arabic.

Other factors that contributed to *Village*'s success were the participation of Israeli actors and accent-sensitive casting. Most of the characters in the play are either immigrants or people from different cultures; therefore, the accents of Gesher's actors sound natural. Critics comment on the role of accents: "Fortunately, the Russian accent does not hurt the trustworthiness of the actors. Besides three young *sabras*...the villagers came from Europe, most of them—from Russia" (Ohed 1996). Hebrew-speaking actors, Mark Ivanir and Efrat Ben-Zur, perform the parts of the young *sabras* in the play—Ami and Dassi. In addition, Israeli actors Levana Finkelstein and Adi Etzion-Zak were invited especially for this production. This meant that a casting of the production was truly bicultural, and signaled to Israeli critics greater integration of Gesher into Israeli theatre life.

---

1 Ester and Yitzhak Pekar, Russian-born puppeteers, who came to Israel in the 1970s, prepared puppets, and trained the actors to use them.

Village premiered on February 18, 1996, at the *hangar* in Jaffa. The first performances were attended by Prime Minister Binyamin Netanyahu, Minister of Defense Shimon Peres, other ministers, Knesset members, generals, and Leah Rabin (Oren 1996). A flood of ecstatic reviews greeted *Village*. The critics accepted the show wholeheartedly and without reservations. Michael Ohed declared: "I don't know if it is the production of a year or the production of a decade. I only know that I have never seen a production like this" (1996). Eliakim Yaron confirmed: "This is a wonderful theatre—exhilarating, funny, moving, sweeping, like a real theatre should be" (1996a). Shosh Weitz called Gesher "the best theatre ensemble in Israel." She also gave theatre praise grounded in Zionist ideology: "Arye and his ensemble make a very Israeli show. It's impossible not to be impressed by the good Hebrew of the actors that made *aliyah* to the *Eretz Israel* only a few years ago, and by their ability to construct mythological Israeli characters with a great trustworthiness" (1996a). In another review she continued:

> In *Village*, Gesher made a new and important step forward. Before *Village*, their repertoire was comprised of plays that matched the cultural-European background of the ensemble. This time they "made *aliyah*." The play by Sobol is Israeli not only because it was written in Israel, but because it deals with the Israeli mythology....The world of images that the director and the leader Yevgeny Arye builds, are borrowed from his theatrical vocabulary, but they fit the subject well. The performance, as usual in Gesher, is excellent. The fact that the actors' Hebrew improved a lot is very conspicuous. It allowed them to be convincing as they create the Israeli experience. (Weitz 1996b)

As in the reception of earlier shows, Weitz's evaluation is influenced by the perceived assimilation of the theatre-makers, their choice of topic, and their Hebrew proficiency.

Haim Nagid's review also gives an identity-driven evaluation. He admires Arye's success in rendering an atmosphere he did not experience personally (as if it is a requirement for a good production):

> *Eretz Israel*...is still kept in the memory of the audiences, but not of the director and the actors. They came to Israel to build and to get settled[2] only six years ago. Despite that, in his genius touch, the director succeeded to reconstruct the atmosphere of that period, the nuances of gestures and body language, familiar to those who lived in that time. (Nagid 1996)

2 "To build and to get settled" (in Hebrew *livnot ulehibanot*) was a slogan of *halutzim*, the Jewish settlers of Palestine at the beginning of the twentieth century. Today, it is an expression infused with Zionist ideology.

Shi Bar-Yakov from the newspaper *Tel Aviv* gives a different praise. He sees *Village* as an embodiment of the modern (as opposed to post-modern) culture, homage to the old-fashioned values, such as life-affirming optimism. He compares the deep optimism of Arye's production to the pessimism of contemporary Israeli playwright Hanoch Levin, and it causes the critic "to reconsider the cynical and stylized line of the 'post' culture, presenting pessimism and artistic coldness as a condition for meaningful art." He continues: "Despite the fact that the work of Yevgeny Arye and Gesher is funny and full of naughty spirit, it is much more than hedonistic entertainment. It is deep theatre, meaningful and moving" (1996a).

Michael Handelsaltz also writes positive reviews of the show, but he is the only critic whose interpretation is ironic, even though his irony refers mostly to Sobol's play rather than to Gesher's performance: "Sobol does not refrain from a single symbol of Zionist nostalgia: the threat from the Germans, and a romance with a Brit, and good relationship with the Arabs, and a young solder, falling in a battle for establishment of the state" (1996a). But Handelsaltz sneers at the show itself too, produced "with pathos and naiveté" (1996b). He does not buy into the story: "The director turns it into affective celebration...with touching actors, so that for a moment one can forget that it is superficial, beatified, and fake" (Handelsaltz 1996a). However, Handelsaltz predicts that Gesher "will tour abroad with this production on the emissary mission"[3] (1996a), implying that the show is lip-service to the establishment.

Indeed, the nostalgic narrative of *Village* does not turn into a sugary melodrama only due to Gesher's superb acting and directing. The play does present an idealized picture of the past, where the only disagreement between Arabs and Jews is a quality of manure, where prisoners-of-war sing Italian arias, where even after death the characters continue to live on stage. True, *Village* used the full arsenal of the ideological clichés and symbols. However, these overused images bothered neither audiences nor critics; on the contrary, their presence in Gesher's production had a pacifying effect. In *Village*, Gesher's outlook on Israeli history did not pose a threat, did not mock the dusty icons, and did not stir a controversy, only rendered a heroic past through tragic-comic personal memoir. The fact that the story was remote in time from the contemporary audiences also helped its unproblematic reception. Gesher's production was not about life in contemporary Israel, it did not speak on behalf of the Israelis, threatening to misrepresent them. Due to their cultural identity, Gesher received a symbolic mandate to speak for the founders of the

3 Israeli Ministry of Foreign Affairs sends *shlihim* [emissaries] to different countries on proselytizing ideological missions of promoting *aliyah* to Israel.

state of Israel, who were also Russian immigrants, like the Gesher theatre-makers themselves.

However, when the critics realized that *Village* could be interpreted as a nostalgic idyll, they assumed a defensive stance. Almost every review makes a point of explaining why the production is *not* nostalgic. Sarit Fuks: "There is nostalgia and there is nostalgia. Gesher's nostalgia is realistic. It is not a romanticized, kitschy, and escapist idealization. It is a realistic nostalgia that shows the way people were attached to the place before the spread of nationalism and chauvinism" (1996a).

Eliakim Yaron also feels compelled to refute nostalgia. Yaron asserts, "The director does not mount a production about nostalgia. Moreover, the humor and delicate irony create a sort of anti-nostalgic screen, and every time there is a moving mise en scène, the director ends it with an alienating and poignant cut" (1996a).

Shosh Weitz makes a similar move. She claims that "a wonderful direction of Yevgeny Arye, and a remarkable performance of the entire ensemble save the nostalgia from the danger of oily kitsch" (1996a). Shi Bar-Yakov agrees: "In the hand of another director, this play could have become a basis for sticky and stunned production, like *Kineret, Kineret*[4] from the time of the World War II and a struggle with the British during settlement of Israel. But in hands of Yevgeny Arye this play turns into one-of-a-kind magical theatre" (1996a).

Haim Nagid noticed that the production is full of familiar symbols: "*Village* personifies our fathers' legacy, 'back-to-the-land' idealism, with all the socialist and Zionist meanings, which once were full of substance and enthusiasm, and since then moved to dusty archives" (1996). However, for him those are not just dated overused symbols, but rather lost ideals. Nagid is unaware that his warm tone actually demonstrates that these "socialist and Zionist meanings" are not in the archives yet, but rather, are still active in his judgment.

After the *Village* success at home and abroad, Gesher's popularity reached such dimensions that prime ministers felt compelled to have a photo shoot with the Gesher actors. *Yediot Ahronot* featured a photograph of Binyamin Netanyahu with Arye, Kamenko (in a costume of Indik) and Heilovsky (dressed as Clara) ("Mar'eh" 1997). Three years later, the Tel Aviv local newspaper *Tzfon Hair* featured a photograph of Ehud Barak, also surrounded by the Gesher actors in *Village* costumes ("Stutzim" 2000).

---

4 *Kineret, Kineret* is a popular play by Israeli poet Natan Alterman about the Jewish settlement of Palestine.

The popular success was followed by professional recognition. *Village* won the Israeli Theatre Award in all the main categories: Best Production, Best Director, Best Actor (Israel [Sasha] Demidov), Best Stage Designer (Alexander Lisiyansky), and Most Promising Actress (Efrat Ben-Zur) for the year 1996. The same year Gesher won the Yigal Alon Award.

Gesher toured abroad extensively with *Village*. The sweeping success of the production abroad was due to the unique combination of cultural specificity and universal humanity of the story. Audiences accustomed to a reserved acting style, were taken by Gesher's "acting from the guts," and by the emotional theatre it created. The visual and musical aspects of the production helped to cross over the linguistic gaps. The timing also helped–the upcoming 50th anniversary of the state of Israel was commemorated abroad by cultural events and festivals. *Village* was a natural choice for such occasions.

In May 1997, Gesher went on tour to the UK. *Village* was received enthusiastically at the Brighton and London Festivals, as well as in several other cities. The tour culminated in a triumphal performance at Lyric theatre, one of the oldest theatres in London. Andy Lavender from *The Times* announced that Gesher is "one of the more remarkable companies in world drama" (1997). Michael Coveney from *The Observer* stated: "Gesher is the top company in Israel." He also compared Gesher to the theatres of Lev Dodin, Peter Brook, Robert Lepage, and Katona Josef, concluding: "The company constitutes today one of the world's leading ensembles" (1997).

In March 1998, *Village* was presented at the Berlin Festival *50 Jahre Israel* [50 Years to Israel], and later toured in several other cities in Germany. It was received remarkably well both by critics and audiences. *Der Tages Spiegel* wrote that Gesher "creates a magical world on stage" (Matthes 1998). *Berliner Zietung* called Gesher "a quintessential original theatre in contemporary Israel" (Koberg 1998).

In July 1998, marking the 50th anniversary of Israel, *Village* opened the annual Lincoln Center Festival in New York (where *Adam Resurrected* was performed as well). "The play is *Our Town* reimagined by Marc Chagall," wrote Peter Marks from *The New York Times* (1998). He suggested that the show was a critical and popular hit in Israel because of the timing of the production and the identity of the theatre makers: "A company of recently arrived exiles, in a land of refugees deep in reflection about its first 50 years of nationhood, struck a responsive nerve with a play" (1998). Francine Russo from *The Village Voice* wrote: "Gesher Theatre's *Village* is like a towering Chagall mural, a swirl of bustling, dreamlike images" (1998). Realizing the limitations of a nostalgic narrative, she particularly appreciated the humanity of the show: "Though *Village* contributes little new to the Middle East debate, it overflows with the ordinary—love and sex and shit and death—heightened by passion, memory, and imagination" (1998). Linda Winer from *Newsday* admired "remarkable images in the Gesher Theatre's joyfully haunting and rhapsodically theatrical production," as well as the ensemble work: "The company...works with the sort of visceral magnificence that comes only with long-term ensemble life" (1998). The reviews by Clive Barnes from *The New York Post* (1998a), as well as Alisa Solomon from the *Village Voice* (1998) admired the production.

In the fall of 1998, *Village* was performed at the Rome Festival in Italy. In October the same year, *Village* participated in the Melbourne Festival in Australia, and a year later, in the Dublin Festival in Ireland. Reviews in *The Australian* (Christofis 1998), *The Age* (Ross 1998), *The Irish Times* (Colgan 1999), and *The Irish Independent* (Gorman 1999) raved. Ironically, Handelsaltz' cynical prophecy about Gesher as an emissary of the Ministry of Foreign Affairs came true. Indeed, the Ministry subsidized and supported these tours.

Village met not only critical and audience success in Israel and abroad, but also was instrumental for the financial well-being of the theatre (see Table 1). Gesher ended 1996 with the budget of over 11 million NIS, out of which over six million came from public subsidy (a million more than in 1995), and nearly five million NIS from ticket sales (including collective and individual ticket sales). Later, in 1997, the theatre made $175,000 touring abroad with *Village* (Dayan 1997).

From Russia with Love Redux: *City (Odessa Stories)*

After the triumphal success of *Village*, Gesher started rehearsing a new production. Echoing the juxtaposition of rural and urban, the new production was titled *City (Odessa Stories)* in contrast to *Village*. In *City*, like in *Village*, Gesher turned to the events of the past, this time not in Palestine, but in Odessa, a center of Jewish life in pre-revolutionary Russia.

City was based on five short stories and a play by Isaac Babel, a Jewish Soviet writer. In his short dense stories, Babel recreated the life of his native Odessa at the dawn of the century. Odessa was a port and a cosmopolitan city. It was one of the few places in Tsarist Russia where Jews were allowed to settle, as a result it was a very Jewish city. The Jews, Russians, Ukrainians, Romanians, and Greeks who lived there spoke a peculiar dialect, a juicy mix of languages and idioms, based on southern Russian and Ukrainian with a strong influx of Yiddish and Hebrew expressions. Babel's characters, populating Odessa's underworld, mostly Jewish mafia, spoke in this dialect, mixing styles and registers, using high- and low-brow idioms in ungrammatical, but expressive and communicative language.

Babel's prose stood out in the era of socialist realism, when literature was called to create a positive picture of a new communist reality. Babel's characters: gangsters, pickpockets, merchants, prostitutes, and beggars, could hardly qualify as protagonists of Soviet literature; yet he depicted them with sympathy and affection. Babel paid dearly for his creative credo. He perished in the Soviet prison, and even though the charges against him were dropped during post-Stalinist era, in the Soviet Union his books have not received official recognition for decades.

In Soviet Russia Babel's romanticizing depiction of criminals was vetoed, but in Israel his depiction struck a nerve (so much that *Odessa Stories* was staged by the Habima theatre in 1986). The Jewish gangsters defied the stereotypes of oppressed diasporic Jews. They were active, powerful, and brutal; also charismatic and masculine. Far removed from a traditional Zionist hero, an Odessa gangster still partakes in the redefinition of a powerless Jew into a strong Hebrew.

When Arye decided to stage *Odessa Stories*, he faced a question: How to dramatize a collection of short stories with motley characters and no unifying plot? Arye also wanted to preserve as much of the original text as possible. Thus, instead of a conventional play, he created a theatrical version of the stories, where dramatic action was interwoven with the voice of a narrator. Like the original, Arye's adaptation was written in Russian. That posed the next question: How to translate Babel's unique language?

Nily Mirsky, an Israeli translator of Babel's work, and Mark Ivanir, resident linguistic expert at Gesher, translated Arye's adaptation into Hebrew. But modern Hebrew does not have a dialect analogous to that of Babel's characters. Mirsky and Ivanir had to invent a new language. They created a new dialect of Hebrew, full of ungrammatical, but picturesque, expressions and idioms lifted from Yiddish, mixing high- and low-brow language. The second problem was the actors' accents. Ivanir and Mirsky explained that because of the accents, the ungrammatical sentences could sound as if the immigrant actors just made grammar mistakes in Hebrew (Shapiro 1996). Translation was tricky: the intentional character of the ungrammatical constructions had to be vivid to the audience. Thus, the idiolect of *City* was created: awkward, uneven, bizarre, but vibrant and endlessly funny.[5]

5 In contemporary American literature, Jonathan Safran Foer emerges as a linguistic heir of Babel. In his novel *Everything Is Illuminated*, the Odessa-born character uses such ungrammatical but colorful expressions as "promenading into things" or "having shit between brains" (2002, p. 1–2).

Like other Gesher productions, such as *Village* and *Adam Resurrected*, *City* does not have a traditional dramatic structure. The narrative structure of the production defined a directorial concept of story-theatre, a metatheatrical device, which allows characters on stage speak simultaneously in the first and third person, switching back and forth between their own perspectives and the perspective of Babel, the narrator. Several plots emerge from the exchange between a photographer Hershkovich (Dror Keren), and a matchmaker Arye-Leib (Boris Achanov). In an opening scene, when Hershkovich and Arye-Leib look at old pictures, small stages are stacked vertically like scaffolding. On each small stage actors pose motionless, like in a snapshot. As Hershkovich shows a photograph to Arye-Leib, the spotlight shifts to a new scaffold, creating the magical effect of still images coming to life.

Most of the plots revolve around Benya Krik, a king of the Jewish criminal world in Odessa (Igor Mirkurbanov). He is a cross between Robin Hood, Al Capone, and Tevye, the Milkman. Dashingly charming and sharply dressed, he has a strong sense of social and aesthetic justice, as well as commitment to his ethnic roots. A Jewish Mafiosi, he plots his escapades during the prayer at the synagogue. In one story, his father Mendel (Leonid Kanevsky), falls in love with a sexy *shiksa* [derogatory Yiddish for a gentile woman] (Efrat Ben-Zur) and plans to run away with her. To protect his family from shame and destitution, Benya fights his own father, and occupies his place of leadership in the criminal hierarchy. Later, Benya reinforces his royal status through marriage with a daughter of another gangster, Froim Grach (Yevgeny Gamburg).

The assault on the rich store-owner (Vradimir Halemsky) nicknamed *Jew-and-a-half* reveals Benya's magnanimity. When a sales clerk gets accidentally killed during the robbery, Benya arranges a lavish funeral, and takes care of the welfare of the poor clerk's mother.

Besides Benya Krik, other dramatic characters populate *City*. A heartbreaking love story unfolds between Jewish photographer Ilya Isakovich (Yevgeny Terletsky) and Russian prostitute Margarita (Natalya Voitulevich-Manor), two lonely aging souls.

In a phantasmatic plot, Arina, a fertile Russian maid (Natalya Voitulevich-Manor) begs Jesus for a solution to her problem of constant pregnancies. Jesus sends her an angel (Israel [Sasha] Demidov) who can share her carnal pleasures, but cannot get her pregnant. However, Arina's happiness does not last long. She accidentally strangles the angel in her sleep, and resigns herself to her old ways.

The final plot of *City*, based on real events, is a story of Babel's own survival of a pogrom. The plot culminates with a scene when young Babel (Yevgenya Dodina) loses his grandfather, his doves, and also his childhood.

Figure 7: *City (Odessa Stories)*. Left to right: Yevgeny Gamburg, Slava Bibergal, Klim Kamenko, Igor Mirkurbanov, Amnon Wolf, and Nelly Gosheva
(Courtesy of Gesher Theatre)

Visually, the production is a celebration of strong bright images drawn from the traditions of magical realism and primitivism. The sets, the costumes, and the makeup are exaggerated and graphic. In the scene of a pogrom, a giant blood-colored sun is setting in the background. In other scenes, a rich mural painted after Pirosmani,[6] adorns the stage background. The metal work of the sets is reminiscent of a nineteenth century train-station and of birdcages. Following the railway motif, trolleys rapidly roll on and off the main stage. These trolleys are small stages set as either Froim Grach's cart, or Benya' red convertible, or a policemen's horse, or a bed on which Benya is serviced by a whooping prostitute.

A live brass orchestra in crisp white uniforms accompanies the show. The stylized music, mixing motifs of klezmer melodies, Odessa folk songs, and tunes famous at the dawn of the twentieth century, add to the visual celebration.

6 Niko Pirosmani, an outstanding primitivist painter, was famous for bright emotional images of people and landscapes of his native Georgia at the dawn of the twentieth century.

As the production moves through several plots, the actors play multiple roles. Each character has a distinctive style of speech and body language. Benya Krik, a brutal and powerful figure, unexpectedly stutters. Due to this speech defect, Benya says precious little, causing others to be attentive to his every word. For his high school entrance exam, young Babel recites Pushkin's poem in Russian with a painfully embarrassing *shtetl* accent. As he recites, he flails his limbs with awkward intensity—a brilliant Jew in a world that will humiliate him.

The premiere of *City* took place on December 24, 1996, at Gesher's *hangar*. Even though Gesher produced both Russian and Hebrew versions of *City*, the official premiere was in Hebrew. Gesher knew better than to advertise its Russian version.

Although successful with the audiences, *City* has not enjoyed the same triumphant critical reception as *Village*. The critics disagreed over the significance of the Russian-Jewish topic, evaluation of Gesher's theatrical style, and the political meaning of the production.

The critics who hailed the show attributed its success to the fact that Gesher went back to its Russian-Jewish cultural roots. The critical appreciation of the topic went hand in hand with the acclaim of the style of the production. Thus, Michael Handelsaltz gives praise to acting, design, and staging, calling the show "an amazing, exciting, fascinating vision" (1996c). Even though Handelsaltz complains about the pursuit of special effects, he concludes that Gesher presents a remarkable production. He attributes the artistic success to the familiar topic: "When they [Gesher's theatre-makers] deal with their own Russian-Jewish materials, they are unbeatable in their scope and talent." In another review he restates that Gesher is at its best "when dealing with the Russian-Jewish materials" (1997).

Avi Gurfinkel from *Yerushalaim* expresses the same idea: "This time it [Gesher] deals with the topic which is custom-tailored to fit. Indeed, is there a theatre in the world, which is suited to deal with the life of Jews in Russia better than Gesher? The familiarity of the creators with the topic is evident, and it adds power to the production" (1997). Both Handelsaltz and Gurfinkel arrive at seemingly favorable conclusions. Yet, these conclusions are also implicitly restrictive. By praising Gesher for dealing with the Russian-Jewish topic, they hint that the theatre-makers should know their place and limit themselves to familiar topics.

As with *Adam Resurrected*, *The Lower Depths*, and *Tartuffe*, Gesher's emotional exaggerated style becomes an object of criticism. Eliakim Yaron argues that Arye is addicted to the richness of his style and "gets swamped with it" (1996b). Shosh Weitz appreciates the story-theatre concept of the production, rich visual imagery, imaginative staging, and coordinated ensemble work, and calls *City* "a celebration" (1996c). However, like Yaron, she complains that Arye gets carried away with his carnivalesque style, forgetting about the ideas of the play:

> With of the plentitude of flavors, decorations, and fireworks, the reason for celebration is forgotten....The style becomes a style for its own sake, and it seems that Arye is in love with his own ability to control the style and the stage, much more than a text requires. The result is that the production is too long and too busy. (Weitz 1996c)

Shi Bar-Yakov condescendingly remarks that "the intensity of their success went to Arye's and his ensemble's heads" (1996b). According to him, Gesher's theatrical style "turned into means to celebrate the virtuoso ability of the actors, designers, musicians, and especially the director, without sufficient justification of this stylized effort" (1996b). Following in the footsteps of *Village* reception, Bar-Yakov interprets *City* as an expression of nostalgia; however, in contrast to *Village*, Bar-Yakov assesses this nostalgia negatively. He also blames it on Gesher's cultural identity: "It is with Russian-Jewish Babel, that is so close to his origin, that he [Arye] gets dragged to kitschy nostalgia." The production is "a gigantic void drowning in the excessive nostalgia and style" (1996b).

Sarit Fuks also disapproves of the style of the production, which she mocks as "a demonstration of tiresome beauty and tedious genius" (1996b). Like Bar-Yakov, she argues that *City* presents "a nihilistic fantasy"—an expression of Arye's nostalgia. This nostalgia "does not carry any meaning besides its beauty. It does not touch upon critical issues of life and death, and does not connect to the present of the audience, let alone its future" (1996b). Fuks contrasts *City* with *Village*, which she interpreted as "realistic nostalgia" (1996a), which inspired hope for the future and was relevant to the Israeli audience. For Fuks, *City* is "a quest for identity" on behalf of Arye and his ensemble. Fuks's interpretation inevitably evokes ethnic and cultural agendas. Thus, she claims that the dramatic tension of the production stems from the sexual tension between Jews and gentiles, a tension apparently familiar to Gesher Theatre members (whose Jewishness the media constantly questioned).

Guy Cohen from the newspaper *Hair* also sees the production as nostalgic: "*City* is a pining for the long-lost world, for the innocence, romanticism, respect, simplicity, joy of life and humanity" (1996). He claims that *City* is not only the best Gesher production, but also the best production of Israeli, and perhaps even international, theatre. Cohen attributes its success to "the great Russian soul." Cohen sees the Russian topic and style of the production in the most positive light; but his interpretation still relies on exposing ethnic and cultural agendas.

One point of disagreement between Fuks and Cohen concerns the political meaning of the production. According to Fuks, the production capitalizes on the audience's Jewish complexes: on memories of anti-Semitism and feelings of self-pity. *City* portrays a touching picture of Jewish life in Russia, and culminates with a scene of a pogrom, which implicitly justifies the founding of the state of Israel. Thus, *City*'s topic is closely connected to the history of Zionism and Israeli forefathers. In this way, argues Fuks, the production's compliance with the Zionist ideology makes it politically conservative. She adds that the production values of *City*, its visual imagery, creative staging, and superb acting, along with the conservative topic, make this production commercial.

Cohen is aware that *City* can be perceived as conservative: "One could think that *City*...pets the establishment on the head." Yet, Cohen disparages this point of view. He argues: "*City* is an oppositional production....Its opposition is in its humanity, and in a complete lack of what was once called 'message'." As for the humanity of the show, Cohen explains that *City* probably was unsettling for the politicians and government officials who attended the show, because the humane portrayal of the diverse characters emphasized the essential humanity of the Other, and, therefore, went against the grain of the Israeli politics of discrimination against Palestinians. As Cohen expresses it: "It's difficult to fall in love with some Russian *goyah* [gentile woman] from a hundred years ago [Arina] and then go and humiliate Arabs" (1996). As for the "lack of message," Cohen does not intend to say that the show is meaningless, rather, he says that it lacks a hegemonic ideological message. By placing the humanity and aesthetic dimensions of the show beyond such a 'message', Cohen rejects the widely accepted *agitprop* function of theatre in Israel. In this way, Cohen's position is hybrid. His interpretation is both complicit with and resistant to the dominant ideology. It is complicit because his interpretation, like that of other critics, relies on ethnic and cultural agendas. Yet it is resistant because Cohen rejects the presence of ideological 'message' as a valid criterion of judgment.

These different interpretations of the production can be explained by the dynamic of mutual colonization engendering ambivalent attitudes to the Other. One aspect of the colonization process is represented by critics such as Fuks and Bar-Yakov, who condescend to Gesher. Their critiques are based on the ethnic and cultural identities of the Gesher theatre-makers. However, other critics take a colonized position. Thus, Cohen's interpretation brings up the Israelis' nagging feeling of inferiority as he attributes Gesher's artistic achievement to its rich cultural heritage: "This is the secret of their success. Besides the great Russian soul, they have a cultural depth" (1996).

These different positions converge in Cohen's conclusion:

> Thank you very much, wonderful actors, and other creators of the show. It is difficult for us to say their names, they are too long, too melodic, and too complicated for our militarist,[7] abrupt, and choppy language. But thank you for the warmness, and the feelings, and for the innocence. Thank you for the great streams of love that are transferred to us, the audience. (Cohen 1996)

Here, Cohen begins by presenting Israeli culture as inferior to Russian: he juxtaposes melodic sophisticated Russian to gruff Hebrew; warm, sensitive, loving theatre-makers to presumably crude and thick-skinned local audiences. Yet, by the end he reverses his position, and presents the Gesher actors as "noble savages"—sincere and innocent.

In the late nineties, this attitude became increasingly popular with some of the critics. Fabiana Hefetz, in her preview titled "Fancy Bridge [*Gesher*] Above Shallow Waters" exhibits the same attitude: "They [Gesher's actors] are wonderful again. The water in the title refers to the rest of the [Israeli] theatres" (1996).

Such adulating attitude angered some critics and theatre-makers. For instance, Shohat quotes Dror Keren, one of the *sabra* Gesher actors: "I protest against the blind worshipping [of Gesher]. This worshipping poses the theatre as members of cultural elite, who throw several trinkets to the natives in banana republic" (1996). In his mocking complaint, Keren captured the dynamic of colonization. He even used traditional colonial language to describe relationships between the theatre and the critics.

As Gesher was working on *City*, the political climate in Israel changed drastically once again. After the assassination of Yitzhak Rabin in November 1995, and the temporary leadership of Shimon Peres, the right-wing Binyamin Netanyahu became Prime Minister (in May 1996). Under Rabin's auspices, a Ministry of Culture, Science, and Sports, headed by a secular, progressive, and active Shulamit Aloni, was separate from the Ministry of Education. Under Netanyahu, the government's priorities shifted. Culture fell under the jurisdiction of the Ministry of Education once again. Zvulun Hammer, a right-wing religious leader, received the education portfolio and became the Minister of Education and Culture. Theatre, an outpost of secular culture in Israel, increasingly lost its priority in the eyes of the establishment. The

---

7 In the Hebrew original Cohen describes Israeli language as *tzahali*, literally "of Israeli Defense Forces."

funding and management reforms initiated by the Shelach Committee never came about.

Political elites still attended Gesher premieres and exhibited their nominal support, but Gesher continued to receive the lowest funding among all public repertory theatres in Israel (Goren 1998). Gesher's budget still grew, but very slowly. By the end of 1997, it had reached over 14 million NIS, out of which the public funding was 7.2 million NIS—an increase by only 1 million as compared to 1996. The main growth came from the theatre-generated profits: the ticket sales (in Israel and abroad) and private donations (see Table 1).

Like *Village*, *City* toured extensively abroad. In March 1998, Gesher took part in the festival of Israeli Culture at the Kennedy Center in Washington, D.C. called *Art of the State: Israel at 50*. Babel's widow and grandson[8] attended the first performance. For once, the reception pattern abroad matched the reception in Israel. The audiences' reception was warm. The critics acknowledged the high production values of *City*, but were reticent about the saturated style: "As a cynical loving vision of a lost world, *City* has many strengths. As a theatrical piece, it's a little clumsy and overlong, though always imaginatively staged and beautifully acted" (Rose 1998).

In June 1999, *City* was performed at the Barbican Festival BITE: 99 in London. Like American reviews, the British reviews in both *The Times* (Cliff 1999) and *The Guardian* (Gardner 1999) praised acting and staging but criticized the overwhelming style of the production. In November 1998, Gesher presented *City* in Paris, France, and, a year later, at the Theatre Festival in Berlin.

In Israel, *City* won the Israeli Theatre Award for 1997 in the categories of Most Promising Actor (Amnon Wolf), Best Stage Designer (Alexander Lisiyansky), and Best Costume Designer (Anna Chruscheva). However, the production had to be removed from the competition in the Best Director category because Arye had won it twice in a row, and the rules of the competition forbid winning it in the three consecutive years.

By 2001, *City* was performed 194 times: 145 in Hebrew and 49 in Russian. Despite the controversial critical reception, *City* became the third most popular Gesher production (after *Village* and *The Idiot*). It remains in Gesher's repertoire as of this writing.

If *Village* marked the ultimate success of Gesher, then *City* reaffirmed it. Both productions became long-running Gesher hits at home and abroad. Paradoxically, despite Gesher's apolitical non-ethnic motto, both *Village* and

---

8 As fate would have it, Andrei Malaev-Babel, a grandson of Isaac Babel, was a director of Stanislavsky Theatre Studio, a Washington-based theatre founded by Soviet immigrants, an American "Gesher."

City productions were based on the original dramaturgy engaging Jewish or Israeli themes. These productions were easily marketed abroad, and international success in turn fed into greater popularity at home. Consequently, Gesher found itself in an ambivalent position: it simultaneously rejected the importance of its cultural identity and was compelled to emphasize it. In turn, Gesher's cultural difference simultaneously attracted and repulsed critics and audiences alike.

• CHAPTER EIGHT •

Into the Valley

Accented Stars

By 1997, the exchange between the Gesher actors and the Israeli cultural producers was under way. The number of Israeli actors in the Gesher troupe increased, and the Russian-born Gesher actors started to take part in Israeli TV and film productions. For the first time in Gesher's history, a journalist referred to it as "a theatre of Russians and Israelis" (Melamed 1997). Unlike reductive references to Gesher as immigrant or Russian theatre, this inclusive reference emphasized the hybrid character of the company. However, this process of cultural exchange was not devoid of problems.

Israeli actors encountered at Gesher a style of artistic work different from what they were accustomed to. Membership in the Gesher troupe was demanding. It required unlimited work hours, full dedication, and maximum resources. Israeli actors perceived this as a Russian approach to theatrical work. Interesting and alluring at first, for some of them it proved exhausting and alienating. Out of several young Israeli actors who joined Gesher in 1996–97, only two, Efrat Ben-Zur and Amnon Wolf, remained in the troupe. Dror Keren, Dorit Lev-Ari, Nadav Aviknin, and Eli Danker[1] left, unable to withstand the pressure and the totality of work at Gesher. Miriam Yahil-Wax explained: "We have difficulties with some of our Israelis because of that [Gesher style of work]. Everyone in Israel is used to more freedom and more space, and more time for yourself. In Gesher it does not exist. Time, your life—everything belongs to the theatre" (1999b).

If it was difficult for Israelis to get adjusted to Gesher, Russian-born actors who started participating in Israeli film and television productions also ran

1 Eli Danker, cast to play Vershinin in *Three Sisters* left only after one month of rehearsal. Keren Dror left in 1997. Dorit Lev-Ari and Nadav Aviknin left in 1999.

into problems. Yevgenya Dodina appeared in several Israeli films,[2] the most famous of them being 1996 feature *Clara Hakdusha* [Saint Clara], directed by Ari Folman and Ori Sivan. She appeared in several TV serials, such as *Balash Beyerushalaim* [Detective in Jerusalem] and *Bat Yam–New York*. Israel (Sasha) Demidov also appeared in *Saint Clara*, and later in the acclaimed TV serial *Florentin*. Natalya Voitulevich-Manor appeared in the films *Eretz Hadasha* [New Land] by Orna Ben-David and *Zikron Dvarim* [Things] by Amos Gitai. In all these films the Gesher actors were restricted to the parts of immigrants or foreigners: they could not overcome the limitations of their accents.

Natalya Voitulevich-Manor publicly disapproved of such typecasting: "The parts offered to [female] immigrant actors are usually the parts of cleaning lady, maid, or a prostitute. Don't they think that it's time to diversify?" (Bahir 1997). She added that since the Israeli filmmakers offer her such limited choice of roles, she rejects most of the offers. For her, like for other Russian-born actors, Gesher remains the most interesting professional arena. Outside of Gesher, they also enjoy professional and popular recognition; yet, they are permanently marked by their cultural identity. In Gesher, Demidov, Dodina, and Voitulevich-Manor are stars, whereas outside of Gesher they remain, using Naficy's (2001) term, "accented." Thus Gesher becomes a golden cage.

No one was more marked by his cultural identity than Yevgeny Arye. His media representation centered completely on the politics of identity, and particularly on his status as a new immigrant. He was expected to fit the ideological Zionist norms. But Arye both reaffirms and challenges these norms. Some characteristics of his public persona are consistent with Zionist ideology. He is a director of a Hebrew-language theatre, which facilitates successful absorption of the immigrant actors. Effectively, he takes part in the production of Israeli culture: his shows are popular with Israeli audiences, and are reviewed by the major media. Moreover, he is highly regarded by the Israeli establishment. Yet other characteristics of Arye's public persona challenge the Zionist norms. Arye's immigration to Israel was motivated by personal and professional, rather than Zionist, interests. He does not know Hebrew, and relies on Russian and English in his daily life. Moreover, he takes a great pride in his cultural heritage, and gives little sign of moving towards cultural assimilation. As a result, Arye occupies an ambivalent position in Israeli culture: he is simultaneously an insider and an outsider, a marginal and a central figure.

2 *Jentele* by Agur Shaif, *Sof Hamishak* [End of the Game] by Yoni Darmon, and *Kitzur Toldot Haahuvim* [Short History of Loved] by Ytzhak Tzefel-Yeshurun.

And yet, Arye's media representation pushes him to one of the two extremes: he is presented as either complicit with, or resistant to, the Zionist norms. In earlier profiles and interviews, Arye is framed as a timid greenhorn on his way to becoming an assertive Israeli:

> Gesher today is an Israeli theatre in the full meaning of the word, and so is its director. When I met him at one of the first shows of Gesher, he was embarrassed and withdrawn. Today he is not hesitant to give his opinion, to point to the weaknesses of Israeli theatre, to suggest, and to criticize. (Shohat 1994a)

The critic presents Arye as a "good" immigrant, whose behavior is consistent with an Israeli ethos. She applies an ideological yardstick to Arye, imposing on him a system of Zionist values.

As the time went by, the critics grew impatient with Arye. In 1997, the same Shohat described him as an "alien" who "still does not speak Hebrew" (1997c). According to the critic's logic, in his first years in Israel Arye's lack of Hebrew was forgivable, but after seven years this cultural dissent is unacceptable. Arye violates the Zionist norms of commitment to learning Hebrew and assimilation to Israeli culture, and the critic ought to call him into compliance.

Similar attitude is expressed in another interview, when the journalist asks Arye: "Everyone knows your issue with Hebrew, that you didn't have time to learn it. So, do you feel attached to the life in Israel or do you live in a bubble?" (Shapiro 1997). The phrasing of the question poses attachment to Israel in opposition to complete separation from it, ruling out other possibilities.

Only one writer, Ariana Melamed, represents Arye's linguistic situation as a personal and professional drama, devoid of ideological meanings:

> English with journalists, Russian with actors, [Hebrew] with the help of crutches of translation....It looks like part of Arye's extra adrenalin has its source in his constant fear that his comments will not pass exactly; that the nuanced language of such a verbal person as he, will not cross the double barrier of Hebrew and local culture. "And it will be like that for the rest of their lives," he says sadly about his Russian actors who do heroic work and manage not to sound like a parody of the early Habima. About the rest of his life and his own linguistic limbo, he does not talk. (Melamed 1997)

But even Melamed's sensitivity comes to an end as soon as she starts discussing the relationships between Russian and Israeli cultures. She claims that the Russian pedigree of Israeli culture created space for a troupe like Gesher:

> In any other place in the world a phenomenon like Gesher wouldn't have survived....Would it seem possible to imagine native New-Yorkers storming the doors of a theatre which performs either in a very foreign language, or in heavy accents of new immigrants? Only in Israel, a place that is still attached by its umbilical cord to Russian culture, or at least to a certain image of the Russian culture, [it is possible]. (Melamed 1997)

According to Melamed, Gesher succeeded in Israel due to its Russian roots. As a matter of fact, Gesher succeeded in Israel despite (and not due to) its cultural origin. Since its first days, the Israeli audiences were reluctant to accept the Gesher actors' accents. The Israeli critics exoticized Gesher as "ethnic" or "immigrant" theatre and judged its productions by how well the theatre-makers met ideological expectations.

Melamed also gives credit for Gesher's success to the receptive Israeli public. She cannot imagine a similar reception elsewhere in the world. Melamed probably would have been surprised to learn, for instance, about the critical and popular success of Washington-based Stanislavsky Theatre Studio, an American ensemble founded by immigrants from the former Soviet Union.[3]

The cultural positioning of Gesher is a stumbling point of almost every article about Arye. Melamed's attitude is stated already in the title of the article: "[Arye] Will Show You What Is *Kultura*." For this threat she chooses the Russian word *kultura* [culture] over the Hebrew *tarbut* for its European "cultured" sound. Having claimed her attitude, she criticizes the ethnocentrism of the Soviet immigrants:

> When the leaders of immigrant intelligentsia point out to the Israelis that they [Israelis] are only descendents of the [Russian] culture, whereas they [Russian immigrants] are bearers of the thousands years of *kultura* [culture], too many Israelis tend to nod in agreement. (Melamed 1997)

Melamed charges the Russian intellectuals with colonizing Israeli culture, and sneers at Israelis who willingly take the colonized position. She asks Arye, "Maybe Chekhov is a part of your colonization program? An attempt to show how to do Russian culture correctly?" In response, Arye appeals to the presumed universality of art: "'There is no program,' he admits, 'Chekhov is not Russian, just as Shakespeare is not English'" (Melamed 1997). Refuting his "colonization program," Arye relies on the universal value of Western art that transcends the boundaries of national cultures. It escapes both the journalist and Arye that his examples, Chekhov and Shakespeare, represent the Western cultural tradition, rather than crossover cultural universals.

---

3 For further information, see the studio's web-site <www.sts-online.org>

Here, and in other interviews, Arye presents himself as an expert from a cultural center. It is from this position that Arye expresses his concern over the provinciality of Israeli art, about incompetent theatre training, and ineffectual criticism (see, for instance, Shohat 1997c). Unfortunately, there is a remarkable symmetry in Arye's and his critics' reciprocal condescension.

The Mutual Disappointment: *Three Sisters*

During the entire year of 1997, Gesher worked on the rehearsals of *Three Sisters* by Anton Chekhov. First produced in 1901 by the Moscow Art Theatre, *Three Sisters* has become one of the best known dramas of the twentieth century, and an indispensable part of European theatre repertoire. The main characters—sisters Olga, Masha, and Irina, stuck in the Russian province, are longing to return to Moscow, the city of their dreams. Moscow for them is not just a geographical location, it is their hopes for a better future, and their nostalgia of happy past. But as time passes, it becomes clear that the sisters will never leave, and that for each of them Moscow will remain an unattainable state of mind. Olga (Natalya Voitulevich-Manor), is sapped by her job as a teacher in a local school. Masha (Yevgenya Dodina), stuck in a frustrating marriage, is in love with Vershinin (Igor Mirkurbanov). But he is married, and their affair leads nowhere. Irina (Efrat Ben-Zur), the youngest, attempts to escape the dullness of her life by marrying Tuzenbakh (Nadav Aviknin). But her fiancée is killed in a duel, and her prospects are ruined. In the meanwhile, Natasha (Dorit Lev-Ari), their manipulative sister-in-law, is taking control over their weak-willed brother Andrei (Israel [Sasha] Demidov), and subsequently over the entire household. At the end, the three sisters are left as they were in the beginning, still clinging to their hopes for a better life.

Arye wanted to produce *Three Sisters* for some time, but he had his reservations. Yahil-Wax explained: "*Three Sisters* and *Uncle Vanya* are Arye's favorite plays by Chekhov, but he hasn't produced them until now because he tries to avoid the self-obvious, and to stage Chekhov in a Russian theatre is a bit expected" ("Shalosh Ahayot" 1997).

When Arye finally approached Chekhov's play, he gave it an unusual interpretation. Arye remained faithful to his style of impressive visual images, atmospheric music, choreographed movement, and emotional acting. Instead of long pauses and loaded innuendos, Arye produced Chekhov with unreserved emotions. In his staging, the characters' feelings were embodied in their movements, body language, tone, and actions. For instance, in the original text, Irina fells into deep distress when Tuzenbach dies; in Arye's version, Irina attempts suicide.

The sets (by Alexander Lisiyansky) create a powerful vision, combining realistic and symbolic elements. The house where the action takes place is hovering in the air, moving slowly in different angles, giving the impression of instability and insecurity. The costumes are realistic: the sisters' elegant floor-length dresses, the officers' uniforms, and the servants' folk garb. In his music, Avi Benjamin includes sad and moving excerpts from Gustav Mahler's *Fifth Symphony*.

The premiere of *Three Sisters* took place on December 6, 1997. Its reception by both Israeli critics and audiences was one of the biggest disappointments for Gesher's theatre-makers. The actors and the director believed in their work, and felt that *Three Sisters* was a truly meaningful production. Chekhov's text had almost a religious quality for them, and the rehearsal process, which lasted almost a year, was lengthy and thorough even by Gesher standards. Yet, this effort fell flat. The audiences complained about the duration of the show (almost 4 hours), and critics rejected the unconventional interpretation of Chekhov's play. Few reviewers were supportive of the productions, and even their reviews were relatively cool.

Shosh Weitz (1997) praised the sets, the music, the visual images, and the ensemble work. But she did not find Arye's interpretation particularly convincing. Shi Bar-Yakov (1997) also admired the visual richness of the production; however, he criticized the indiscriminative casting of Russian- and Hebrew-speaking actors, which highlighted the difference in their Hebrew pronunciation. Yehudit Orian was the only journalist whose review testified to her deep appreciation of the production:

> I am sitting through four hours of sweet sadness, of passionate desire "that there is no place in the world like Moscow," of identification with Olga, Masha, and Irina. There is no similarity between their history and my history, but I feel their pain, and I am longing to see what would happen to them, and I care for them much more than I care for female characters in the contemporary plays. (Orian 1998)

This sympathetic account clearly shows that the journalist was moved by the performance. Yet, this review does not carry the same weight as reviews by tenured critics, (such as Handelsaltz, Weitz, Fuks, and Shohat), because Yehudit Orian is not a theatre critic. She runs a column in *Yediot Ahronot* reviewing various cultural events from a personal perspective.

In contrast to the limited positive responses, the negative reception was extensive, articulate, and argumentative. Two closely related issues were at stake: Gesher's theatrical style and Arye's role as a director.

Figure 8: *Three Sisters*. Left to right: Yevgenya Dodina, Nadav Aviknin, Efrat Ben-Zur, and Igor Mirkurbanov
(Courtesy of Gesher Theatre)

Gesher's theatrical style is the main subject of Eliakim Yaron's review. He starts with venting his unfulfilled expectations: "I hoped that Gesher would mount the ultimate Chekhov production. Who if not they?" (1997). Yaron considered Gesher and Chekhov an ideal combination, and now cannot conceal his disappointment. Despite "a wonderful ensemble" and a director who is "a magician, in whose long show there is not a boring moment," the production, according to the critic, does not succeed. It is overloaded with visual effects, loud music, and exaggerated acting. The result is that "Chekhov is lost." Yaron explains: "The director tried to show the level of absurdity in Chekhov, but with that he lost Chekhov's acclaimed irony, and even more terrible, the feeling that we are dealing with human beings" (1997). Yaron refuses to accept Arye's interpretation which goes against the grain of his expectations.

In Sarit Fuks's review, the analysis of the production is reduced to criticism of Arye's directorial style and his cultural identity. This criticism becomes an opportunity for a fierce personal attack. Fuks starts her review with an anecdote: the night of premiere, when Arye was called to the final bows on stage, he looked as if he was in a hurry—in Fuks's interpretation, "as if he needed to go elsewhere." Fuks found that unnerving: "Where he could possibly want to go?" she asked. The reason for her annoyance is that she found his behavior symbolic:

> I am not talking only about his posture but about Arye's essential position. Since he made *aliyah* to Israel, he is not present in this place, but is always on the way...Arye does not really belong. He is an artist who is cut off from his roots, who works within an alien cultural environment, which he does not value. He does not create within his own living culture; yet, he continues to produce theatre that this culture taught him. The further away he is from it [the Russian culture] the more rigid are the patterns that he brought with him from his motherland. This is an advanced process, with a recess of the successes like *Village* or *Lower Depths*....This process culminates in the *Three Sisters*....When Arye looks at us from the stage impatiently, he does not show much respect to us nor to our culture. And justifiably so, too. (Fuks 1998)

Fuks's sketch demonstrates the process of mutual and internal colonization at work. Fuks starts by taking a colonizing position, and putting Arye into an inferior position ("Arye does not really belong"). Further she moves to Arye's vantage point, and ascribes to him the condescending position of a colonizer ("he does not show much respect to us nor to our culture"). Yet, at the end, she makes another shift and concludes by agreeing with Arye: "And justifiably so, too." Internal colonization makes Fuks turn not only against Arye, but also against herself.

Fuks frames the relationship between Gesher and its critics and audiences in terms of an antagonistic dichotomy: Russian culture on one pole, Israeli on the other. She refuses to see Gesher as a hybrid theatre, and Arye as a hybrid cultural producer. Approaching Arye with the yardstick of ideological norms (Hebrew proficiency, attachment to the Land of Israel, and Zionist commitment), Fuks judges Arye by how well (or rather how poorly) he fits the norm. Her verdict is unrelenting: "The relative failure of the *Three Sisters*...is a testimony of Arye's troubled condition" (1998). She argues that Arye chose to produce a play about a dream to go back to Moscow because this theme for him is autobiographical: "Like characters in *Three Sisters* Arye is stuck in a provincial town" (1998). Fuks suggests that Arye sees himself left behind in the provincial Tel Aviv, outside of the great European cultural centers.

But Fuks in her anguish does not blame only Arye. She charges the Israeli public, who admired Gesher too much, with the responsibility for Arye's presumed failure. This is an illustration of how the colonial process gets internalized: Fuks switches from contempt towards Arye to accusations against her own culture. Fuks's inner colonizer scolds her own inner colonized for adulation of Arye and for Israeli cultural inferiority:

> We surrounded him with a cult-like adoration, which was very pleasant to him—oh, how pleasant, but that also gave to his theatre a provincial quality. And in a province...one gets used to low standards, because every Sasha Demidov is Gerard Philippe, and every Yevgeny Arye is Stanislavsky. The fame is reached easily, the criteria are lower and lower, but the expectations from the local deity are so endless, that even a genius director like Yevgeny Arye is prone to screw up. (Fuks 1998)

At the end of her diatribe, Fuks demonstrates yet another shift: as she accuses Israelis, she is dismissive of Arye who, in Fuks's terms, "screwed up."

Fuks's preoccupation with Gesher's cultural identity is expressed even in her criticism of Gesher's tours abroad. She scolds Gesher for both the scope and destinations of the tours. She particularly dislikes the fact that Gesher tours in the US and not in Russia. In her interpretation this fact testifies to Gesher's reluctance to acknowledge its cultural and national origin. Fuks concludes her review by calling on the theatre "to solve the problem of the split identity" (1998). This "split identity"—an expression of hybridity—clearly unnerves the critic. According to her, in order to resolve this problem, Gesher should either resign to being a Russian theatre, including language, location, and cultural affiliation; or to perform a full act of mimicry, and turn into a truly Israeli theatre. It seems that if it was up to Fuks, she would order Gesher to stop staging Israeli plays in Russian style, as well as staging Russian classics in an unconventional interpretations; instead, Gesher should choose which side it is on and stick with it.

In Fuks's review, the discussion of directorial style and the unconventional interpretation of Chekhov's play leads to conclusions that far exceed the realm of theatrical production. Her intolerance of cultural difference and her inability to accept hybridity result in replicating colonial discourse.

Arye's directorial style emerges as a central subject of Michael Handelsaltz's review. According to Handelsaltz, a combination of Gesher and Chekhov should have guaranteed the success of the production. Yet, "the miracle does not happen." Why? Handelsaltz's blaming finger point at Arye's directorial style:

> This is a show that shouts: 'Look, what a wonderful director I am.' Yes, Arye is a director with vision, enthusiasm, and innovative thinking, and he does not spare us a single bit of his great talent....But Arye forgot that sometimes less is more, and more is way too much....All the good qualities of Arye were impressive until now—until he met Chekhov. (Handelsaltz 1997)

His verdict marks a new era of critical reception for Gesher. Chekhov, for Handelsaltz, is the theatre's litmus paper, revealing all the drawbacks of Arye's style.

Later, Michael Handelsaltz published a more extensive review of the production titled "They Didn't Invent the Wheel." This review, seemingly, an analysis of *Three Sisters*, effectively turns into an anti-Gesher manifesto. What is at stake in this review is not the production itself, and not its style, but rather the cultural identity of Gesher's theatre-makers, especially of Yevgeny Arye:

> They [Gesher's theatre-makers] bask in the admiration of the Israeli audience and critics. The attitude of the cultural establishment to them is almost self-demeaning. Judging by the praises—only few of them deserved—addressing their productions and their director, one might think that they invented theatre, and that before their arrival all what was here [in Israel] was a cultural desert. (Handelsaltz 1998a)

This statement results from the dynamic of mutual colonization. The critic is threatened by Gesher's perceived cultural superiority. In his view, Gesher took a condescending position towards Israeli audiences and critics, whereas Israeli audiences and critics took positions of ingratiating admirers. In his attempt to restore justice, Handelsaltz calls both the theatre and its fans to order. In doing so, he takes a condescending position towards the theatre. It does not occur to Handelsaltz that he contributes to the endless tag of war of mutual colonization.

From his condescending position, Handelsaltz exposes the secret of Gesher's success: seemingly, Gesher succeeds only with weak dramatic material, which serves as "a primary material for Arye's theatrical imagination" (1998a). Amongst "primary materials" he lists *Dreyfus File, Molière, The Idiot, Village, City,* and *The Lower Depths*. Handelsaltz explains, "The problem arises when Arye is required to cope with exemplary dramatic creations, which were around for a long time, and survived also productions where directors served the plays and not their creative ego" (1998a). Among such plays he lists *Rosencrantz and Guildenstern Are Dead, Tartuffe* (which he calls "the least successful production in Gesher's repertoire"), and finally, *Three Sisters*. *Three Sisters* presents "powerful, unique, and rich in tradition dramatic material with which one needs to cope with, and not to use it only in order to demonstrate to ignorant Israelis how a great director who came from Russia does Chekhov" (1998a). In this account, Handelsaltz approaches Arye's production not as an interpretation of Chekhov, but as an expression of cultural superiority. Internalizing colonization process, Handelsaltz alone, without any input from Arye, is able to produce both the rhetoric of narcissism and rhetoric of inferiority.

Like other reviewers, Handelsaltz also gives an unfavorable account of the casting, indiscriminative of Russian and Israeli accents: "Their [Israeli actors'] introduction into the ensemble only emphasizes the artificiality of Hebrew in the mouths of the Gesher actors. It was preferable to keep the homogeneity of their Russian-Hebrew accent" (1998a).

Handelsaltz's judgment is indicative of changes in the reception of Gesher's performance in Hebrew and of inclusion of Israeli actors in the troupe, that took place over time. In 1994–95, critics celebrated the inclusion of Israeli actors into the Gesher troupe as a sign of Gesher's openness to Israeli culture. But by 1997–98, the situation had changed. Previously, Israeli actors were cast so that their accents would be instrumental to the plot (like in *Rosencrantz and Guildenstern Are Dead* and *Village*). But in the *Three Sisters* casting relied not on the accents, but rather on conventional casting criteria (such as actors' physique and professional potential), thus, the accent was not accounted for. The critics protested against this; they were fast to remind Gesher about the accent of its actors.

Handelsaltz concludes his review with a personal attack—an expression of irrational anger. According to him, coping with Chekhov "hides the good qualities and emphasizes the weaknesses [of Gesher]. The biggest of them all is lack of modesty, which was never a strength of Gesher people" (1998a). What Handelsaltz is getting at is again a perceived position of cultural superiority. Gesher's theatre-makers do not behave as respectful modest newcomers. They don't step aside; they don't treat Israeli culture with awe. And equally unnerving, they do not exhibit much respect towards "their own" Chekhov. Clearly, the critic's anger is not directed at the style of the production, but at the theatre-makers themselves.

Despite his condescending tone, Handelsaltz's disproval of the production is not convincing. Paradoxically, when he describes the stage and the acting, his words testify to his sincere sympathy with the characters, and his appreciation of the staging:

> The show starts with Olga's monologue. [She is] the oldest sister, who recalls the funeral of their farther, general Prozorov, a year ago, on a birthday of the youngest sister Irina. But at the beginning of the production we don't see the sisters. The stage looks like a kind of a cemetery, covered with a thin layer of snow. In the background, a military band is playing, but we see only its shadows, we hear rifle salvos [like at a military funeral], and then Olga's voice sounds. Only when she completes her monologue, the shadows of a funeral disappear, and the band marches off. What first appeared to be tombs slowly rises and becomes a façade of the house, floating in the air. (Handelsaltz 1998a)

After reading this description, it is difficult to take at face value Handelsaltz's diatribe about the loud, emotional, busy style of the production that betrays Chekhov's spirit. This example shows that what is at stake is not the style and interpretation of the production, but rather the identity of the theatre-makers, and the dynamics of cultural exchange that engage critics into the process of mutual colonization.

Three Sisters did not survive in the Gesher repertoire for long. The unfavorable reception was exacerbated by the fact that the show did not travel well. The sets were heavy and difficult to assemble, which meant that outside of the *hangar* in Tel Aviv, the production could tour only big halls, such as Jerusalem Theatre. In 1999, after only 62 performances, *Three Sisters* was taken off the repertoire.

During 1993–1997, Gesher received high critical acclaim and recognition of the theatre community. The reception of *Three Sisters* indicated a new period in the life of Gesher—a period when Gesher's shows received neither rave reviews nor multiple prizes. What caused such drastic change in the critics' hearts?

Israeli critical discourse is characterized by the colonial hierarchies of power. The praise of Gesher backfired. Gesher, in the context of the identity-driven Israeli criticism, is perceived as "a Russian theatre," or "a new immigrant theatre." Thus, a review of a production turns into a political and cultural debate. If the critics praise Gesher, that means that they admire Russian culture it represents, and consequently, look down on the Israeli culture. The negative reception of *Three Sisters* was nothing but a defensive response of the critics to their self-imposed position of subjugation to the 'Great Russian culture'. The critics fell prey to their own colonial discourse. They created a monster, got scared of it, and decided to fight it. They reacted by swinging completely to the other side, staking for themselves a position of superiority and confining Gesher to inferior position. The negative reception of *Three Sisters* prepared the soil for the critical disregard for Gesher that would last several years.

A New Generation on Stage: *Don Juan*

In mid-1997, Gesher started working on the new project—a theatre studio, an acting school for future generations of Gesher actors. The conceptual basis for such a studio had emerged long before. As early as 1993, Arye criticized the acting schools in Israel: "I cannot see any connection between this school [Beit-Zvi acting school] and what is happening in the practice of theatre life in Israel" (Milshtein 1993). He advocated for greater connection between the existing theatres and actor training. For Arye, training had to be theatre-specific, reflecting the philosophy, artistic approach, and style of work of a particular company: "As for me, there is no such thing as a good acting school....Acting school can only be good for a specific theatre" (Milshtein 1993). Arye urged Israeli theatre-makers to focus their efforts on training the younger generation: "If we don't develop young actors, then...we, ourselves will not be able to produce good theatre" (Milshtein 1993). Later, Arye continued to be vocal in his criticism: "I think that there is a gap between the working theatres and acting schools. Directors, who work in the theatre, have no connection to actor training" (Shohat 1994a).

In 1997, when the Gesher-2 project was under way, Arye became even more explicit in his critique: "I don't like the system of actor training in Israel, where people who teach theatre don't work in the field" (Shohat 1997c). Arye wanted to establish not just an acting studio, but a school of followers who could continue his artistic agenda. Miriam Yahil-Wax adds another rationale to Arye's idea: "The future generation of Gesher will be Israeli. It is impossible to import actors from Russia" (Lev-Ari 1998). Gesher had to coach the new generation.

Lena Kreindlina, an assistant director who left Gesher back in 1995 as a part of Maltzev's team, came back to Gesher inspired by the idea of the new studio. She believed that if there was no 'fresh blood' in the troupe, the theatre would cease to be interesting: "It is important to give [an old] theatre a push and to revitalize it" (Lev-Ari 1998). Kreindlina became an initiator and coordinator of the new project. In October 1997, Gesher founded a studio for young actors called Gesher-2. Kreindlina became the principal studio teacher of the group, and Arye's assistant director for the Gesher-2 production.

According to the plan, the young actors would go through a training program, at the end of which they would produce an independent show. According to the original plan, Gesher-2 would stage a play by Alexander Ostrovsky *Diary of the Scoundrel*. However, it's turned out that Habima planned to stage the same play, and Arye decided to stage *Don Juan* by Jean-Baptiste Molière, translated by a renowned Israeli poet, Natan Alterman.

The project was financed from the modest budget of Gesher Theatre, with the financial support of Cellcom company, one of the most powerful hi-tech companies in Israel. The cost of the project was reported to be 500,000 NIS (Lev-Ari 1998).

The young actors flocked to Gesher. They were in awe of the renowned director, and were flattered to be part of the artistically acclaimed theatre. In October of 1997, when Gesher auditioned actors for Gesher-2, 235 candidates showed up (Shohat 1997b). Only 14 finalists were selected, and already by January 1998 the group was reduced to 11 members, who effectively formed the core of the new studio. They came from a variety of cultural backgrounds: five Israel-born actors, four Russian-born, one actor from Uruguay, and one from Germany. All of them had acquired theatre training and/or professional experience in Israel.

In November of 1997, the Gesher-2 actors gathered for the first meeting with their new mentors. In a press-release, Michal Scheflan reported that Arye emphasized the importance of young actors as future heirs of Gesher (Scheflan 1997). The group started rehearsals, working mainly with Kreindlina. In January, after the premiere of *Three Sisters*, Arye joined the group to work on the rehearsals of *Don Juan*. The rehearsals with Gesher-2 quickly revealed mismatched expectations and mutual misunderstandings. Gesher's leadership had very specific ideas about theatre training: it required hard work, full dedication, and willingness to put up with long hours, poor compensation, and absolute dictatorial authority of a director. For Arye and Kreindlina, young actors had to learn through a military-like basic training, almost a boot camp. Kreindlina gives her philosophy: "It's known that the actor has to be hungry. One cannot work on a full stomach. We told them in advance that it is going to be very difficult, that they won't earn a lot of money, that they wouldn't be able to do projects on the side and act in commercials" (Lev-Ari 1998).

The Gesher-2 actors were an ambitious, hardworking bunch, eager to learn and to succeed. But they did not foresee the level of dedication to theatrical work that Arye and Kreindlina expected from them. Miriam Yahil-Wax implicitly links this convention to Russian theatrical tradition, explaining that it is uncharacteristic of theatre in the West:

> In Israel, theatre is similar to Western theatre. Work of Arye is based not on a schedule, but on total dedication. We, in Israel, don't work like this. There is a schedule, and one can participate in a movie during a rehearsal period. Here, in Gesher, it is impossible. (Lev-Ari 1998)

This demand of complete dedication became a point of contention between the Gesher-2 actors and their mentors. Another point concerned the emotional involvement of the Gesher veterans, especially Arye, with their work. Arye was notorious in the Israeli theatre circles for his bad temper. During the rehearsals, he swings from rage to kindness and back in a matter of seconds. His voice rises to thunderous heights in anger, and then switches to a child-like excitement, the curses intermingled with terms of endearment. The Gesher-2 actors had heard the gossip, but they were not prepared to work in such high emotional voltage. Yahil-Wax explained:

> At first, actors were scared of Arye, they were not used to such temperament, they took it personally, until they understood that this is the way he is, always at a

> maximum, always at a peak of energy and focus, 16 hours a day, and he thinks that everyone is like that. (Lev-Ari 1998)

These points of contention surfaced even before, when Gesher started employing Israeli actors. However, with the establishment of the Gesher-2 group, a new conflict emerged. Due to the tight budget and ill-defined status of the Gesher-2 actors, they were hired on special contracts with fewer benefits. The Gesher management did not see a problem with that; for them Gesher-2 were students, who instead of paying tuition, actually received something of a stipend. However, the Gesher-2 members, most of them graduates of different theatre schools in Israel, with prior professional experience, saw themselves as paid professional actors. This clash of expectations resulted in a serious organizational conflict. The members of the Gesher-2 group battled with the management for fair conditions of employment. But the battle was futile. One of the Gesher-2 actors expressed to me the collective anger and frustration:

> Yes, I belong to Gesher-2, to the second-class actors. They took us as "young actors," but indeed they took people who have already acted before...and now we have a contract that is not legal, we don't have real positions, that's why we don't have rights—only responsibilities. We have no vacations and no severance pay. I am terribly angry, we are fighting and fighting, but here—it is not like a normal place, when you come and you know the conditions, everything is unclear and one needs to wait...and if you are not content here—then you are a traitor, and if you are earning at another place—you are a traitor, everything is like a family, and in the family it is not nice to demand and to fight. (Gesher-2 actor 1999)

Besides the unfair contracts, resulting in "a second class" status for the Gesher-2 actors, this account brings up another sticking point—the family-like style of relationships in the Gesher company. The Israeli actors were accustomed to the model of the contemporary Habima or Cameri theatres, where the cast is production-specific. In contrast, Gesher was a permanent ensemble with its own rules and ethics. Clearly, many of the young actors did not realize what they were getting themselves into. The actor quoted above bitterly describes the limitation imposed by the family rules and ethics. Family mores render business negotiation nearly impossible.

At the same time, in contrast to the anonymous and temporary setting of an average Israeli theatre, the family style of Gesher offered some advantages. The same actor admits:

> There are many advantages to this theatre; there is something very home-like, family-like in this company, something that envelops you, because they take care of all the details...I feel comfortable, and we spend a lot of time here, and there are wonderful

people here, feeling people, good people. In the theatre I feel beloved, and it's very comforting to me. (Gesher-2 actor 1999)

For the Russian-born actors the model of theatre-family, theatre-home, is traditional. But for the Gesher-2 actors it was new. It induced contradictory feelings: they appreciated the personal connections within the troupe, but also were repulsed by the manipulative possibilities that the family style allows, conveniently proscribing legal or financial discussion in the theatre.

The idea of a studio for young actors has roots in Russian theatrical tradition. In fact, Habima grew out of one of the studios of Stanislavsky's theatre. When Arye discussed his plans, he located the idea within the context of Russian theatre: "I would like very much to have a school, in the way Lev Dodin[4] does with the Maly [theatre], and I am starting a workshop for young actors" (Coveney 1997). However, the foundation of Gesher-2 coincided with the establishment of studios for young actors at the two other major Israeli theatres: Habima and Cameri (Shohat 1997a). With the establishment of the Gesher-2 studio Arye simultaneously continued the Russian theatrical tradition and successfully positioned Gesher within the Israeli theatre context.

The establishment of the new studio provoked media interest. Several previews and interviews appeared before the premiere of *Don Juan*. As expected, the media representation of Gesher-2 was centered around the issue of cultural identity. The reportage emphasized the Israeli cultural identity of the young actors: "All of them speak mostly Hebrew, and define themselves as Israelis" (Lev-Ari 1998). Gesher-2 quickly became known as "an Israeli group" within "the Russian theatre" (Bar-Yakov 1997). For journalists, the establishment of a new group meant "a change of image from a Russian theatre to Israeli" (Lev-Ari 1998). For his part, Arye, time and again, protested against the ethnic framing of his theatre by saying, "Gesher is not a Russian theatre" (Lev-Ari 1998).

Another aspect of the identity-focused media representation of Gesher-2 was the issue of cultural differences between Russians and Israelis. Journalists were eager to know how the young Israelis were getting along with the Russian maestro. Arye was reluctant to recognize the significance of cultural differences. He downplayed them and focused on professional differences, ignoring their cultural roots: "I don't see a big problem with cultural difference. As for me, the problem in Israel is that young actors don't understand that every professional work demands if not their entire life, than at least a big part of it" (Lev-Ari 1998). He sneered at the Israeli 'doing the minimum' attitude to work (for which Israelis often chastise themselves). But

4 Lev Dodin is one of the most innovative and respected contemporary Russian directors.

for him, it was not a problem of cultural difference, only of work ethics. Since, according to Arye, the Gesher-2 actors had the right attitude ("they are ready to be part of the troupe and to work hard"), he did not admit to any conflict between them.

Language also became part of the discussion. Journalists asked how Arye, who does not speak Hebrew, worked with the young Israeli actors. Arye, as usual, was reluctant to acknowledge the linguistic limitations of his work, he kept saying: "If you really want to express yourself, you'll succeed regardless of language" (Lev-Ari 1998). He denied the significance of linguistic and cultural differences: for him, theatrical work is universal; it transcends cultural boundaries.

Only indirectly does Arye admit the cultural differences between himself and the Gesher-2 actors by acknowledging different realms of their experiences: "I said to my actors, not only it is interesting for them to work with me, but also it is interesting for me to work with them; they know things that I don't know" (Lev-Ari 1998). There is a hint of this recognition in another statement too: "The young group interests me—they are my connection to the surrounding reality" (Shohat 1997c).

Several previews greeted the upcoming premiere of *Don Juan*. In addition to preoccupation with the cultural identity of Gesher and its new studio, the critics insisted on a political interpretation of Gesher's repertoire choice. Shi Bar-Yakov drew an analogy between Don Juan's morals and Israeli sensibility:

> [Maybe] our whole society is governed according to the immoral laws of the jungles? Behind the chutzpa and the brazenness, and lack of boundaries, we too, like the last Don, are looking for the disappearing authority that will tell us, hey guys, you can't behave like that! (Bar-Yakov 1997)

The mechanism of internal colonization is at work in this account. Bar-Yakov internalized the complaints of Russian immigrants about "rude" and "uncultured" Israelis and then took a self-deprecating position. He chastised Israelis for the qualities of "chutzpa and brazenness" acceptable in the Israeli ethos.

Another preview takes a position of self-deprecation: "In contrast to many Israeli directors, Arye is not hesitant to return its European roots to the story of the world-famous lover and to introduce the explicit Catholic motifs, that emphasize the moral conflict in the play" ("Don Juan" 1997). This preview juxtaposes Israeli directors to Arye, whose cultural background enables him to cope with the European roots and Christian motifs of the classic play.

The premiere took place on February 21, 1998. *Don Juan* was the third meeting between Gesher and Molière, after *Molière* by Mikhail Bulgakov and *Tartuffe* by Jean-Baptiste Molière himself. Like in these productions, Arye used

Figure 9: *Don Juan*
Left to right: Glenda Sevald, Sami Samir, and Tamara Shtern
(Courtesy of Gesher Theatre)

the device of metatheatre, turning *Don Juan* into the play-within-the-play. He brought in the character of a Prompter (Limor Itshaik) who functions as a narrator. Like in *Adam Resurrected* and *Tartuffe*, metatheatre allows for a sophisticated treatment of the theatrical fabricated reality, and the theme of artistic creation. In *Don Juan*, metatheatre highlighted the fact that this production was a version of a classic play, not a 'real life' story.

Don Juan continued Molière's criticism of the hypocrisy of the religious establishment. Its main character, Don Juan (Sami Samir), is not only a lover, driven by passions, but also an atheist and a libertine, declaring that he believes in a rational mind and personal freedom. Assisted by his loyal servant Sganarelle (Alexander Senderovich), Don Juan conquers the hearts of noble Dona Elvire (Michal Weinberg/Natalie Shilman) and peasant girls Charlotte (Tamara Shtern) and Maturine (Glenda Sevald). The settings of the play change rapidly, from tavern to beach, from town to mausoleum. Don Juan escapes from the most dangerous situations, turning them into further opportunities for amorous adventure. He masterfully manipulates both the virtuous women and the vindictive men. However, none of his escapades is rebuked by the heaven's wrath. It is only when Don Juan decides to pretend a conversion to religion, and becomes a pious hypocrite himself, that he is punished.

The production process of *Don Juan* brought together the diverse group of Gesher-2 actors, and the veteran creative and technical staff of the main Gesher troupe. The production bore the imprint of Gesher's theatrical style, rooted in metatheatre and the Russian tradition of expressive staging.

The media's initial interest in the Gesher-2 project and its participants gradually subsided. By the time of the premiere, the interest had died out almost entirely, and *Don Juan* did not gain much publicity. Discussion of Arye's directorial style became the main topic of a few reviews. The only unequivocal praise came from Yuval Zohar from the newspaper *Yerushalaim*. He admired Arye's directorial style full of "effects and gimmicks," which had become a trademark of Gesher Theatre. According to Zohar, *Don Juan* was produced "in Gesher's best tradition—the dynamic and sparkling production" (1998).

Other reviews were less sympathetic. Even though Michael Handelsaltz cooled down after his demolishing reviews of *Three Sisters*, he still maintained his criticism of Arye. Handelsaltz praised the play and the acting, but not the direction: "Even if there are good ideas, and Arye is a director with vision and sweep...it looks like he is lacking a sense of taste and proportion, and this lack spoils the rest" (1998b). Handelsaltz also acknowledged the work of the Gesher-2 actors, who are "an interesting and a serious group, and skilled in its majority." The review concludes indulgently, "Despite the direction, the production was for me an interesting night at the theatre" (1998b).

Eliakim Yaron was even more critical of the directorial style: "The process, which the director Yevgeny Arye started in *Three Sisters*, when he drowned an important play in a flood of loud music and hyper-active movement, gains momentum in *Don Juan*" (1998). According to Yaron, the effects "strangle" the show. He also argues that the theatrical style chosen by Arye hinders the young actors: "The director was immersed in himself and did not notice the actors." Yaron concludes in a patronizing tone: "The actors are young, some of them are talented, but this whole business goes over their heads" (1998).

Shosh Weitz seconds both Handelsaltz and Yaron. Even though she praises the actors, she disapproves both of Arye's choice of play, which she considers antiquated, and his interpretation of it. First, Weitz fails to appreciate the concept of metatheatre. She criticizes the character of a Prompter, which, according to Weitz "just slows the show down." Second, she argues that the stage design, including the revolving and moving stage, was pointless: "Style and theatrical means, beautiful as they are, cannot substitute for interesting material and clear interpretation." Her conclusion is condescending: "As theatre training it is maybe good for the students, but not so much for the audiences" (1998).

In short, the critical reception of *Don Juan* was not encouraging. The storm clouds were gathering above the Gesher-2 studio. The clash of expectation between Arye and Kreindlina on the one hand, and the Gesher-2 actors on the other, resulted in mutual hard feelings. The young actors felt increasingly discriminated against: the conditions of their contracts were unfair, their status tenuous, and their participation in the other shows only occasional. Arye and Kreindlina, on the other hand, felt that the Gesher-2 actors failed to appreciate the opportunity of training that they were offered. All these factors posed questions about the future of the Gesher-2 project. What should be the status of Gesher-2: should the young actors "graduate" and enter the main troupe? If the project was to continue, should Arye and Kreindlina work with the same actors, or should they admit a new class? And, finally, from what sources could it be financed? These questions lingered unanswered, and the young actors' group started gradually to disintegrate. At the very end of 1999, Gesher made another attempt to mount a production intended to engage mostly Gesher-2 actors. A comedy titled *Sea* premiered in January 2000. It was an adaptation of a classic play by Carlo Goldoni (*Le Baruffe Chiozzotte*). However, this production gained neither critical acclaim nor popularity with the audiences, and only facilitated the disintegration of the Gesher-2 project.

Overall, *Don Juan* had performed 90 times. It won the Israeli Theatre Award in the categories of Most Promising Actor (Alexander Senderovich) and Most Promising Actress (Tamara Shtern). In May of 1999, *Don Juan* was taken off Gesher's repertoire, and in 2000 Gesher-2 as a project ceased to exist. Most of the young actors left Gesher for good; few remained in the company. They joined the main troupe and achieved better contracts with standard benefits. As of this writing, only Michal Weinberg and Alexander Senderovich still remain in the troupe.

Was the attempt to create a young actors' studio at Gesher a success or a failure? This question remains controversial. If the goal was to establish a studio, which would function on a permanent basis and serve as a training school for new Gesher actors, the project failed. However, if the goal of Gesher-2 was to replenish the current Gesher troupe by training several young actors, and to inject "fresh blood" into the company, then the project succeeded.

• CHAPTER NINE •

All the Way Down

The Critical Demolition: *Eating*

Gesher finished year 1998 with a budget of over 16 million NIS, only half of which came from public subsidies (see Table 1). The rest came from self-generated profits: besides individual and collective ticket sales, Gesher had revenues from private donations, commercial sponsorships, and other sources (such as hall rentals). Gesher's public subsidies were still at a level of 50%, which is about 10% less than other major public theatres in Israel (Levy 2001). Additionally, Gesher continued to be in an insecure position with its housing. The *hangar* was rented to Gesher one year at a time, and rumors circulated about the intentions of the landlord (an Armenian archdiocese) to use the building differently. Gesher was constantly in danger of becoming homeless without much notice. The lack of technical equipment and space at the *hangar* became increasingly problematic as well, as the theatre produced shows with more elaborate sets (such as *Three Sisters*).

Therefore, when in late 1998 Noga hall became available for long-term rental, Ori Levy jumped at the opportunity to make it Gesher's home. Noga hall was a large modern theatre in downtown Jaffa, right next to the heart of Tel Aviv nightlife and trendy neighborhoods. It was a well-known location for cultural events and performing arts. The building had only one stage, but it offered potential for the necessary theatrical facilities, such as a stage tower. The audience hall seated 800, and was relatively new and in an acceptable condition. However, Noga also had its drawbacks. It did not have the unique atmosphere of the *hangar* in Jaffa port, and the audience hall was twice the size of the *hangar*, which was threatening. Ori Levy complained: "Maybe if they built it especially for us, it would have been built differently...there was no theatrical atmosphere at all" (2001). Yet, the prospect of gaining a permanent home was so appealing that Gesher's management decided to trade the charm and atmosphere of the *hangar* for the security of Noga.

When Gesher prepared to move to Noga, in late 1998, the building was still privately owned (by Tzabar family) and had to be rented. The Tel Aviv municipality supported Gesher by paying two-thirds of the rent; Gesher had to pay only one-third. In addition, Gesher still had an access to the old building at Nachmani Street, which continued to serve as a second rehearsal stage and as a workspace for the crew of set designer Alexander Lisiyansky. Later, the municipality calculated that it made more financial sense to buy the building for Gesher and own it, in the same way that the municipality owns the buildings of Cameri and Habima theatres. In November 2000, the municipality purchased Noga hall, and it officially became Gesher's permanent home. According to the arrangement with the municipality, Gesher was allowed to occupy the building as long as the theatre existed. In addition, Gesher continued to rent the building at Nachmani Street.

In late 1998, before the move, Gesher had to invest in renovations of the building: to change the design of the audience hall, to improve the acoustics, to install sound and light systems. After an investment of 3.5 million NIS that came from Gesher's budget and from private donations, the hall was ready to accept its new tenant. In January of 1999, Gesher moved to Noga hall.

The consequences of this move for Gesher were two-fold: on the one hand, the move had positive consequences. First, the theatre gained stability and security, especially after the municipality purchased the building. Second, the move also brought about organizational changes: from now on, the offices of the manager, the director, the publicist, the dramaturge, the marketing director, and other administrators were housed under the same roof with the artistic and technical staff (with the exception of Lisiyansky, whose workspace remained at Nachmani Street, and the technical crew that worked in workshops in the Tel Aviv suburb of Rishon-le-Tzion). This change led to better integration between the staff and the administration, opened up natural channels of feedback, and facilitated a smoother work process. This was especially crucial for the publicist and the marketing director, who have to work in close cooperation with the other theatre members. Third, the grand building in such a central location reaffirmed the respectability of Gesher's status in Israel and reiterated the support of the establishment for the theatre.

On the other hand, the move was detrimental. First, this visibly prestigious location came to signify the change of Gesher's position from almost a fringe status—a small theatre housed in the artsy *hangar* in the bohemian part of Jaffa—to a well-established venue. This change induced even more jealousy from both Israeli and immigrant cultural producers than ever before. Second, the bigger hall changed the interactive dynamics between the audience and the performers. Now, instead of the intimacy, warmth, and individuality of the *hangar*, the audience found themselves in a well-equipped, modern, but large and anonymous Noga hall. Besides portraits of Gesher's director and actors in the foyer, Gesher's cultural uniqueness and its ambiguous position of both insider and outsider in Israeli culture was not marked in the building. Third, the sheer size of the audience hall put more commercial pressure on the theatre, which now had to almost double its sales. Gesher's management promptly realized that it had to limit the size of the audience to avoid at least the subjective feeling of "mass production" and to diminish the pressure to fill the hall. Consequently, part of the hall was closed, and it was decided that a show was "sold out" if 620–650 seats were full (Binder 2000). But even with part of the hall closed, this commercial pressure was still significant. Gesher, which was always opposed to a subscription system, now allowed Zvia Binder to institute a mini-subscription (a series of two shows) and to market it to collective buyers. In short, the theatre increasingly lost its underdog position along with all its advantages and disadvantages, and despite its unique cultural profile took on the appearance of a typical Israeli public theatre.

On January 30 of 1999, Gesher celebrated the move with the grand opening of the production *Eating* that had premiered just recently (on January 6, 1999). As the elections planned for May 1999 were nearing, the opening was well attended by politicians and public figures, including left-wingers, such as the future Prime Minister Ehud Barak; right-wingers, such as Avigdor Liberman; politicians with a Russian-immigrant agenda, such as Minister of Absorption Yuly Edelstein (himself Russian-born); and politicians without specific ethnic agendas, such as Tel Aviv mayor Ron Huldai, as well as several Knesset members and high-rank officials from different ministries. As in previous times of crucial political decisions, attending Gesher was their way for showing their support for Russian immigrants.

Eating was the third play by an Israeli playwright staged by Gesher. Originally written in 1975, the play borrowed its storyline from the Hebrew Bible. Like other Israeli dramaturges of his generation, Yakov Shabtai saw the Bible as a secular national epic. In *Eating*, he adapted a biblical passage (First Kings, 21:1) telling the tragic story of Naboth the Jezreelite, to create a political satire of Israeli colonization of Palestine. Naboth (Yevgeny Gamburg) has vineyards beside King Ahab's palace. The action is set in motion when Ahab (Amnon Wolf) becomes obsessed with the idea of using Naboth's land for a vegetable garden. Ahab approaches Naboth with an offer to buy the vineyards, but Naboth refuses to sell his ancestral inheritance. Seeing how upset Ahab is about Naboth's refusal, power-lusting Queen Jezebel (Yevgenya Dodina) decides to take advantage of her husband's whim and entices him to acquire the vineyards through political conspiracy. She recruits the king's advisor (Vladimir Halemsky) and the high priest (Leonid Kanevsky) to fabricate a charge against Naboth claiming that he has cursed god and the king. As a result, Naboth, an honest man and a devoted citizen, is executed, allowing Ahab to finally lay his hands on the vineyards. Ahab's appropriation of Naboth's land is a metaphor for Israeli occupation. In Gesher's interpretation, this metaphor is also realized through costume and scenery: Naboth wears an Arab headdress, and in the scene of his main monologue, footage of a landscape that looks like the West Bank is screened at the background.

Another metaphor that structures the production is the act of eating as an expression of an insatiable urge for power. Almost all action on stage takes place during feasts, where the evil rulers devour immense amounts of food. In a final scene, Queen Jezebel, unable to consume more food, vomits violently, as if she is poisoned with power.

Israeli critics demolished the production. *Eating* was a highly-professional, visually and musically entertaining show. It was performed 56 times over the 1999–2000 season, which is not exactly a success, but not a failure either. *Eating* was even nominated for the Israeli Theatre Award in the category of Best Actress (Yevgenya Dodina). However, the critics fiercely attacked the production. What were the reasons for such critical response?

Critics interpreted Arye's production as an attack on Israel. Indeed, *Eating* criticized contemporary Israeli politics. However, the main satirical message of the play, which was aimed at the Israeli colonization of Palestine, even though subversive in 1975 (when the play was written), had become by 1999 commonplace. Therefore, critics were infuriated not by the satirical message, but by the mere fact that a bunch of 'new immigrants' allowed themselves to produce a political satire of Israeli society and culture.

Also, the critics interpreted the production as a criticism of national and popular culture in Israel. The critics unanimously decided that *Eating* was a mockery of Israeli culture because of the Mizrahi music[1] accompanying the show, and the unmistakably Israeli communication style of the king and his court. The critics remained oblivious to the symbolic costumes and the mannerisms of the characters, mixing and matching elements from the

1 Mizrahi music, with its Arabic melodies and originally Arabic lyrics, has been a controversial subject in Israel for years. Mizrahi music was interpreted by Ashkenazi elites as "primitive" and unworthy of public distribution and presentation. Even though Mizrahi music has been popular in Israel since the 50s, only in recent years was it incorporated into mainstream TV and radio programming, and did its stars receive official recognition.

Figure 10: *Eating*
Yevgenya Dodina as Queen Jezebel and Amnon Wolf as King Ahab
(Courtesy of Gesher Theatre)

different cultures and eras. This hodge-podge of cultural references was a tribute to the cultural hybridity of the troupe. For instance, the king's advisor looks remarkably like Lavrenti Beria, Stalin's chief of security; Queen Jezebel resembles both Nefertiti and an MTV pop-star; the high priest mimics an Israeli orthodox rabbi; and the feast includes decisively non-kosher gourmet foods (such as oysters).

The most notable aspect of the reviews of *Eating* is that they are written from the position of a colonizer. In her review in *Haaretz*, Batya Gur (1999) does not analyze the actual production; instead, she focuses on the mere fact that Gesher staged an Israeli satire. Her position is stated in the title: "Big Show-off of Israeliness" and the subtitle: "From the Gesher members' point of view, the *Eating* production...is a statement of their seemingly complete integration in Israeli theatre. They present the terrible story of Naboth as a satirical cabaret, which is nothing but a lip-service to their new identity." Gur's interpretation demonstrates the ambivalence of colonial discourse: she interprets the theatre's choice of the play as an act of political mimicry—as an affirmation of their Israeli identity, consistent with the Zionist expectation of such mimicry, she denies the theatre its choice by denigrating the production to the status of "lip-service."

The same vacillation between mimicry and menace occurs in her further argument. Gur disparages the critical impetus of Gesher's production as a "manipulation." She argues that *Eating* results from theatre's "desire to align itself with the forces critical [of Israeli society] by all means." Clearly, Gur is unable to take seriously the critical content of the show; instead, she interprets it as a conspiracy against Israeli society, uncovering ulterior motives in Gesher's artistic choices that, according to her, aim to criticize Israel "by all means." This interpretation denies the theatre its right to have a critical voice. Time and again, Gur returns to Gesher's choice of the play, a choice she clearly sees as illegitimate. After explaining that Yakov Shabtai represents "the best of Israeli culture" she argues:

> The meaning of producing Yakov Shabtai's play is to make a statement that the troupe members...succeeded to present both the pinnacle of Israeliness and the universal evils of power (which even Israelis suffer from). Therefore...Gesher chose the play with direct and explicit political meanings, which they made even more extreme. (Gur 1999)

Insisting on Gesher's political and national motives for producing this play, Gur rejects the theatre's right to critique "afflictions of power" in Israeli society. It is interesting that her phrasing "even Israelis" alludes to the myth of the egalitarian nature of Israel that apparently makes it immune to corruption known by other societies.

Like other reviewers, Gur also criticizes Gesher for its carnivalesque style. She claims that the show's genre, which she defines as "satirical cabaret," is inappropriate while telling a "terrible story" based on a biblical plot. The biblical origin of the play gains the status of a sacred cow, which Gesher desecrates. Besides this comment, Gur's review provides very scarce analysis of the actual performance of *Eating*, substituting argument for a condescending tone.

Ironically, she concludes by critiquing Gesher for putting political goals ahead of artistic ones: "*Eating* is a lip-service to 'correct' Israeliness, where political correctness and not artistic endeavor is a top priority." Clearly, the same critique applies to Gur's own review.

Shi Bar-Yakov gives the exact same interpretation as Gur: "The new production signifies the most significant attempt of the troupe to integrate into local cultural reality" (1999a). For him, as for Gur, the choice of the play is meaningful. One would think that such an attempt of mimicry should please the critic, since it is consistent with the requirements of Zionist ideology. But he foresees the threat of this mimicry. Bar-Yakov reacts to this threat: "This attempt proves a huge gap between the Russian poetic imagination of Yevgeny Arye and between the poignant and rough reality of life in the Middle East." Taking the position of a colonizer, Bar-Yakov uses a stereotypical cultural reference ("Russian poetic imagination") to remind the reader that Gesher, despite its toying with Israeli topics, is not Israeli. Therefore, it does not have a license from critics to represent Israeli reality. If it is legitimate for the Israeli playwright "to challenge the national myths in the mirror of cynical reality," not so for Gesher. Further, Bar-Yakov reinforces his argument by claiming that the production of *Eating* exposed "the failure of director Yevgeny Arye to relate to Israeli humor."

Bar-Yakov continues with the discussion of food in the production. He claims that obsessive eating on stage, symbolizing an urge for power, is portrayed as "a European feast including oysters and variety of meats. Due to this sophistication, the performance fails to disgust the audiences even in the moments of forced eating and vomiting." Bar-Yakov stresses, "Yakov Shabtai wrote about animalistic devouring in the culture of pita with *schwarma* [grilled meat] and dripping tahini." This apparently gastronomical comment is, in fact, evidence of the mutual colonization process at work. First, Bar-Yakov reminds the reader that Gesher comes from the "European" background and hints that Gesher takes a condescending position towards Israeli culture. Then, having read condescension into Gesher's stage interpretation of Shabtai's play, Bar-Yakov goes on the preemptive defensive. He emphasizes the cultural otherness of the Gesher theatre-makers. Try as they might, he is saying, they are still not in the same league with Israelis, and they still have a lot to learn. How can they critique Israeli society or politics if they do not know such elementary realities as the local food staple of pita with *schwarma*? This comment, insisting on the cultural incompetence of Gesher, devalues the critical impetus of the show. As a conclusion to his argument, Bar-Yakov exudes half-threat and half-prophecy: "[Gesher] will have to work very hard in order to find the right connection between themselves and Israeli culture" (1999a). His colonizing voice sounds especially strong in this conclusion.

Giora Yahalom-Rimshon (1999) from the newspaper *Yerushalaim*, is in complete agreement with both Gur and Bar-Yakov. In his main argument, Yahalom-Rimshon treats theatre members not as artists or cultural producers, but as immigrants, explaining their artistic choices by their cultural and national identities: "If until now his actors and he himself [Arye] were not confident enough in their Israeliness, currently they have been long enough in Israel, and thus are able to critique it. Right?" Yahalom-Rimshon continues by giving a negative answer to his question, disputing Gesher's ability to critique Israeli reality: "This is the problem of *Eating*. The staging is too hesitant, fearful of opening up old wounds, of saying things that are really important." This critique may seem to be a reference to the staging and directorial interpretation. However, in Israeli social and historical context, Yahalom-Rimshon's rhetoric has ideological meanings. His comment invokes a stereotypical image of an insecure and hesitant diasporic Jew. In the process of immigrant absorption this neurotic character turns into a strong and confident Israeli. Therefore, by criticizing *Eating* for being too hesitant in its critical impetus, the reviewer is essentially saying that the producers were not Israeli enough to voice their critique yet.

In his final line, Yahalom-Rimshon brings his readers to the same comforting conclusion as other reviewers: Gesher's satire of Israeli society and politics is inadequate and as such should not be considered seriously. The same idea is expressed in a summary of other reviews published by the newspaper *Globes* titled "Hovering Over Israeli Reality" (Barkan 1999). The title of the article not only excludes Gesher from Israeli political and social contexts, but also hints at the seeming arrogance of Gesher (above Israeli reality).

The most glaring examples of the colonizing position come from two reviews by Shosh Weitz. In the first review, she comments: "The acting of Yevgenya Dodina, Leonid Kanevsky, Vladimir Halemsky and Yevgeny Gamburg does not help the performance to approach the ground of Israeli reality. In that sense, Amnon Wolf in the role of Ahab was much more connected to the play and to the place" (1999a). Weitz's critical judgment is based entirely on the cultural identity of the performers. Amnon Wolf is distinguished from the rest of the mentioned actors only by being a *sabra*, a native Israeli.

This review infuriated Yoram Kanuk, author of *Adam Resurrected* and one of the committed supporters of Gesher. He himself did not think that *Eating* was the most successful show; however, he contested Weitz's colonial position. Kanuk wrote that Weitz's "claim that the Russians do not have the same connection to Ahab's Samaria, as native Israelis do, is on a borderline with racism" (1999).

In her second review, Weitz was even more opinionated. Its title "What Is Gesher Attached to?" capitalizes on such common coins of Zionist discourse as *attachment to the Land of Israel* and *attachment to the national values*. The rest of the review epitomizes the critic's colonizing position:

> In these days, Gesher Theatre moves into its new home, the Noga hall, and puts on stage the premiere of *Eating* by Yakov Shabtai. These two events symbolize, apparently, the process of the theatre's integration in Israel. While moving to Noga reaffirms the place and the status that the theatre obtained in the Israeli society,

> establishment, and culture, the *Eating* production demonstrates the foreignness and distance of the theatre from the Israeli experience...the onstage interpretation of *Eating* by Yevgeny Arye shows not only a lack of understanding of the play and its poignant political message, but also of reality in the Middle East, where the play is taking place and in which we all live. (Weitz 1999b)

Weitz's "we" is two-fold: it includes Weitz's assumingly Israeli readers in the "reality in the Middle East," simultaneously excluding from it Gesher's theatre-makers, as unable to understand the play, and the surrounding reality.

But according to Weitz, it is Gesher that takes a colonizing position in respect to Israeli culture. She charges Arye with using colonial images:

> [Arye creates] an oriental Levantine world built in the best traditions of colonial images....But Eastern-Western[2] interplay doesn't contribute to the play, the political message of which is disguised and dissolved. However, it discloses the European-Western arrogance of the ensemble and its inability, especially of Yevgeny Arye, to give expression to the Israeli experience. (Weitz 1999b)

Now, that Weitz has convinced herself that Arye tries to 'colonize' Israeli culture, she responds to this perceived threat by shifting positions from colonizer to colonized. Taking the colonizing position herself, she now has the opportunity to express her disregard for Arye and Gesher. She insists on their inability to represent the 'Israeli experience', which is unavailable to inferior newcomers. According to Weitz, there is one and only one kind of 'Israeli experience', and she holds ownership over it.

In order to gain such crucial experience, Weitz recommends Gesher to "benefit from exuberant Israeli spirit." Here Weitz both restates Gesher's non-Israeli identity and encourages Gesher's theatre-makers to assume the position of the colonized—to mimic the 'Israeli exuberant spirit'. Unexpectedly, Weitz concludes that there is a place in Israel for a theatre "from a different world," as long as, she forgets to add, it adheres to the ideological norm of complete assimilation.

Weitz's review provoked a polemical response, this time from Miriam Yahil-Wax affiliated with Gesher. The debate between Weitz and Yahil-Wax became a real terrain of struggle over the questions of national identity and cultural production. In her response, also published in *Yediot Ahronot*, Yahil-Wax accuses Weitz of criticizing Gesher as not "Israeli enough" and insists on the universal cultural value of theatre production:

> There is no contradiction between being Israeli and being universal. Not in principle and not in the context of our show. All we are doing is Israeli theatre, and it succeeds

2 Here, Weitz refers to East and West in an Israeli sense. The East is associated with Israel and the West with Russia, even though it is not geographically correct.

> both in Israel and in the rest of the world. And our agenda here is an entertaining and sarcastic production of the forgotten play, not the cornerstone of our being Israelis, and not even the cornerstone of theatre in Israel. (Yahil-Wax 1999a)

Even though Yahil-Wax disagrees with Weitz, her argument remains largely within the framework of hegemonic Zionist discourse. She makes an argument for the universal appeal of the show, but it is still important to her that Gesher should be considered an "Israeli" theatre. Yet, she is sensitive to the fact that the defensive critical response to *Eating* was out of bounds:

> The outburst of gatekeepers of Israeliness against Gesher is ridiculous....Excuse me, what is going on here? Is the attack justified? Yes, we are different, we are intercultural theatre, we are bilingual and multi-ethnic. Why do they want to straighten us in a line, so that we become like everyone else? In art, diversity is a key word. (Yahil-Wax 1999a)

In their respective responses to Weitz, both Kanuk and Yahil-Wax picked out the same stumbling block of the critique—Gesher's cultural identity.

In his reviews of *Eating*, Michael Handelsaltz (1999a; 1999b) repeats the same praises of acting and the same objections to Arye's style familiar from his reviews of other Gesher productions. He does not pass up the chance to remind the reader about Gesher's cultural identity: "One thing Gesher brought with them [from Russia]—their control over their tools—body and voice. Even with the Russian intonation, their acting is well done, in full control, even when it is exaggerated to the extreme by their director" (1999a). As usual, Handelsaltz criticizes the grotesque staging. Describing *Eating* as a "blown-up exaggerated spectacle" (1999a), he claims that Arye is unable to work with Shabtai's simple and straightforward play. According to Handelsaltz, Arye's interpretation of conflict between King Ahab and Naboth is overly political. He is upset by Naboth's character who wears *kafiya*-style headdress and pronounces Hebrew prayer on stage. This combination of Palestinian and Jewish cultural references is deeply unsettling for the critic. It leads Handelsaltz to a damning conclusion, "Either interpretation of the play in political terms doesn't work, or its performance is just a random collection of theatrical effects and tricks, which doesn't look right in regards to this specific play" (1999b). Handelsaltz's condescending tone testifies to his dismissal of Gesher's interpretation. In sum, Gesher does not have a mandate from some sort of *politburo* of the Israeli critics to represent the local society and politics.

Eliakim Yaron makes similar critical claims about Gesher's artistic style: "Yakov Shabtai wrote a short play based on a political fable. Gesher Theatre strangled it with songs and dances, sometimes bordering kitsch" (1999a). Like

Handelsaltz, Yaron claims that Gesher is unable to convey the political meaning of the play, which "has no connection whatsoever to what is happening in the performance." The specific points of references in Yaron's critique are not clear; his resentment of the production is.

Critics, acolytes of the Zionist ideology, hold an antiquated idea of *agitprop* art serving the ideological needs of society. They act as gatekeepers to the dominant ideology, with its national priorities of commitment to Hebrew language and Israeli-Zionist culture, as well as vigilant attention to the politics of identity. Thus critical discourse becomes colonial—a means of replicating dominant ideology—foregoing the empowering potential endowed in their judgment. What is at stake here is not the negative reception of *Eating*, but rather status of criticism in Israel in a broader sense, since even the most effusive reviews of other Gesher productions were also fully aligned with the hegemonic ideology.

Yevgeny Arye vs. Critics

The critical demolition of his recent productions, especially of *Eating*, visibly upset Arye. As a media interview reflects, he clearly understood the reasons for the negative reception of *Eating*:

> In the play by Yakov Shabtai I did what was not acceptable to critics....It is interesting to me to look for serious problems common for all of us in a political anecdote. But critics see the things in different terms than I. For them, this is politics, which is why [in their minds] I broke all the laws that I was supposed to follow. (Katz 1999)

By staging a satire of Israeli society, Arye broke the unspoken rules and, as a consequence of this heresy, he took the punishment. In this and other interviews Arye expressed his disillusionment with the Israeli critics.

In another interview in *Maariv*, Arye also commented on the emerging negative media reception of Gesher: "Because we are foreign, there was a wave of adulation towards us, and now there is another wave—a lack of appreciation. They ask,...Why? Don't we have our own theatre?" (Avidar 1999). Essentially, Arye describes the effects of mutual colonization. Gesher's popularity and high status became threatening, as critics read cultural superiority into it. The threat triggered a defensive reaction. As a result, the critics attempted to reaffirm their cultural superiority ("Why? Don't we have our own theatre?"). This shift of positions results in a critical demolition of Gesher.

Other topics that loomed large in these interviews were Arye's cultural identity and the relationship between Russian and Israeli cultures. The first interview quoted above (Katz 1999) focuses entirely on the politics of identity. The journalist's questions emphasize Arye's non-Israeli cultural identity: "Do you have a dialogue with Israeli theatre?", "What do you like in Israeli art?", "How is your theatre attached to Israel?", "Do you miss Russia?" But Arye downplays the identity issue. He laughs it off ("I have a wonderful Hebrew, and it helps"), or just brushes it away, focusing on the "universal" aspects of his work, which, according to him, transcend cultural boundaries. In another interview, Arye's responses painted a more complex picture:

> I understand how right I was to leave everything behind and to immigrate to Israel. Not because of Gesher's success, but because everything that is happening there [in Russia] does not belong to me any more. While visiting Russia I missed it here, despite the fact that my literature and theatre are still not here, but there, in Russia. (Avidar 1999)

Arye's self-representation is ambivalent. His approval of his immigration to Israel is complicit with the Zionist ideology. However, his allegiance to Russian culture contests the Zionist norms. Thus, Arye's hybrid identity both reaffirms the authority of the hegemonic ideology and disrupts it.

Arye's outlook on the relationship between Russian and Israeli cultures is ambivalent as well. On the one hand, Arye renounces cultural hierarchies and stereotypes:

> Yevgeny Arye does not like generalizations like 'Russians' or 'Russian theatre', he is also against the generalization of 'Israelis'. He protests when I ask him whether he is partial to the complaints of Russian immigrants that native Israelis are less cultured than Russians: 'I hate such thinking, but it touches upon a painful subject....If Russians think they are so cultured, I'd like to challenge them. Maybe they say it as a defensive response, because their process of absorption was so difficult and painful. (Avidar 1999)

On the other hand, Arye's statements perpetuate colonial hierarchies of cultures. Arye's criticism of Israeli society indicates his colonizing position. When Tamar Avidar asks what bothers him in Israel, Arye responds: "Junk that people leave behind, little towns that are covered with garbage, dogs whose owners don't clean after them. El-Al [Israeli air flight company] airplanes that look like dumpsters after the flight" (1999). This may sound like an environmental concern; however, in Israel such rhetoric usually aims at housing developments populated by Mizrahi Jews. In Arye's complaint, "garbage" stands for the lack of civilization of the people who produce it, their low stage of cultural development. Arye's words echo colonial rhetoric.

The most outrageous exchange between Arye and a journalist took place on the pages of *Anashim* magazine. If journalists from more respectable publications are constrained by "the good taste" that their bourgeois audiences expect, nothing holds back Goel Pinto from *Anashim*. He asks Arye: "When you read negative reviews, do you think sometimes that if you were not Russian, they would not have written such review?" Arye agrees: "I am not talking about the fact that I am Russian, but that I am an immigrant—an other. I don't think that they [critics] are consciously writing [negative reviews] because I am a foreigner, but it definitely influences them" (1999).

As the interview proceeds, Arye starts confronting Pinto. Arye takes an ambivalent position: he criticizes the media that perpetuate the cultural hierarchy, yet he joins in himself. He asks Pinto: "[Why] does the fact that we receive great press all over the world mean nothing for Israeli critics?" For Arye, "all over the world" stands for the international cultural centers of London, New York, Paris, and Berlin. Using references to the international critics' authority, Arye takes a superior position, and puts Israeli critics into a position of subjugation.

When Pinto asks Arye about his take on sour relationships between Russian immigrants and veteran Israelis, Arye's position is also ambivalent. On the one hand, he tries to put things into perspective:

> Both sides [Russian immigrants and native Israelis] have problems. When the Russians say that there is no culture in Israel, they essentially are saying that the Israelis themselves are not cultured. I never thought so. Israelis have the same problem, when Israelis think that all the Russian women are prostitutes. (Pinto 1999)

Arye recognizes the mutual character of stereotyping between the two sides. But after scolding the Russian immigrants who say "there is no culture in Israel," he easily restates it himself in his explanation of Gesher's credo:

> I still believe that we are fighting [a battle] over at least a little bit of culture in this country, which...is not in a good condition in that respect. We are trying to struggle with TV and movies, we are trying to be unique, and we need help in order to achieve it. (Pinto 1999)

Arye takes upon himself the role of a missionary, the role enabling him to alleviate the assumed deficiencies of the "natives," who without him would lose even the meager "little bit of culture" he is struggling to maintain. After statements like this, it is no surprise that some critics and audiences find Arye's tone condescending.

But the most heated exchange results from a discussion of music in *Eating*. The journalist tries to force clear cultural categories onto Arye, who time and again resists these attempts:

> [Pinto asks:] "When a Russian director, in a Russian theatre, adds Mizrahi music to a play, does it have a special meaning?" [Arye replies:] "I never think in terms of Russian director and Russian theatre. The problem is that after we have been performing in Israel for eight years, you are still asking me such questions. For you, we are still not among the rest of the theatres, and not because of our art, but because of our [cultural] background. For you, we are still foreigners here." [Pinto asks] "And you feel Israeli?" [Arye replies] "I am already not Russian, but not yet Israeli. I am Israeli because I live and work here, but I am different, because I have not been born here. My childhood and my [world of] associations are different. I will be different until the end of my life, but there is a big difference between the way I see myself and the way others see me." (Pinto 1999)

Arye wants to be accepted the way he is, neither quite Israeli nor quite Russian. As he asserts his hybridity, he protests against Israeli critics who constantly drag him to either one cultural identity or the other.

However, this manifesto of hybridity only further infuriates the journalist. Pinto goes into a direct attack on Arye: "Why are you staying here? I am sure that if you go to France, everyone there will fall to your feet." Arye's answer testifies to his great desire to be accepted in Israel: "I've worked in France....The problem is that in France I will always be an alien, but if here I will also remain foreign forever, that will be truly bad."

Pinto is unrelenting: "But you are foreign! You haven't even learned Hebrew." Arye flies into a rage: "This is not the critics' business whether I am conducting rehearsals in Russian or in Hebrew. If they want to criticize me for that, then they might as well criticize me for the fact that I am fat, or that I have a big beard....When you ask me why I don't know Hebrew, I ask myself, why does it bother you?" They've reached an impasse.

CHAPTER TEN

The End of the Old Road, the Start of the New

The Season of Love and Death: *River* and *Love and Intrigue*

After the devastating reception of the Israeli satire, Gesher decided to stage a European classic drama. The choice fell on *River* (*Dowryless Bride* in the original) by Alexander Ostrovsky and *Love and Intrigue* by Friedrich Schiller. The two shows premiered almost simultaneously and were promoted as a "package." Indeed, the plays had significant similarities: both were European classic dramas based on love stories; both combined elements of tragedy and comedy; both examined romantic private love in the context of a corrupt and coercive society; both ended with the violent deaths of protagonists. Gesher's publicist Michal Savel (1999b) promoted these new shows as "The season of Love and Death." The two new productions substituted the poignant political critique of *Eating* with melodramatic plots appealing to the universal human themes of love and death. The threat of the newcomers from Gesher critiquing the cornerstones of Israeli society was removed.

The two productions also served to provide at least a partial solution to the problem of employing the Gesher-2 actors, whose position in the troupe had become more and more tenuous with time. By summer 1999, the Gesher-2 vehicle *Don Juan* was running only once a month, and the rest of the time the Gesher-2 actors were left to their own devices. Luckily, both *River* and *Love and Intrigue* had several scenes where the Gesher-2 actors could be engaged, although only in the minor roles.

River was scheduled to premiere first. This play occupies a different place in Russian and Israeli cultures. In Russia, *Dowryless Bride* and other Ostrovsky's plays are considered classic dramas; their plots are widely known, and the characters are familiar. *Dowryless Bride* is a staple of repertory theatres. The play was also adapted for cinema—the first time, as a silent *Bespridannitsa* [Dowryless Bride] directed by Yakov Protazanov (1937), and later as *Zhestokyi Romans* [Ruthless Romance], directed by Eldar Ryasanov (1984), which was a real hit. In contrast, in Israel Ostrovsky's plays are not popular, and *Dowryless Bride* (in Rina Litwin's translation—*River*) is neither widely read nor staged.

In this, as well as his other plays, Ostrovsky criticized the cruelty and narrow-mindedness of a Russian province, where with the spread of capitalism, the power of new capital takes over individual freedom. In *River*, young Larisa (Efrat Ben-Zur) falls prey to the coercive forces of capitalist society and market economy. The action takes place in a provincial town on the Volga River. Beautiful but poor, Larisa was abandoned by Paratov (Israel [Sasha] Demidov), when he left the town a year ago. Larisa's enterprising mother (Natalya Voitulevich-Manor) finally convinces her heart-broken daughter to marry out of desperation. Larisa picks a teacher Karandyshev (Michael Teplitsky).

When the engagement is settled, Paratov unexpectedly returns, and wins Larisa over again. He convinces her to spend a night with him cruising on the Volga. Despite the societal conventions, trustful Larisa is all too happy to follow Paratov. In the morning she discovers that he had no intentions of marrying her; rather, he has plans to marry money. In the meanwhile, a swarm of Larisa's other admirers, the local merchants and nouveau riches, are already dividing her between themselves, as they realize that Larisa's name is ruined by a night cruise, and that they can now take advantage of her situation. Only a gunshot fired by her desperate fiancé interrupts their plans. Larisa dies.

Arye's interpretation relied on the concept of metatheatre. Like his previous productions (such as *Dreyfus File*, *Adam Resurrected*, and *Tartuffe*), the show presented the play-within-the play, when a plot emerges from a story told on stage. In the opening scene, an old destitute actor (Yevgeny Terletsky) is thrown into the river. Standing knee-high in the water, he starts reading the prologue of Ostrovsky's play. As he reads out loud the words, "One can hear the distant sound of the steam-ship's whistle," the whistle indeed sounds, the curtain raises, and the action begins.

The sets are instrumental to the directorial concept, which uses cinematographic montage and filmic blackouts. The whole left portal of the sets is designed as a fragment of a steamship—a symbol of spreading industrial capitalism. A deck is on top; underneath it is exposed machinery—a giant plunger moving in wide and powerful sweeps. And finally, at the very bottom, a sweating stoker is shoveling more and more coal into the red flames of an open furnace, which looks like a greedy mouth. The deck is lit, but the coal storage is dark, lit only by flashes of fire. The focal point of Arye's production is the power of capitalism, its grip on society and the individual, and its ability to ruin someone's life. The production starts and ends with the image of the engine at work, demonstrating the powerful sweep of the machine, the inhuman force of capital, unstoppable, once set in motion.

Most of the action in *River* takes place on the pier sidewalk, which in other scenes turns into the deck of a ship, or the backyard of Larisa's house. The surface of the sidewalk moves slightly, as if it floats on the river water (the audience can see the real water as well).

In addition to sets integral to the story, the production presents several stunning mise en scènes. In one, Larisa, in a bright yellow dress, sings a heart-piercing gypsy song. As she is singing, she is swaying on a long swing, her voice filling the whole theatre. Paratov first pushes the swing, but then unable to resist the poetry of the moment, joins her on a swing, and the song ends with an embrace. Another mise en scène quotes from a famous love scene in Hollywood's *Titanic*. Standing on the front deck of the steamship, Paratov and Larisa embrace, the wind blowing back her scarf and his hair. Every now and then a picturesque bunch of gypsies (Gesher-2 actors and musicians from Avi Benjamin's team) appear on stage with a performance of folk music and dance. The original Roma songs adapted by Avi Benjamin are performed live.

Despite the stunning visual images and magnificent music, the production was not a great success. There was nothing revealing in the play's criticism of the power of capital or gender inequality. The acting, as usual with Gesher, was emotional and psychologically credible. Yet, the play dictated Larisa's character as one-dimensional, a beatific victim—a damsel in distress, falling for the false promises of dashing Paratov. Paratov, despite Demidov's charm and electrifying stage presence, did not become a complex character either. Nothing in this production connected to the contemporary Israeli context, nothing explained or justified this production at this particular place and time.

Paradoxically, it is this remoteness from the contemporary Israeli context that defined the positive critical reception of *River*. The politics of identity again were at the heart of critics' appreciation: like with the reception of most of Gesher's previous "Russian" productions, the cultural identity of the theatre-makers worked in their favor. Critics were relieved that Gesher had left behind the satire of Israeli politics, which pressed on sensitive spots, and returned, instead, to the safe territory of Russian classics. The critics were generous, almost indulgent, in their reception, as if they were expressing an implicit gratitude to Gesher for leaving the sacred cows of Israeli politics alone. As a result of this dynamic, critics praised virtually every aspect of the production: the choice of the play, the acting, and the set design, making exception only for the familiar critique of the carnivalesque directorial style.

Critics were upfront stating the reasons for their approval of repertoire choice: "In *River* the director Yevgeny Arye returns to his Russian origin, and demonstrates that with this material he is beyond competition," claimed Shi Bar-Yakov (1999b). Bar-Yakov also acknowledged the significant role the sets played the in performance.

Yuval Shahal of *Zman Tel Aviv* wrote an overwhelmingly positive review—though without analyzing or even describing the production. His main argument is that the criticism in the play is relevant to the current Israeli context: "'province', 'hedonism', 'nouveau riche', 'a woman in trouble', 'money-money-money', etc., those are not only issues of Russia in nineteenth century, they are here and now of many Israelis" (1999).

Michael Handelsaltz joined in praising the sets, the play, and Demidov's acting. But, as usual, Handelsaltz claimed that the only drawback of the show was "the director's attempt to take the play in the direction of exaggerated comedy." This style resulted in "grotesque" acting and the lack of "the depth and diversity of the [original] play" (1999d).

Like other critics, Eliakim Yaron admired the beauty of the sets and mise en scènes creating "an unforgettable poetic picture" as well as Demidov's acting, succeeding "to maintain the conquering humanity" (1999c). Yet, like Handelsaltz, Yaron aimed his critique at the directorial concept and stylized acting of other cast. Because of these, the production remained "cold" and failed to move the audience. "Indulgent to the eyes, but far from the heart," Yaron concluded.

Unlike *Eating*, *River* did not provoke controversy. Just the opposite, it almost failed to register with critics. This production stirred very little interest, and the published reviews were brief and shallow. *River* enjoyed a moderate reception with the audiences. By 2001, it was performed 80 times. *River* won the Israeli Theatre Award in the category of Best Stage Designer (Alexander Lisiyansky). It was a quality show; neither a failure nor a success, it did not bring Gesher back to the peak of fame.

Only a month after the premiere of *River*, Gesher released the new show, *Love and Intrigue* by Friedrich Schiller. For the first time in its official history[1] Gesher invited a guest director, Leander Haussman—an *enfant terrible* of German theatre. Leander Haussman was an artistic director of Bochum Theatre in Germany, as well as an independent filmmaker (*Sonnenallee* [Alley

---

1 As mentioned earlier, in actuality, other directors, besides Arye directed Gesher's productions before: Vladimir Portnov directed *Balaganchik* (1991) and *Contract* (1991); Igor Voitulevich directed *Small Demon* (1991).

of the Sun], 1999). Haussman, famous for his unconventional interpretations of classic drama, was an interesting and, in the Israeli context, scandalous character. Haussman, then 40, grew up in Eastern Germany. He was vocal about his family history: his grandfather was a passive supporter of Nazi regime, and his grandmother, though Jewish by birth, was a true believer of Nazi ideology (and also Herman Hesse's wife in her first marriage). Haussman also did not conceal his eagerness to use alcohol and recreational drugs of any kind, and took pride in his confrontational behavior with colleagues (Karpal 1999). Clearly, he made these confessions public in order to shock the Israeli audiences. What was even more shocking was Gesher's choice to invite Leander Haussman as a visiting director. Every theatre-maker and critic in Israel was positive that if Arye finally invited a visiting director, he would choose either an Israeli or Russian director. However, Arye invited a German.

Arye explained this choice: "I wanted to bring to Gesher a director with fresh blood and a different vision. From what I've seen in Germany, he does dangerous projects, and I liked him" (Karpal 1999). The media and theatre professionals were visibly disappointed with Arye's choice. Arye was asked: "Do you know that you are creating an unpleasant atmosphere when you bring a guest director from outside, after the fact that you haven't worked with a single Israeli director?" (Katz 1999). Arye was not taken aback by this attack and responded with sarcasm: "Finally, there will be a good production at Gesher, so that everyone will see what a terrible job Arye is doing, and what a great job a German director is doing. I am almost positive that this will be the [critical] response" (Katz 1999). Arye continued explaining his choice in a more serious tone, "I was looking for someone totally different from me, but someone professional and interesting. Therefore I chose to take a completely different approach and style" (Katz 1999). In this explanation, Arye, as usual, refuted the considerations of national or ethnic identity in his choice of director, and emphasized his professional reasons.

As the premiere approached, the expectations of critics and audiences mounted. There was a sense that after so many years of complete artistic monopoly over Gesher, Arye couldn't have possibly released it for just any director. The pressure was on: the German *enfant terrible* had to deliver.

The production process of *Love and Intrigue*, which became a site of complex cultural and linguistic negotiation, is worth a separate discussion. *Love and Intrigue* was produced by a multicultural and multilingual team. Haussman arrived in Israel in June 1999 for six weeks of intense rehearsals. The preliminary work, such as reading and learning texts, was accomplished before his arrival. Haussman brought with him his own crew: the costume designer (Miro Paternestro), the set designer (Bernard Cleber), and his assistant (Folker Tille). The rest of the staff was from Gesher. Haussman and his crew spoke German, and to different extents English. (Brazilian-born Paternestro was also a native Portuguese speaker). The theatre had to find ways for productive cross-cultural teamwork.

During the routine production process, Gesher managed with one translator (usually, Arye's personal assistant), but now, with two productions in the works, and with the multilingual staff, one translator was not enough. Since the Gesher troupe members were both Russian and Hebrew speakers, at least two translators were needed: one with Russian-German (and ideally some Hebrew) language proficiency, and the second with Hebrew-German (and ideally some Russian) proficiency, both of them competent in English. The task to find such translators was not easy. The translators had to be familiar with theatrical work, and with the specifics of its style and vocabulary. To top these requirements off, the translators had to be available and willing to work around the clock, in a stressful environment, and for little money (Gesher was already stretching its budget working on two productions simultaneously).

Two translators were finally found. In compensation for harsh work conditions and low pay, both of them were officially appointed as director's assistants. Sivan Schiffer, a theatre student at Tel Aviv University, an Israeli of Swiss origin, became a Hebrew-German translator. Andrea Vigger, a sociology student, whom Gesher members met on their tours in Germany (and who translated for them at that time) became a Russian-German translator. Schiffer was a theatre professional who fit the job perfectly. Vigger was not a theatre professional, but she possessed a unique set of skills: a native German speaker, she learned both Hebrew and Russian for her academic work, which dealt with Russian immigration to Israel (Vigger 1999). As a result of her unfamiliarity with theatre work, Vigger often translated from German literally, causing numerous misunderstandings between the Russian-speaking actors and the German-speaking director. The imperfect translation led, in turn, to the exasperation of Russian actors, who felt that they couldn't communicate with the director.

The rehearsal scene was a true tower of Babel. The Hebrew translation of *Love and Intrigue* differed from the original text: the Hebrew version was much shorter and did not lend itself to lengthy elevated monologues. Referring to this terse and succinct character of Hebrew translation of the classic Schiller's play, Haussman joked that he staged "Israeli Schiller." Because of these differences, he had to work not only with the original play, but also with its reverse translation from Hebrew into German. The actors on stage performed in Hebrew, but addressed the director in Hebrew, English, or Russian, mediated through translators. Haussman and his crew spoke mainly in

German, with occasional ventures into English. The translators, Andrea Vigger and Sivan Schiffer were standing by, simultaneously translating back and forth everything that was being said in either language. Therefore, at any given moment, whenever someone spoke, at least three voices sounded in three different languages. This situation led to numerous confusions.

Sometimes, when Vigger failed to render the meaning of Haussman's directions into Russian, one of the younger Gesher actors, who was competent in both Hebrew and Russian, would take over, and translate from Hebrew (using Schiffer's translation from German as an original) into Russian for the older Gesher actors, whose Hebrew competence was still insufficient. Even for the hardened Gesher actors this work took a stout effort. Arye was used to multilingual work: staging in Hebrew, using a play in Russian, and communicating with actors either in English or through translator. He was familiar with both Hebrew intonations and with the conventions of Israeli theatre (such as what is considered overacting). However, this multilingual, multicultural work was new for Haussman, who had to learn it in the limited time of the rehearsals.

In addition to the translators, Gesher had to increase the number of linguistic coaches. In the past, Gesher rehearsed one production at a time, for which one or two coaches were enough. Mark Ivanir, with the help of Miriam Yahil-Wax, and later Adi Etzion-Zak did the job. But now, with Mark Ivanir on sabbatical in London (he left in June 1999), and with the two productions in the works, Yahil-Wax and Etzion-Zak were overwhelmed. The actors and the coaches had to work on the texts in advance in order to allow Haussman start rehearsals right away. Therefore, two more specialists joined the ranks of Gesher coaches. As a result, by the time Haussman arrived, the actors had full control over text.

The strict timeframe, the work with an unfamiliar director, and linguistic gaps between the visiting crew and the Gesher cast made the work excruciatingly stressful for everyone. The drama was unfolding not only on stage, but also behind the scenes and in the greenroom. Rarely did a rehearsal finish without an emotional outburst or crisis.[2]

The relationship between Haussman's crew and Gesher's technical and supporting staff was tense. The Gesher staff members had been together for years; they had formed a cohesive family-like social structure where inside membership was highly valued, and where hierarchy of power was well established. Work with the outsiders, especially ones in positions of authority,

2 Zak Berkman's injury on the set, and the urgent surgery on Haussman's partner, were among the crises during the production process.

was new and threatening for Gesher's technical and supporting staff. Besides plain linguistic misunderstanding, these new power relations and different work ethics resulted in additional stress and mutual disappointment. Both Gesher's staff and the visiting crew had to adjust to each other, and find a way to work together under tremendous time pressure.

An additional tension was caused by Haussman's choice of play. Not everyone at Gesher was content with his choice. *Love and Intrigue* was produced in Hebrew only once, in 1939 by Ohel Theatre (Savel 1999). Since then, Israeli theatres had not expressed much interest in staging German romantic drama. Miriam Yahil-Wax openly expressed doubts whether Israeli audiences will find a German "bourgeois drama" from the eighteenth century contemporary and relevant (1999b). But Arye decided to trust the guest director and his reputation, and went along with his choice of the play.

Like *River*, *Love and Intrigue* is a melodramatic love story ending in death. Ferdinand (Zak Berkman), the son of Von Walter, the prime minister at the court of a German prince (Leonid Kanevsky), falls in love with Louisa (Tamar Kenan), a daughter of a music teacher, a man without means and pedigree (Vladimir Halemsky). But Von Walter has major political plans for his son, which Louisa does not fit. He conjures an intrigue intended to part the lovers and pressures Ferdinand to marry Lady Milford (Yevgenya Dodina), a Prince's mistress, whom Ferdinand furiously rejects. Simultaneously, Von Walter imprisons Louisa's father in order to pressure Louisa to give up Ferdinand. Cornered by the power of the rulers and losing hope in their future union, the young lovers kill themselves.

Both Russian- and Hebrew-speaking actors appeared in the production. However, after an unsuccessful attempt to engage actors in *Three Sisters* regardless of their accents, the casting of *Love and Intrigue* was mindful of accents. Hebrew-speaking actors (one of them from Gesher-2) played the young lovers, whereas Russian-speaking actors played the older characters.

The stage for *Love and Intrigue* was elegantly designed in pastel colors. The stage space was left mostly open, with only few scattered objects indicating different locations. But the sets only appeared simple. The inner part of the stage was tilted and narrowed towards the backstage, creating the illusion of perspective, of a grand hall, where the court scenes took place. The big table, indicating Louisa's family dining room popped in and out of the floor within seconds of a blackout. In another scene, the whole stage was transformed into the lush residence of Lady Milford by rotating only the left panel of the sets. The elegant costumes, even though not accurate historically, were inspired by the dress of Schiller's epoch. There were also breathtaking special effects. The audience gasped when old Miller's cello burst into flames.

In hindsight, the choice to stage *Love and Intrigue* proved to be disastrous. Like other romantic dramas of the time, *Love and Intrigue* features high-pitched poetic monologs, explicating at length the characters' love, hate, despair, and other extreme emotions. In Germany, audiences familiar with the conventions of romantic drama, and perhaps with several stage interpretations of the play, can relate to Haussman's choice and appreciate his radical interpretation. Hebrew theatre does not encompass the romantic tradition. The Israeli audiences and critics are familiar with romantic tradition but, generally, not through personal experience. Thus, Haussman's sophisticated parody of romantic drama, in Israel did not really have a target. Instead, his interpretation was misleading. For example, mocking romanticism, Haussman directed the actors to be exaggeratingly dramatic in certain scenes: Ferdinand and Louisa ran around and shouted on stage, giving the impression of an overly dramatic amateurish performance. In another scene, Haussman, who was also a music editor for this production, incorporated contemporary pop song into the scene of Louisa's death (*Love Will Never End* by *Hear'say*). For Haussman, this choice was intended to emphasize the collision of the contemporary pop culture and the past drama tradition. Yet, for Israeli critics and audiences, this scene did not have the intended effect. The ostentatious display of romantic feelings performed in contemporary Hebrew was increasingly contrived and jarring to the Israeli ear. The text of the translation (by Shimon Zandebank) was also antiquated, and even though it was modified by Yahil-Wax during the production, it maintained its florid elevated tone discordant with the down-to-earth Israeli ethos.

Haussman's agenda did not strike a cord with the Israeli sensibility. Haussman protested against high-brow art and welcomed popular culture. He publicly scorned people who read Hegel, and sneered at people for whom "music stopped with Schonberg" (Karpal 1999), insisting that for him the music continues with the *Rolling Stones*. No one would have argued with him in Israel. But Haussman was not familiar with Israeli audiences who did not perceive Schonberg in opposition to the *Rolling Stones*. Haussman's production did not deliver: it was produced in terms of one cultural system and interpreted in terms of another.

Predictably, the critical reception was negative. The critics pinpointed the problems with both the repertoire choice and the directorial concept. Eliakim Yaron argued that the play was so antiquated that "it does not cross over the boundaries of its epoch" (1999b). He explains that the only reason to resuscitate such a play is a contemporary interpretation of a director. However, Haussman's interpretation was lost on Yaron. Instead of the contemporary interpretation, Yaron sees "an embarrassing attempt to mount an antiquated play" (1999b).

Shosh Weitz also reports a feeling of embarrassment. She realized that the show is "a parody that intends to ridicule the play and the traditional style in which the play is performed in Germany" (1999c). But this realization does not make her appreciate Haussman's concept. On the contrary, she interprets his concept as an expression of European cultural superiority and it sends her into defensive frenzy: "Because of my Mediterranean education I did not have a chance to develop familiarity with the traditional style of German theatre, which becomes a basis for parody at Gesher Theatre" (1999c). She frames herself in self-deprecating terms, describing her education as "Mediterranean" (read—not European). She alludes to the perceived feelings of Israeli cultural inferiority in respect to European high culture. At the end, Weitz asks, not without reason: "Why ridicule a play from the eighteenth century, when it is possible just not to stage it?" She continues: "*Love and Intrigue* is an excellent example of [cultural] misunderstanding. Maybe in a different place and with different audiences it would have been a successful show." Yet, Weitz charges Gesher management with the responsibility for this failure:

> Leander Haussman is the first guest director at Gesher. The fact that his production is foreign, strange, and alienated, speaks not only about him, but also about the artistic management of Gesher. They should have identified the problems with staging such an interpretation of Schiller's play during the rehearsals, or even before that. (Weitz 1999c)

Michael Handelsaltz was the only reviewer who thought that Gesher deserves "compliments for staging classic German drama." He also seems to understand the directorial concept and appreciate the acting: "The style of acting is beyond parody, and maybe that's right, since a play which is full of pathos is not going to be credible today anyhow" (1999c). His conclusion, though far from unconditional praise, was not a death sentence either: "All and all [the production] is very strange, in some moments unbearable, and in other impressive. Surprisingly, the plot still works. There are miracles in the theatre" (1999c).

The production of *Love and Intrigue* was a real failure with the audiences. By December 1999, after only 19 performances, it was taken off Gesher's repertoire. It was not until much later, in June 2001, that the theatre finally enjoyed an appreciative reception of the production. Weitz's words, "Maybe in a different place and with different audiences it would have been a successful show" (1999c), turned out to be prophetic: the production, indeed, became a big hit at the Schiller Festival in Manheim, Germany. Gesher resuscitated the show for the festival, and finally, three years after the premiere, in different cultural and historical circumstances *Love and Intrigue* found its audience. Indeed, the production's failure in Israel was predicated on the lack of cultural relevance.

Gesher finished the year 1999 with a budget of over 18.5 million NIS; however, the public subsidies remained at the 1998 level (see Table 1). The growth came from private donations, commercial sponsorships, and other sources. Work on two productions simultaneously put a dent in Gesher's budget that needed to be repaired.

"The season of Love and Death" turned out to be a dead season. The two productions did not succeed to reverse the critical trend: Gesher was sliding further and further down from the peak it had reached with the production of *Village*.

Postscript: Gesher after 2000

In the several following productions (that are beyond the scope of this research but will be addressed briefly here) Gesher made attempts to try different artistic strategies in order to regain the love of audiences and appreciation of the critics. The first attempt aimed to engage the Gesher-2 actors. As mentioned before, at the beginning of 2000, Gesher produced a comedy by Carlo Goldoni titled *Sea* (in contrast to *River*). However, this production gained neither critical acclaim nor popularity with the audiences, and only exacerbated the disintegration of the Gesher-2 project.

By 2000, Arye had given up on his aspiration to find understanding with the Israeli critics and audiences. At the same time, the Russian-speaking audiences started to feel "betrayed" by Arye and by Gesher, who seemed to try too hard to become accepted in Israel. Gesher management sensed that productions in Hebrew, especially the ones dealing with Israeli topics (such as *Eating*) loosened Gesher's connection with its Russian-speaking audiences. These factors resulted in Gesher's attempt to return to the Russian language and drama. The theatre even hired a public relations agency specializing in advertising on "Russian Street." In March and May of 2000, Gesher presented two productions in Russian: *Mr. Brink* and *Moscow–Petushki*. *Mr. Brink*, a play by Paul Osborn, was staged by a guest director from Russia, Mikhail Mokeev, and later revised by Arye. *Moscow–Petushki*, based on a Russian cult book by Venedict Erofeev was directed by Igor Mirkurbanov (one of the leading actors of Gesher) as his solo-performance. Later, *Mr. Brink* was produced in Hebrew as well, whereas *Moscow–Petushki* remained only in Russian. Both productions were received favorably, especially on "Russian Street." Yet, Gesher still struggled financially. Its budget remained lower than that of other public theatres of comparable size. Gesher applied to the Ministry of Education and Culture for additional funding. This application inadvertently led to the eruption of the most significant crisis for Gesher since its foundation.

In March 2000, a high-rank official from the Ministry of Education and Culture said in an interview in *Yediot Ahronot* that Gesher should not receive the additional subsidy that it requested. He added that Gesher's fiscal crisis should lead to Arye's removal from the theatre, and that it was time to realize that Gesher is a failure (Shrir 2000). Almost immediately after that, *Haaretz* offered its readers a scoop on the salaries of the major artistic directors of Israeli theatres, giving vastly inflated numbers for both Ori Levy and Yevgeny Arye (Shohat 2000a).

Gesher's management, backed by some Israeli politicians and cultural producers, saw these publications as an unreasonable and angry attack not only on Gesher, but also, by extension, on the Soviet immigrant community. Once again, Gesher became a political card that politicians skillfully played. Gesher appealed to its friends and supporters among Israeli public figures, and the debate ensued. Major Israeli cultural and political figures, such as Yoram Kanuk, Leah Rabin, the Minister of Absorption Yuli Tamir, and even the Prime Minister Ehud Barak, got involved. The debate focused both on the role of Soviet immigration in Israeli society, and on cultural policy, specifically on the responsibility of the government to support cultural production. Finally, with the involvement of the Prime Minister and the Minister of Finance, the crisis was resolved, and the government decided to grant Gesher additional support, the sum of a million NIS (Shohat 2000b). This drama showed that Gesher remained a cultural representative of Soviet immigrants, and, like at the time of its foundation, this position was exploited both by the establishment and by the theatre toward political ends.

After Gesher recovered from the crisis, Arye undertook a new attempt to reestablish Gesher as a top-ranked theatre. He went back to his plan to stage the now classic novel by Mikhail Bulgakov *The Master and Margarita*. This production titled *Satan in Moscow* was unprecedented for Gesher. Firstly, it was an opera, a new genre for both Arye and the troupe; second, a limited number of performances was planned (the production was to run only for three months); and finally, several opera singers and well-known actors were invited especially for this production, the most famous of them Haim Topol (known for his leading role in the 1964 Israeli hit movie *Sallah Shabati*). For these reasons, *Satan in Moscow* provoked a lot of interest from critics and public, and received vast coverage. The premiere was set as a true media event. The show was sold out, but the critical reception was split between those who appreciated the show, and between those who acknowledged the production values (*Satan in Moscow* was the most expensive show that Gesher had produced so far), but denied its artistic contribution. In sum, the grandiose endeavor of musical theatre starring famous actors brought Gesher back to the spotlight, but it did not reestablish Gesher as top Israeli theatre. *Satan in Moscow* received the Israeli Theatre Award in six categories, all of them reflecting its high production values (Best Composer, Best Costume Designer, Best Stage Designer, Best Movement, Best Lighting Designer, and Most Promising Actress).

In the summer of 2001, for the first time in its history, Gesher invited an Israeli director. Yosi Israeli directed *Mademoiselle Julie* by August Strindberg, a classic play of European repertory theatre. It was a passing show, neither a popular nor a critical success, which was quickly taken off Gesher's repertoire.

Gesher's fate did not change until the fall of 2001, when Arye produced Shakespeare's *Midsummer Night Dream*, which earned excellent critical responses. For this production Gesher received the Israeli Theatre Award in the categories of Best Director, Best Actress, and Best Lighting Designer. Gesher reached the peak of success again with the production of *The Slave* by Isaak Bashevis-Singer in 2002, which also was hailed by both critics and audiences. It received the Israeli Theatre Award in the categories of Best Director, Best Production, Best Actress, Best Stage Designer, and Best Lighting Designer. In the year following its premiere, *The Slave* was performed over 200 times, becoming one of the most popular shows in Israel. This success is particularly important in the context of growing political uncertainty, when the governmental support for theatres is undergoing considerable budget cuts. *The Slave*'s popularity (and resulting sales) allows Gesher to survive the current budget cuts. At a time when some theatres in Israel are forced to reduce their staff, and others are under the threat of closing, Gesher continues to function as usual. This relative financial well-being comes, of course, at the price of over-performance of the production and the actors' increasing weariness. *Three-Penny Opera* by Bertold Brecht and Kurt Weil premiered the same year. Musical and colorful show, it was not as successful as *The Slave*.

Other recent events at Gesher include a new attempt to establish a studio for young actors, this time, in a different format than Gesher-2. The project started in the spring 2002, when Arye saw a production by a graduating class at the Nissan Nativ acting school. He instantly loved their work, and invited them to come to the theatre as a group and to mount their own production (under his supervision but their own direction). He made only one condition—this production has to generate profits, so that the studio would be self-sustaining. The offer was accepted, and seven young actors formed the Studio-Gesher.

Arye had to work hard convincing Ori Levy and the board to accept his idea in the times of budget cuts and economic uncertainty. However reluctant, they went along with his plan. Like in the good old times, Gesher found an old warehouse in southern Tel Aviv, promptly converted it into a modest but functional performance space, and called it *hangar*. Meanwhile, the new group rehearsed *Unidentified Human Remains and the True Nature of Love* by Brad Fraser under the direction of one of the members, Ido Mosari. The premiere took place at the newly renovated space. *Unidentified Human Remains* instantly became popular with both audiences and critics due to the dynamic, contemporary script and the young talented ensemble. More evidence of the studio's success is that four members of Studio-Gesher are engaged in *Shosha*, the most recent production, two of them are starring in the main parts. *Shosha* by Isaak Bashevis-Singer, which premiered in June 2003, was also a success. In summer 2004, Gesher brought both *The Slave* and *Shosha* on tour to New York. The show goes on.

• CHAPTER ELEVEN •

Retracing the Journey

In this book, I applied cultural and critical studies to the analysis of the cultural practices of Gesher Theatre and emergent discourses in the theatre's media reception. So, how is Gesher positioned within the Israeli scene of cultural production, and how is this position reflected in Gesher's reception over the years?

Gesher is a hybrid theatre. Gesher is located in Israel, it performs in Hebrew, its organizational structure and budget are similar to other Israeli theatres. Yet, its style, its mode of artistic production, and hierarchy within the troupe definitely have Russian sources.

Gesher's style is distinctive in the context of Israeli theatre. Some theatres mount large-scale Broadway-style productions. Some theatres work in the docu-drama tradition, involving the audience and making the text relevant to their community. Outside of the institutionally supported theatre, there are experimental fringe productions. Gesher produces neither Broadway-style shows, nor docu-drama, nor fringe productions.

Gesher continues the Russian theatrical legacy. Like Goncharov, Arye unites the traditions of the Russian actors' theatre with the full control of a director's theatre. He synthesizes the psychological approach derived from Stanislavsky's method, with Vachtangov-style theatrical poetry, and with the principles of Meyerhold's montage. Following Stanislavsky, the work of the theatre is based on long systematic rehearsals of a permanent ensemble and a small number of productions. The actors are encouraged to inhabit the world of the play, to act with both psychological and physical precision. Gesher's acting style remains in the Russian tradition, distinct from the Israeli acting style that is generally understated, realistic, and often minimalist in its emotional expressiveness. Under the influence of Vachtangov's 'theatre as celebration', Gesher creates on stage brightly emotional theatre, often incorporating elements of cabaret. These characteristics lead to a subversive aesthetic of the carnivalesque—to the principle of "grotesque realism" (Bakhtin 1984/1965). Under the influence of Meyerhold's constructivism, Gesher uses 'active scenography' and multimedia techniques (such as film).

Yet, whether the scenic effects, sound, and lighting are realistic or symbolic, they are concept-driven. One of Gesher's concepts is a metatheatre that over the years became a trademark of the theatre. This device allows Gesher to continuously problematize the process of artistic creation and the position of the artist in society.

Gesher is a theatre of superb production values, yet it is not a commercial theatre that caters to the tastes of conservative audiences. Israeli theatre is increasingly experiencing the influence of the market economy and the conservative values of collective subscribers. Gesher, following the Russian tradition, does not see theatre as entertainment. The company is motivated by an idealistic perception of the high moral and educational value of theatre arts, which forces the audience to think, to suffer, to go through significant personal experiences, and, rephrasing Stanislavsky, to 'work on themselves'. In that, Gesher identified with the tradition of Russian and European theatre.[1]

Gesher also has distinctive dramaturgy. Emanuel Levy classifies the repertoire of Israeli theaters into three major categories: Israeli plays, Jewish plays, and what he calls "universal plays" (he means classical and contemporary European plays) (1980, p. 39). Apparently, Gesher's repertoire is structurally similar to those of other Israeli public theatres (see Table 4). In the years 1990–1999, Gesher mounted three Israeli plays, two Jewish plays, and ten "universal" plays. Importantly, six out of the ten "universal" plays were written by Russian or Soviet playwrights. Gesher's Israeli plays, like the rest of Israeli drama, draw from political events and local sensitivities. Thus, in its repertoire choice, like in other aspects of artistic production, Gesher is a hybrid theatre: it is simultaneously similar to and different from other Israeli public theatres.

Gesher's seemingly apolitical agenda actually resists the idea of socially useful *agitprop* art, and rejects the identity-driven theatre criticism in the mainstream media. Gesher's example makes possible an interesting reversal, when "art for the art's sake" emerges as an expression of resistance to the hegemonic ideology, while critical discourse discussing the theatre in political terms replicates the hegemonic ideology.

Gesher's media reception evolved parallel to the development of the theatre itself. This reception can be divided into several periods. The years

---

1 *Yiddishkeit* was not part of Gesher's culture. By the time Gesher's actors and director were trained, the traces of GOSET and other Yiddish theatres were erased from the Soviet cultural memory. The only link from Yiddish theatre to Gesher was the late Gregory Lyampe, whose influence was limited.

1990–1992 were the initial period when Gesher was founded, and its structure, funding, artistic profile, as well as repertoire and language policy were established. During this period the critics considered Gesher a novel and interesting troupe; yet, already this early reception shaped the main points of critical debate surrounding Gesher: fixation on the cultural identity of the theatre-makers, obsession with the questions of language and, consequently, with the legitimacy of public funding. In 1993, the production of *The Idiot* marked a new era in Gesher's history. The Russian cultural identity of Gesher worked in its favor, and the production received the highest critical acclaim.

This successful period was punctuated by the 1995 crisis within the Gesher company, which brought up questions of the definition of the theatre in the context of Israeli culture and policy all over again. However, Gesher overcame the crisis, and during the years 1995–1997 Gesher reached the peak of its fame, despite the fact that the critics were still brooding over the questions of cultural identity. This period culminated in the production of the nostalgic Israeliana *Village*, which enjoyed a resounding critical and popular success and became a trademark of the theatre. *City (Odessa Stories)* was the last production of that famed period. The reception of *Three Sisters* in 1997 indicated a new period in the life of Gesher—a period when Gesher's shows received neither rave reviews and multiple prizes at home, nor offers of tours abroad. This period was marked by mutual disappointment between Gesher and the critics, who consistently failed to fulfill each other's expectations.

This period included the foundation of the Gesher-2 project, an acting studio for young actors. However, Gesher-2's production of *Don Juan* (1998) did not change the critical trend. The year 1999 became a year of a complete critical demolition: Gesher's productions, namely *Eating* and *Love and Intrigue*, were savaged by critics, who assumed condescending and vindictive positions towards Gesher. Gesher's director, put on the defense, publicly responded to this reception with equal condescension. The theatre's fate did not change until the fall of 2001, when Gesher produced *Midsummer Night's Dream*, which finally regained an excellent critical response, and *The Slave* succeeded even beyond this.

Only two of Gesher's productions encountered unproblematic critical reception: *The Idiot* and *Village*. *The Idiot* presented "Russian culture in Hebrew" in a way that threatened neither the critics' sense of Israeli identity, nor their preconceptions about Russian art. The production was foreign, but not too foreign. For critics, *The Idiot* was a production of "Russian theatre."

Conversely, *Village* presented a story from the Israeli past, but also in an unthreatening way. It achieved just the right amount of mimicry, without it turning into menace. The characters in *Village*, mostly immigrants and exiles, were consistent with Gesher's identity as "immigrant theatre." Thus even these unproblematic receptions fit Gesher into the mold of ideological norms and ethnic stereotypes.

Gesher is situated between Russian theatrical tradition and the Israeli cultural context. However, Israeli critics consistently ignore this hybrid position, fixating instead on the ideology-driven questions of identity politics. Paradoxically, that means that Gesher inadvertently becomes a political theatre.

Political theatre is usually understood as the theatre with social concerns geared toward awakening awareness and facilitating social change. But mostly, political theatre is associated with expression of resistance to the dominant forms of oppression. One notable alternative is an "art for the art's sake" approach to theatre. Such an approach deemphasizes the social significance of art, and reduces theatre to pure aesthetic form.

But art is always political (Wolff 1993). Gesher represents an interesting illustration of this point because its nearly religious approach to theatre, with the artistic production as the top value, becomes political in the Israeli cultural context. Critics see Gesher in political terms, and refuse to ground discussion in aesthetic criteria. As one critic noted, "Gesher is in itself a political text" (Ben-Nun 1994). In doing that, critics align themselves with the hegemonic Zionist ideology prioritizing national significance of art over artistic values. Thus critical discourse perpetuates hegemonic ideology.

Gesher's media reception reveals the complex interrelations between culture, ideology, and discourse in Israel. The dynamic of mutual and internal colonization shaped the media discourse about Gesher. The discourse of both the critics and of the Gesher theatre-makers are characterized by shifting positions of colonizer and colonized and by the ambivalence contained within each position.

When critics take the colonizing position towards Gesher, two things happen: first, the critics fixate on the cultural identity of the theatre-makers; second, the critics then use a condescending, patronizing tone towards both the production and the theatre-makers. This puts Gesher into a bind. On the one hand, if it yields to the demands of the critics (representing mainstream ideological discourse) and performs an act of mimicry (e.g., transitions to Hebrew, stages Israeli plays), the mimicry becomes too menacing. The critics then attack its productions, trying to emphasize Gesher's cultural difference. On the other hand, if Gesher gives up mimicry and positions itself as an Other (e.g., performs in Russian, avoids Israeli plays), it is also attacked, since the refusal to be a colonial subject is threatening. At best, Gesher is left to walk a tight rope (as with *The Idiot* and *Village*).

However, when the positions shift, and Gesher takes the colonizing position towards the critics (and by extension to Israeli culture), the situation does not improve. When critics perceive the threat of subjugation, they attack Gesher even more vehemently. Thus, whether they take colonizing or colonized positions, both discourses, that of Gesher and that of the critics, remain within the framework of mutual colonial subjugation, thereby replicating the colonial hierarchy of monocentric aesthetics. To cut short the vicious circle, the discourse needs to break free of cultural hegemony and step towards what Ella Shohat and Robert Stam (1998, p. 27) call "polycentric aesthetics" opening up multiple narratives and trajectories of artistic creation. Following Bhabha's argument about the transformative potential of hybrid agencies, I suggest that it is cultural hybridity that would allow a way out of this colonial lose-lose situation. Specifically, I hope that the hybrid in-between discourses recently emerging in Israel (such as that of Gesher) will destabilize the hegemonic discourse, and help critics to get over the monocentric system of values.

In conclusion, I'd like to briefly discuss the theoretical contributions of this research. My study contributes to several areas, among them cultural studies, research on immigration, rhetorical criticism, studies of diaspora, cultural policy, and post-colonial discourse analysis.

I approach theatre from the perspective of cultural studies. Within this discipline, excellent work has been done in transcultural visual culture, particularly on film and visual art. The performing arts have been somewhat less studied, especially drama theatre. The few existing studies of "accented" or hybrid theatre examine it from a strictly theatrical point of view (e.g., Pavis 1996) without situating theatre within a broader cultural context. I approach Gesher as a cultural phenomenon positioned at the intersection of 'high' and 'low', European and Middle-Eastern, Russian and Israeli, as well as national and popular cultures. Such an interdisciplinary approach to the theatre makes it a fitting site for posing the questions of cultural production and exchange.

My research also approaches the topic of Soviet immigration and interethnic relations in Israel from the vantage point of cultural studies. The existing body of literature is written from the sociological perspective (e.g., Gitelman 1982; Leshem and Lissak 1998). My application of cultural studies to the study of immigration allows me to give a close reading to the cultural practices and discourses of immigrants and veteran Israelis, as well as to uncover regimes of power and normative knowledges active in the site of local cultural production.

This research also makes a contribution to rhetorical criticism by problematizing questions of critical judgment (particularly in the genre of journalistic theatre review). Considering the relations between aesthetic and ideological criteria of judgment, I show how even the discussion of such an 'aesthetic' domain as directorial style becomes an arena of an ideological 'terrain of struggle'. Gesher becomes an example of a reversal of habitual categories, where the specific context of artistic production and critical reception renders seemingly apolitical theatre political.

This research also problematizes the concept of diaspora. As William Safran (1999) has shown, diaspora has become a fluid concept. Soviet immigration to Israel provides an interesting example of such fluidity. In Israel, diaspora is defined through ideology. For example, due to the ideological concept of Jewish immigration as "homecoming," the Soviet immigrants in Israel are not considered to be a diasporic community *de jure*, even though they constitute one *de facto*. But the concepts of diaspora and homecoming are not mutually exclusive. Relinquishing one diaspora may only mean beginning a new one.

This research offers some conclusions on a practical level. It serves as a launching pad for a discussion of cultural policy. In Israel, the ideology of Zionism provides criteria for public funding, guarding against any potential disintegration of social consensus. Throughout its history, Gesher Theatre has occupied an ambivalent position vis-à-vis hegemonic ideology, simultaneously perpetuating and resisting it. Studying Gesher's particular history helps in tracing connections between cultural policy and political economy within the context of Zionist ideology.

Finally, on a theoretical level, this research adds a new dimension to post-colonial discourse analysis. Extending the colonization trope to a context of immigration, my research widens the understanding of the colonial relationship. In contrast to previous theorizing, my model of Mutual and Internal Colonization emphasizes two distinctive processes: first, the discursive process of mutual colonization, when the roles of the cultural colonizer and the colonized shift, leading both immigrants and their hosts to colonize each other, and second, the discursive process of internal colonization, when colonial subjects ultimately colonize themselves as the role of colonized turns inwards.

The model of Mutual and Internal Colonization can reveal the ambivalent relationships between two cultural discourses, as they complement and clash within the same subjectivity. Application of this model has the potential to give insight into the internal structure of hyphenated identities in other geo-political and historical contexts.

Appendix

Table 1: Budget of the Gesher Theatre in the Years 1991–1999[a]
(in thousands of NIS, rounded off)

	Collective Ticket Sales (including "external" sales)	Individual Ticket Sales	Public Subsidies	Ticket Sales Abroad	Donations (including Gesher Friends)	Sponsorship and Advertisement	Other Sources (including hall rentals)	Total
1991	NA	512	710	NA	NA	NA	NA	1,223
1992	NA	459	1,397	NA	194	15	NA	2,065
1993	NA	1,390	2,916	NA	258	4	NA	4,567
1994	NA	1,377	5,105	29	279	75	32	6,897
1995	1,621	687	5,257	224	215	57	31	8,117
1996	2,278	2,450	6,238	NA	137	67	137	11.308
1997	2,536	2,900	7,246	437	649	319	145	14,231
1998	2,391	3,670	8,419	683	341	633	198	16,335
1999	5,589[b]	NA	8,538	557	1,708	980	1,248	18,620

[a] Data based on the financial reports of the theatre.

[b] Including individual ticket sales.

Table 2. Repertoire of the Gesher Theatre in Chronological Order[a]

Production	Premiere	Last Performance	Number of Performances[b]		
			In Hebrew	In Russian	Total
Rosencrantz and Guildenstern Are Dead	Apr. 20, 1991	Apr. 10, 1999	59	80	139
Dreyfus File	July 5, 1991	March 2001 (tour)	91	97	188
If Only	Sept. 25, 1991	June, 1992	NA	24	24
Molière	Jan. 12, 1992	Aug. 13, 1994	50	20	70
The Idiot	Dec. 20, 1992	Nov. 1997	180	22	202
Adam Resurrected	June 9, 1993 (Vienna) Oct. 26, 1993 (Tel Aviv)	ongoing	145	43	188
The Lower Depths	Dec. 28, 1994	June 26, 1997	42	NA	42
Tartuffe	July 29, 1995	Sept. 1998	143	35	178
Village	Febr. 18, 1996	ongoing	430	NA	430
City (Odessa Stories)	Dec. 24, 1996	ongoing	145	49	194
Three Sisters	Dec. 6, 1997	May 9, 1999	62	NA	62
Don Juan	Febr. 21, 1998	May 11, 1999	90	NA	90
Eating	Jan. 6, 1999	Sept. 10, 2000	56	NA	56
River	July 9, 1999	July 9, 2001	80	NA	80
Love and Intrigue	July 29, 1999	June 2001 (Schiller Festival)	20	NA	20

[a] Data based on the records maintained by Elena Kreindlina (in 1990-1995) and by Tatiana Suchanova (from 1995 on).

[b] As of 2001.

Table 3. Box-office Success of Gesher's Productions

Production	Performances in Hebrew	Performances in Russian	Total
	Most Successful (over 100 performances)		
Village	430	NA	430
The Idiot	180	22	202
City (Odessa Stories)	145	49	194
Adam Resurrected	145	43	188
Dreyfus File	91	97	188
Tartuffe	143	35	178
Rosencrantz and Guildenster Are Dead	59	80	139
	Moderately Successful (50–100 performances)		
Don Juan	90	NA	90
River	80	NA	80
Molière	50	20	70
Three Sisters	62	NA	62
Eating	56	NA	56
	Least Successful (under 50 performances)		
The Lower Depths	42	NA	42
If Only	NA	24	24
Love and Intrigue	20	NA	20

Table 4. Repertoire of the Gesher Theatre by Cultural Origin of Drama

Production	Performances in Hebrew	Performances in Russian	Total
	Russian Classic and Contemporary Drama		
If Only	NA	24	24
Molière	50	20	70
The Idiot	180	22	202
The Lower Depths	42	NA	42
Three Sisters	62	NA	62
River	80	NA	80
	Western Classic and Contemporary Drama		
Rosencrantz and Guildenstern Are Dead	59	80	139
Tartuffe	143	35	178
Don Juan	90	NA	90
Love and Intrigue	20	NA	20
	Israeli Contemporary Drama		
Adam Resurrected	145	43	188
Village	430	NA	430
Eating	56	NA	56
	Jewish Drama		
Dreyfus File	91	97	188
City (Odessa Stories)	145	49	194

Table 5: Gesher Theatre's Tours Abroad

Production	Date of Tour	Destination
Rosencrantz and Guildenstern Are Dead	Jan. 1992	Festival of Israeli Culture, Brooklyn Academy of Music, New York (USA)
	Aug. 1993	Festival D'Avignon (France)
	Aug. 1993	*Welt in Basel* Festival, Basel (Switzerland)
Dreyfus File	March 2001	Chicago, Detroit, New York, Philadelphia, Washington, D.C. (USA) Toronto (Canada)
Molière	Oct. 1992	Zurich (Switzerland)
The Idiot	Sept.-Oct. 1993	*City of Drama* Festival, Manchester (UK)
Adam Resurrected	June 1993	Vienna Festival (Austria)
	Sept. 1993	*Welt in Basel* Festival, Basel (Switzerland)
	Oct. 1994	Berlin, Dresden, Erfurt (Germany)
	July 1998	Lincoln Center Festival, New York (USA)
Village	May-June 1997	Brighton Festival, London Festival, Newcastle, Cambridge, Manchester (UK)
	March 1998	*50 Jahre Israel* Festival, Berlin and tours in other cities (Germany)
	July 1998	Lincoln Center Festival, New York (USA)
	Oct. 1998	Rome Festival (Italy)
	Oct. 1998	Melbourne Festival (Australia)
	Oct. 1999	Dublin Festival (Ireland)
City (Odessa Stories)	March 1998	*Art of the State: Israel at 50* Festival, Kennedy Center, Washington, D.C. (USA)
	Nov. 1998	Paris (France)
	June 1999	Barbican Festival BITE: 99, London (UK)
	Nov. 1999	Theatre Festival, Berlin (Germany)
Love and Intrigue	June 2001	Schiller Festival, Mannheim (Germany)

Table 6: Gesher Troupe in the Years 1991 and 1999

	1991[a]	1999[b]
Artistic Director	Yevgeny Arye	Yevgeny Arye
Manager	Slava Maltzev	Ori Levy
Actors	Yevgeny Gamburg	Yevgeny Gamburg
	Vladimir Halemsky	Vladimir Halemsky
	Michael Asinovsky	Michael Asinovsky
	Mark Ivanir	Mark Ivanir
	Boris Achanov	Boris Achanov
	Natalya Voitulevich	Natalya Voitulevich-Manor
	Sasha Demidov	Israel (Sasha) Demidov
	Yevgenya Dodina	Yevgenya Dodina
	Lilian Heilovsky	Ruth (Lilian) Heilovsky
	Yevgeny Terletsky	Yevgeny Terletsky
	Roland Heilovsky	Nelly Gosheva
	Shaul Alias	Leonid Kanevsky
	Lora Kvetner	Igor Mirkurbanov
	Igor Voitulevich	Vladimir Portnov
		Klim Kamenko
		Svetlana Demidov
		Adi Etzion-Zak
		Vladimir Vorobyov
		Efrat Ben-Zur
		Slava Bibergal
		Levana Finkelstein
		Amnon Wolf
Administration and Production	Lena Kreindlina	Lena Kreindlina
	Roman Kvetner	Roman Kvetner
	Avi Nedsevetsky (Benjamin)	Avi Benjamin
	Tatiana Suchanova	Tatiana Suchanova
	Anton Romanovsky	Anton Romanovsky
	Yuri Suchanov	Yuri Suchanov
	Anna Itskovich	Anna Itskovich
	Sergey Novitsky	Sergey Novitsky
	Tatiana Terletsky	Michal Savel
	Alena Minkovskaya	Alexander Lisyansky
	Maria Kataeva	Miriam Yahil-Wax

Continued on next page

[a] At the time of the production of *Rosencrantz and Guildenstern Are Dead.*

[b] At the time of the production of *River.*

Table 6—*Continued.*

	1991	1999
Administration and Production—*continued*	Arsen Gotlib	Victor Sokolov
	Alan Bochinsky	Zvia Binder
	Michail Cherniavsky	Victor Riskin
	Nikolai Artamonov	Lena Laskina
	Maria Kraiman	Michael Vaisbrud
	Katya Sosonsky	Arkady Bogdanovich
	Dmitri Krymov	Vitaly Sergeev
	Galina Lioly	Michal Scheflan
		Dmitry Gurevich
		Victor Vinokurov
		Alexander Sikirin
		Eli Atia
		Olga Berezina
		Marina Krasilnikova
		Iana Kuzinets
		Lena Marchinovsky
		Michael Slepner
		Alexander Suvorov
		Olga Arieva
		Olga Kolchin
		Yuli Ziv
		Liron Naigeboren
		Alexander Ushakov
		Alexander Goldin
		Oleg Gusachenko
		Vadim Ilyin
		Andrei Christichenko
		Ilya Levintant
		Yuri Perel
		Alexander Kozhevnikov
		Leonid Kolesnikov
		Michael Rivkin
		Maxim Rosenberg

Table 7: Major Israeli Printed Media Included in the Study

Publication	Profile	Permanent Reviewers	Theatre Reviews[a]
	National Daily Newspapers		
Haaretz	elite (comparable to *The New York Times*)	Michael Handelsaltz Tzipi Shohat	most productions
Yediot Ahronot	popular (comparable to *New York Daily News* and *New York Post*; the most widely read newspaper)	Boaz Evron Shosh Weitz	most productions
Maariv	popular (the second most widely read newspaper)	Sarit Fuks Haim Nagid Eliakim Yaron	most productions
Hadashot[b]	popular	Shosh Avigal	most productions
Davar[c]	popular (originally, a Labor party organ)	Aviva Zaltzman	most productions
Globes	business and finance (comparable to *The Wall Street Journal*)	Michael Ohed Nili Barkan	most productions
	Local Weekly Newspapers		
Hair (supplementary of *Haaretz*)	popular (comparable to *The Village Voice*)	Amir Orion	most productions
Tel Aviv (supplementary of *Yediot Ahronot*)	popular	Shi Bar-Yakov	most productions
Yerushalaim (supplementary of *Yediot Ahronot*)	popular	none	most productions
Zman Tel Aviv (supplementary of *Maariv*)	popular	none	most productions
	Weekly Magazines		
Haulam Hazeh[d]	elite and left-wing; culture, society, and arts	Miri Litvik	some productions
Anashim	popular; entertainment and media (comparable to *People* magazine)	none	few productions

[a] "Theatre Review" column indicates extent of coverage of theatre productions: whether a newspaper publishes original reviews of most productions by public theatres in Israel, some productions, or only few of them.

[b] Closed down in 1993.

[c] Closed down in 1996.

[d] Closed down in 1993.

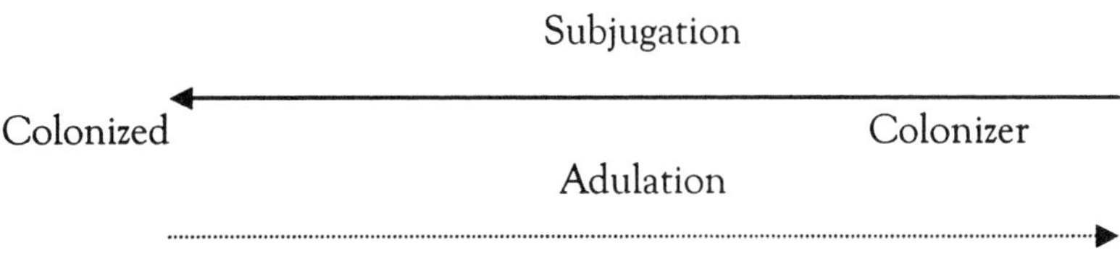

Figure 11: Unidirectional Colonial Relationships
Colonizer subjugates the colonized; the colonized adulates the colonizer.

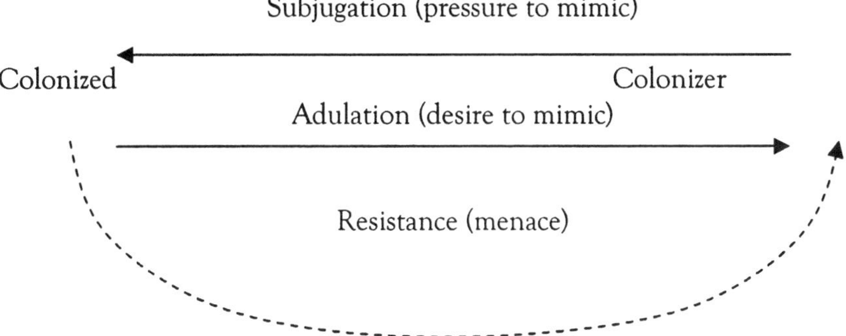

Figure 12: Ambivalent Colonial Relationship
Mimicry of the colonized is charged with the danger of menace for the colonizer.

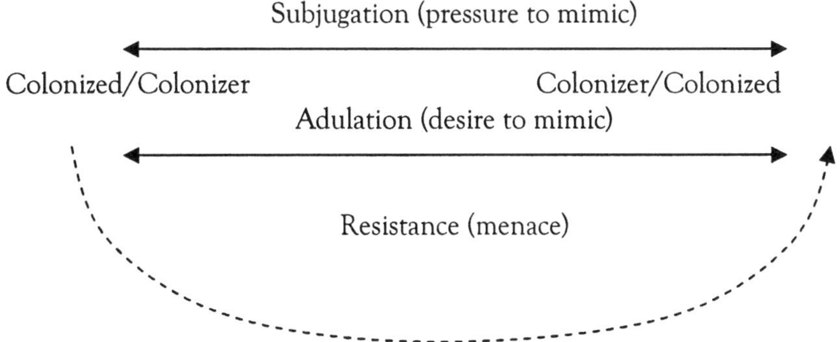

Figure 13: Mutual Colonization
Positions of colonizer and colonized shift; vectors of colonization switch direction.

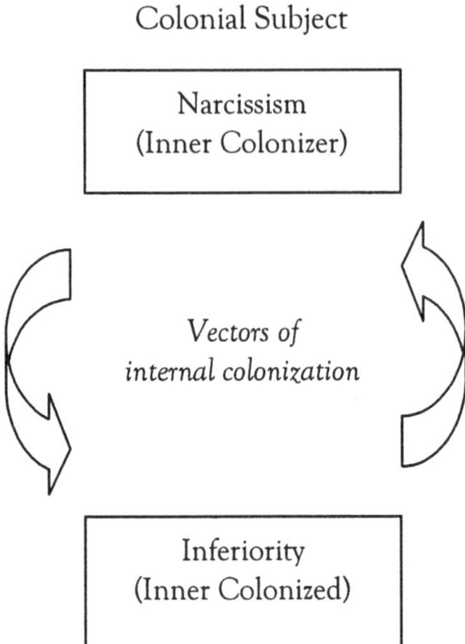

Figure 14: Internal Colonization
A subject contains both colonizer and colonized; positions shift within the subject. Narcissism reflects the position of adulation of one's own culture and subjugation of other's culture. Inferiority reflects the position of subjugation of one's own culture and adulation of other's culture.

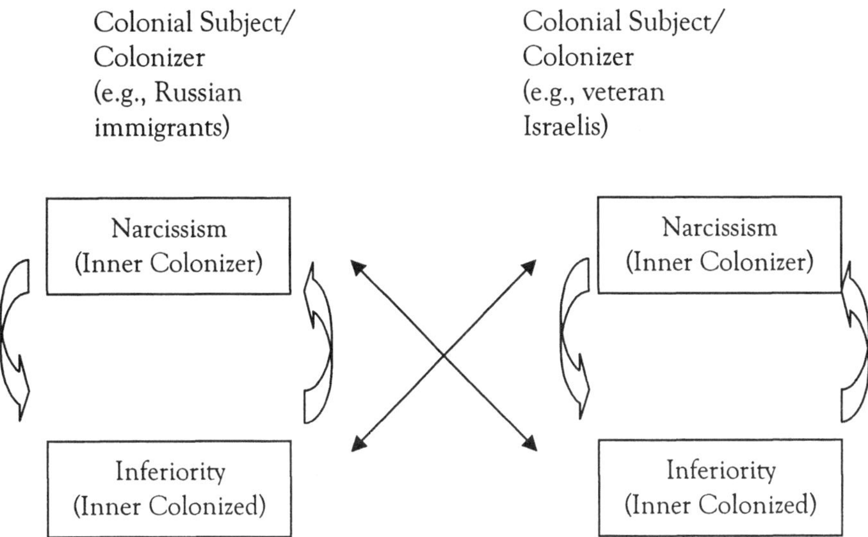

Figure 15: Mutual and Internal Colonization

Mutual colonization results in internal colonization; the narcissistic position of the Inner Colonizer is coupled up with the inferiority of the Inner Colonized. The vectors of colonization cross when the narcissism (Inner Colonizer) of one is engaged into colonial relationships with the inferiority (Inner Colonized) of another.

Interview Guide

The opening question:

"How did you come to Gesher?"

This question was followed only with questions that stemmed from an interviewee's narrative, for instance:

Clarifying questions:

"You said your contract was terrible. What was terrible about it?"

Questions about professional work:

"What were the main components of this marketing campaign?"

Questions focusing on multilingual and multicultural composition of the theatre:

"How is marketing different for the Russian-speaking and Hebrew-speaking audience?"

"How is your work for Gesher different from (or similar to) the theatre in Haifa?"

The concluding questions:

"Who are the closest people to you in Gesher?"

"Where do you see yourself in five years?"

"What do your friends say when you tell them that you work at Gesher?"

Glossary

Aliyah, literally "ascent," means Jewish immigration to Israel. Originally, it meant an ascent to a synagogue's stage to read from the Torah, or a ritual ascent to Mount Zion in Jerusalem. The Zionist movement adopted the term and gave it the new meaning of ideologically motivated repatriation. Today *aliyah* is commonly used in both private and public contexts in Israel, and is juxtaposed to the ideologically neutral term for immigration—*hagira*.

Eretz Israel, literally "the land of Israel," is a biblical trope. When used instead of "Israel" or "State of Israel," it signifies the author's affectionate attitude to Israel and commitment to Zionism.

Halutz (plural *halutzim*), literally "pioneers," refers to the small and ideologically driven group of Jewish newcomers who settled/colonized Palestine at the beginning of the twentieth century. In contemporary Hebrew the term has strong positive connotations. The Zionist discourse glorifies the *halutzim* as national heroes. Their life stories are commemorated in media, education, and museums (see, for instance, Katriel, 1997).

Klitat Aliyah (or just *klita*) literally means "immigrant absorption." Throughout the history of Israeli state, the absorption policy changed from forced assimilation to partial tolerance for difference. And yet, *klitat aliyah* remains a charged term due to the ideological importance of Jewish immigration to Israel. One reflection of this importance is that a whole ministry—a Ministry of Absorption—oversees and governs the process of *klitat aliyah*.

Mizug Galuyot, literally "the mixing of exiles," figuratively means "the melting pot." The policy of *mizug galuyot* calls for the immediate cultural assimilation of new immigrants into Israeli society. As the immigrants blend into the melting pot of a new society, they shad their diasporic culture, and turn from passive Jews into active Hebrews. In that they partake not only in physical, but also in spiritual relinquishing of the diaspora (*Galut*). The traditional meaning of *Galut* is revealing here. In Jewish theology *Galut* is a punishment for the sins of the Jewish people (including uprooting from the homeland, subjection to foreign rule, and alienation from the surrounding society). The Zionist movement adapted the term to emphasize incompleteness of Jewish life in diaspora, and to validate its goal of building a Jewish nation-state. Thus, *mizug galuyot* becomes one of the means of reaching this goal.

Ole, (plural *olim*), literally "ascendant," means "immigrant." In Zionist discourse, *olim* are oppressed diasporic Jews who "ascend" to the Land of Israel in order to build their national home. As such, *olim* are expected to adhere to the ideological norms of first, a Zionist motivation for immigration; second, an attachment to the Land of Israel; third, a commitment to learning Hebrew, and finally, complete cultural assimilation. Zionist ideology, which sets immigrant absorption as a top national priority, sanctifies the positive meaning of the term *ole*. However, in the vernacular Hebrew, it has developed degrading connotations, which point to the incompetence and ineptitude of new immigrants, and emphasize their otherness.

Bibliography

Abel, Lionel. *Metatheatre: A New View of Dramatic Form*. New York: Hill and Wang, 1963.

Althusser, Louis. "Ideology and Ideological State Apparatus." In *Lenin and Philosophy and Other Essays*, 127-186. Translated by B. Brewster. London: New Left Books, 1971.

Avigal, Shosh. "Patterns and Trends in Israeli Drama and Theater, 1948 to Present." In *Theater in Israel*, edited by Linda Ben-Zvi, 9–51. Ann Arbor: The University of Michigan Press, 1996.

Bakhtin, Mikhail M. *Rabelais and his World*. Translated by H. Iswolsky. Bloomington: Indiana University Press, 1984. (Original work published 1965)

Bhabha, Homi K. "The Third Space." In *Identity: Community, Culture, Difference*, edited by J. Rutherford, 207–221. London: Lawrence and Wishart, 1990.

——. *The Location of Culture*. London and New York: Routledge, 1994.

——. "Culture's In-between." In *Questions of Cultural Identity*, edited by S. Hall and P. Du Gay, 53–60. London, Thousand Oaks, New Delhi: Sage Publications, 1996.

Bourdieu, Pierre. "The Forms of Capital." In *Handbook of Theory and Research for the Sociology of Education*, edited by J. C. Richardson, 241–258. Westport, CT: Greenwood, 1986.

Brecht, Bertold. *Brecht on Theatre*. Edited and translated by J. Willet. London: Methuen, 1964. (Original work published 1957)

Brym, Robert J. and Rosalina Ryvkina. *The Jews of Moscow, Kiev, and Minsk: Identity, Anti-Semitism, Emigration.* New York: New York University Press and the Institute of Jewish Affairs, 1994.

Caspi, Dan and Yihiel Limor. *The In/outsiders: The Media in Israel.* Cresskill, NJ: Hampton Press, 1999.

Fanon, Frantz. *Black Skin, White Masks*. New York: Grove Press, 1952.

Feingold, Ben-Ami. "Hebrew Holocaust Drama as a Modern Morality Play." In *Theater in Israel*, edited by Linda Ben-Zvi, 269–285. Ann Arbor: The University of Michigan Press, 1996.

Foer, Jonathan S. *Everything is Illuminated.* Boston, New York: Houghton Mifflin, 2002.

Foucault, Michel. *The History of Sexuality. Volume 1: An Iintroduction*. New York: Vintage Books, 1981.

Fraser, Nancy. "Social Justice in the Age of Identity Politics: Redistribution, Recognition, and Participation." *The Tanner Lectures on Human Values* 19 (1998): 1–67.

Gershenson, Olga. "The Family of Strangers: Metaphors of Connection and Separation in Gesher Theatre in Israel." *Western Journal of Communication* 67, no. 3 (2003): 315–334.

Gertz, Nurith. "From Jew to Hebrew: The 'Zionist Narrative' in the Israeli Cinema of the 1940s and 1950s." In *In Search of Identity: Jewish Aspects in Israeli Culture*, edited by Dan Urian and Efraim Karsh, 175-200. London and Portland, OR: Frank Cass, 1999.

Gitelman, Zvi. *Becoming Israelis: Political Resocialization of Soviet and American Immigrants*. New York: Praeger Publishers, 1982.

Goluboff, Sascha L. *Jewish Russians: Upheavals in a Moscow Synagogue*. Philadelphia: University of Pennsylvania Press, 2003.

Gramsci, Antonio. *Prison Notebooks*. New York: Columbia University Press, 1991.

Jones, Clive. *Soviet Jewish Aliyah, 1989–1992: Impact and Implications for Israel and the Middle East*. London and Portland, OR: Frank Cass, 1996.

Katriel, Tamar. *Performing the Past: A Study of Israeli Settlement Museums*. London and Mahwah, NJ: Lawrence Erlbaum, 1997.

Katz, Elihu and Shmuel N. Eisenstadt. "Some Sociological Observations on the Response of Israeli Organizations to New Immigrants." *Administrative Science Quarterly* 5 (1960/61): 115–24.

Katz, Elihu and Hed Sella. *Culture Policy in Israel*. Jerusalem: The Van Leer Jerusalem Institute, 1999.

Kimmerling, Baruch. *The Invention and Decline of Israeliness: State, Society, and the Military*. Berkley: University of California Press, 2001.

Koestler, Arthur. *The Thirteenth Tribe: The Khazar Empire and its Heritage*. New York: Random House, 1976.

Leshem, Elazar and Judith T. Shuval. *Immigration to Israel: Sociological Perspectives*. New Brunswick, NJ: Transaction Books, 1998.

Leshem, Elazar and Moshe Lissak. "Development and Consolidation of the Russian Community in Israel." *Roots and Routes: Ethnicity and Migration in Global Perspective*, edited by Shalva Weil, 135–171. Jerusalem: Magnes, 1998.

Levy, Emanuel. *The Habima: Israel's National Theater 1917–1977: A Study of Cultural Nationalism*. New York: Columbia University Press, 1979a.

———. "The Role of the Critic: Theater in Israel." *Journal of Communication* 29, no. 4 (1979b): 175–83.

———. "National and Imported Culture in Israel." *Sociological Focus* 13, no. 1 (1980): 37–53.

———. "Art Critics and Art Publics: A Study in the Sociology and Politics of Taste." *Empirical Studies of the Arts* 6, no. 2 (1988): 127–149.

Levy, Shimon. "From Habima to Gesher: The Lasting Impact of Russian Culture on Israel." *International Affairs* 44, no. 6 (1998): 83–89.

Manor, Dalia. "From Rejection to Recognition: Israeli Art and the Holocaust." In *In Search of Identity: Jewish Aspects in Israeli Culture*, edited by Dan Urian and Efraim Karsh, 253–279. London and Portland, OR: Frank Cass, 1999.

Mouffe, Chantal. "Hegemony and Ideology in Gramsci." In *Gramsci and Marxist Theory*, edited by C. Mouffe, 168-204. London: Routledge, 1979.

Naficy, Hamid. *An Accented Cinema: Exilic and Diasporic Filmmaking*. Princeton, NJ: Princeton University Press, 2001.

Nimni, Efraim. *The Challenge of Post-zionism*. London and New York: Zed Books, 2003.

Pavis, Patrice. *The Intercultural Performance Reader*. London and New York: Routledge, 1996.

Porat, Dina. "Attitudes of Young State of Israel toward the Holocaust and its Survivors: A Debate over Identity and Values." In *New Perspectives on Israeli History: The Early Years of the State*, edited by L. J. Silberstein, 157-175. New York and London: New York University Press, 1991.

Roi, Yaacov. *Jews and Jewish Life in Russia and the Soviet Union*. Portland, OR: Frank Cass, 1995.

Rokem, Freddie. "Ideology and Archetypical Patterns in the Israeli Theatre." *Theatre Research International* 13, no. 2 (1988): 122-131.

Safran, William. "Comparing Diasporas: A Review Essay." *Diaspora* 8, no. 3 (1999): 255-291.

Said, Edward. *Orientalism*. New York: Pantheon Books, 1978.

Shohat, Ella H. and Robert Stam. "Narrativizing Visual Culture: Towards a Polycentric Aesthetics." In *The Visual Culture Reader*, edited by N. Mirzoeff, 27-49. London, New York: Routledge, 1998.

Shohat, Ella H. "The Invention of Mizrahim." *Journal of Palestine Studies* 29, no. 1 (1999): 5-20.

Shuval, Judith T. "Israel in the Context of Post-industrial Migration: The Mythology of Uniqueness." *Roots and Routes: Ethnicity and Migration in Global Perspective*, edited by Shalva Weil, 225-244. Jerusalem: Magnes, 1998.

Silberstein, Laurence J. *The Postzionism Debates: Knowledge and Power in Israeli Culture*. New York: Routledge, 1999.

Slezkine, Yuri. *The Jewish Century*. Princeton: Princeton University Press, 2004.

Swirski, Shlomo. *Israel: The Oriental Majority*. London: Zed Books, 1989.

Thompson, Ewa M. *Imperial Knowledge: Russian Literature and Colonialism*. Westport, CT: Greenwood Press, 2000.

Wachtel, Andrew. "Translation, Imperialism, and National Self-definition in Russia." *Public Culture* 11, no. 1 (1999): 49-73.

Weitz, Shoshana. "From Combative to Bourgeois Theater: Public Theater in Israel in 1990." In *Theater in Israel*, edited by L. Ben-Zvi, 101-119. Ann Arbor: The University of Michigan Press, 1996d.

Wexler, Paul. *The Ashkenazic Jews: A Slavo-Turkic People in Search of a Jewish Identity*. Columbus, Ohio: Slavica Publishers, 1993.

Williams, Raymond. *Keywords: A Vocabulary of Culture and Society*. (Rev. ed.). New York: Oxford University Press, 1985.

———. *Marxism and Literature*. London: Oxford University Press, 1997.

Wolff, Janet. *Aesthetics and the Sociology of Art*. (2nd ed.). Ann Arbor: University of Michigan Press, 1993.

Young, Robert JC. *Colonial Desire: Hybridity in Theory, Culture and Race*. London, New York: Routledge, 1995.

Media Materials

Avidar, Tamar. "Haemet he, sheani atzlan, soneh laavod." [The truth is that I am lazy and hate working]. *Maariv*, 10 January 1999.

Avigal, Shosh. "Teudat zehut marshima." [Impressive identification card]. *Hadashot*, 6 December 1991.

——. "Amin velelo patos." [Credible and without pathos]. *Hadashot*, 20 December 1992.

——. "Rutzu lir'ot." [Run to see]. *Hadashot*, 18 January 1993a.

——. "Mashehu bsisi pagum." [Something basic is damaged]. *Hadashot*, 31 October 1993b.

——. "Kitsch orkoli." [Audiovisual kitsch]. *Hadashot*, 10 November 1993c.

Avishi, Mordechai. "Hashefel mitorer lehaim." [The depths are coming to life]. *Davar*, 24 February 1995.

Avrahams, M. "Ma shehamevaker maadif." [Whatever the critic prefers]. *Haaretz*, 2 May 1994.

Bahir, Maya. "Chekhov beirom." [Naked Chekhov]. *Yediot Ahronot*, 7 December 1997.

Barkan, Nili. "Merhafim meal metziut israelit." [Hovering over Israeli reality]. *Globes*, 11 January 1999.

Bar-Kedma, Emanuel. "Halolita vehaidiot" [Lolita and the idiot]. *Yediot Ahronot*, 25 December 1992.

Barnes, Clive. "*Village* Starts out Grave, but Winds up Life-affirming." *The New York Post*, 10 July 1998a.

——. "The Tears of a Clown." *The New York Post*, 20 July 1998b.

Bar-Yakov, Shi. "Mavet bo leluna-park."[Death goes to amusement park]. *Tel Aviv*, 23 February 1996a

——. "Yoter midai sukar." [Too much sugar]. *Tel Aviv*, 19 December 1996b.

——. "Hizayon teatrali piyuti." [Poetic theatrical vision]. *Tel Aviv*, 26 December 1997.

——. "Tzdafot bimkom shwarma." [Oysters instead of shwarma]. *Tel Aviv*, 15 January 1999a.

——. "Havaya teatronit mushlemet." [The perfect theatrical experience]. *Yediot Ahronot*, 20 October 1999b.

Bar-Yosef, Eitan. "Gorky met paamaaim." [Gorky dies twice]. *Tel Aviv*, 6 January 1995.

Ben-Nun, Ran. "Or legoim." [Light for the nations]. *Tel Aviv*, 9 December 1994.

Ben-Shaul, Moshe. "Lo rotzim lehiot bnei-aruba shel kahal rusi." [We don't want to be hostages of the Russian audience]. *Maariv*, 10 May 1992.

Blillngton, Michael. "The Idiot/Manchester." *The Guardian*, 2 November 1994.

Christofis, Lee. "Visitors from K'far Steal the Show." *The Australian.*, 19 October 1998.

Cliff, Nigel. "Tour de Force of Babel." *The Times*, 7 June 1999.

Cohen, Ada. "Leah Rabin: teatron Gesher heeshir meod et hayeinu." [Leah Rabin: Gesher theatre enriched our lives]. *Maariv*, 17 June 1993.

Cohen, Guy. "Enoshi, kimaat enoshi midai bishvileinu." [Humanist, almost too humanist for us]. *Hair*, 20 December 1996.

Colgan, Gerry. "The Village." *The Irish Times*, 7 October 1999.

Coveney, Michael. "The Week in Reviews: Israeli Theatre." *The Observer*, 27 April 1997.

Croyden, Margaret. "Waiting for Hamlet." *The Village Voice*, 8-14 January 1992.

Dayan, Saar. "Ori levy, mankal gesher: 'im kol hahatzlahah, adain ein lanu bait rauy leshmo'." [Ori Levy, Gesher's manager: 'With all the success, we still do not have a decent home']. *Maariv*, 19 June 1997.

"Don Juan." *Maariv*, 20 February 1997.

Elkariv, Yakir. "Pisgat hashefel." [The peak in the depth]. *Tel Aviv*, 23 December 1994.

Evron, Boaz. "Haftaa." [Surprise]. *Yediot Ahronot*, 1 May 1991a.

———. "Lo leolim bilvad." [Not only for the immigrants]. *Yediot Ahronot*, 19 August 1991b.

———. "Hateatron hamikzoi baioter baaretz." [The most professional theatre in Israel]. *Yediot Ahronot*, 26 September 1991c.

"Festival chich veziva, hairuim beitzumam." [Festival of Chich and Ziva, the events are at their peak]. *Maariv*, 5 November 1993.

Fuks, Sarit. "Haulam bli myshkin." [The world without Myshkin]. *Maariv*, 29 January 1993.

———. "Hibuk dov." [Bear's hug]. *Maariv*, 29 April 1994.

———. "Arye." *Maariv*, 13 January 1995a.

———. "Im avanim bemara." [With stones in kidneys]. *Maariv*, 4 August 1995b.

———. "Hayeah hakfulim shel haez Dizza." [The double life of the goat Dizza]. *Maariv*, 16 February 1996a.

———. "Mur'al." [Poisoned]. *Maariv*, 13 December 1996b.

———. "Hashafan hekzistentziali." [The existential bunny]. *Maariv*, 2 January 1998.

Gardner, Lyn. "Theatre Review." *The Guardian*, 7 June 1999.

Gore-Langton, Robert. "Prize Idiot amid the Mayhem." *The Daily Telegraph*, 3 November 1994.

Goren, T. "Matzaveiny hatov rah kol kach." [Our good situation is so bad]. *Hateatron*, 13–17 July 1998.

Gorman, Sophie. "Hebrew Parable Triumphs over Language Barrier." *The Irish Independent*, 6 October 1999.

Gur, Batya. "Hahatzaga hagdola shel haisraeliut." [The big show of Israeliness]. *Haaretz*, 1 January 1999.

Gurfinkel, Avi. "Arig meshubach." [Superb material]. *Yerushalaim*, 25 April 1997.

Gussow, Meil. "Stoppard in Russian from Israel." *The New York Times*, 31 January 1992.

Habim, D. "Adam ben kelev." [Adam Resurrected]. *Hadashot*, 27 October 1993.

Handelsaltz, Michael. "Nitzavim bemerkaz habamah." [Standing in the centerstage]. *Haaretz*, 21 April 1991a.

———. "Zehut bemashkon." [Identity in deposit]. *Haaretz*, 24 April 1991b.

———. "Kartis bikur lesahkanim." [A card for the actors]. *Haaretz*, 11 August 1991c.

———. "Hahatzaga haeevet lehimashech." [The show must go on]. Haarets, 14 January 1992a.

———. "Gesher leshum makom." [Bridge to nowhere]. *Haaretz*, 20 January 1992b.

———. "Teudat kavod lemoreihem." [Appreciation certificate to their teachers]. *Haaretz*, 7 July 1992c.

———. "Shiur beklita vebeteatron." [A lesson in absorption and in theatre]. *Haaretz*, 8 January 1993a.

———. "Hakeev haenoshi besherut haspektakl." [Human pain for the sake of a spectacle]. *Haaretz*, 1 November 1993b.

———. "Hem metzuianim, aval hem lo hemtziu et hateatron." [They are excellent, but they did not invent the theatre]. *Haaretz*, 25 April 1994a.

———. "Hasiim shebashefel." [The peaks that are in the lower depths]. *Haaretz*, 29 December

1994b.

———. "Gesher al maim soarim." [Bridge (*Gesher*) over trouble water]. *Haaretz*, 23 April 1995a.

———. "Molière nitzeach et habamai." [Molière bit the director]. *Haaretz*, 1 August 1995b.

———. "Hatzionut hanostalgit." [The nostalgic Zionism]. *Haaretz*, 19 February 1996a.

———. "Kfar." [Village]. *Haaretz*, 6 June 1996b.

———. "Ulam katan venora." [Small and terrible world]. *Haaretz*, 11 December 1996c.

———. "Yoter midai velo maspik." [Too much and not enough]. *Haaretz*, 24 December 1997.

———. "Hem lo hemtziu et hagalgal." [They did not invent the wheel]. *Haaretz*, 6 January 1998a.

———. "Bdicha leulam hozeret." [The eternal joke]. *Haaretz*, 17 March 1998b.

———. "Hakishateta vegam tishtashta." [Decorated and Blurred]. *Haaretz*, 7 January 1999a.

———. "Mitrahakim min hamakorot." [Departing from the sources]. *Haaretz*, 13 January 1999b.

———. "Gahamot venesim." [Sparks and miracles]. *Haaretz*, 1 September 1999c.

———. "Hasrei naduniya." [Dowryless]. *Haaretz*, 10 October 1999d.

Hefetz, Fabiana. "Gesher mefuar meal maim radudim." [Fancy Gesher above shallow waters]. *Zman Tel Aviv*, 6 December 1996.

Kanuk, Yoram. "Hamachshefim yardu davka lemartef." [The wizards went to the basement]. *Tel Aviv*, 21 June 1991.

———. "Gam ksheeino bemeitavo." [Even when it is not at its best]. *Yediot Ahronot*, 13 January 1999.

Karpal, Dalia. "Yeled ra germaniya." [Bad boy from Germany]. *Haaretz*, 30 July 1999.

Katz, Shiri. "Arye bekaitz." [Arye in summer]. *Maariv*, 9 July 1999.

Kimchi, Alona. "Harusim al Tel Aviv." [Russians on Tel Aviv]. *Tel Aviv*, 19 March 1993.

Kingston, Jeremy. "Black and White Magic." *The Times*, 2 November 1994.

Koberg, Roland. "Das Alte Leben ins Neue Retten." [Saving the old life with the new]. *Berliner Zeitung*, 3 March 1998.

"Laavor et hagesher." [To cross the bridge]. *Haaretz*, 12 August 1991.

Laor, Yitzhak. "Shelo yegamer." [Don't let it end]. *Tel Aviv*, 22 January 1993.

Lavender, Andy. "Wishful Non-political Thinking." *The Times*, 1 May 1997.

Lavi, Eyal. "Mahazeh shoah beohel shel kirkas." [Play about the Holocaust in the circus tent]. *Telegraph*, 27 October 1993.

Lev-Ari, Shiri. "Nivheret hahalomot." [The dream team]. *Haaretz*, 20 February 1998.

Litvik, Miri. "Gesher rotze lehiot teatron Israeli normali." [Gesher wants to be a normal Israeli theatre]. *Haulam Hazeh*, 9 June 1993a.

———. "Kazakov mul gesher: mehir kaved avur hatehila." [Kazakov vis-à-vis Gesher: a high price for fame]. *Haulam Hazeh*, 27 October 1993b.

Lubits, Tami. "Hakirkas haachzari mikulam." [The most cruel circus]. *Maariv*, 14 October 1993.

Luzie, Avi. "Gesher el haolim." [Bridge to the immigrants]. *Haaretz*, 18 December 1990.

"Mahazeh hadash shel Sobol beteatron Gesher." [A new play by Sobol at the Gesher theatre]. *Yediot Ahronot*, 19 October 1995.

Manor, Giora. "Mirsham leteatron amiti." [A recipe for a true theatre]. *Davar*, 1 January 1993.

"Mar'eh meal hagesher." [Vistas above bridge]. *Yediot Ahronot*, 4 September 1997.

Marks, Peter. "Where Past and Future Intersect." *The New York Times*, 9 July 1998.

Matthes, Meike. “Terror, Iddylle.” [Terror, idyll]. *Der Tages Spiegel*, 3 March 1998.

Melamed, Ariana. “Hu yareh lany ma ze kultura.” [He will show us what is kultura]. *Hair*, 5 December 1997.

Merten, Von J. “Gott war wohl zigaretten holen.” [God went out to buy cigarettes]. *Berliner Morgenpost*, 24 October 1994.

Michman, Y. “Michtav lemaarehet.” [Letter to the editor]. *Haaretz*, 15 August 1991.

Milshtein, Avishai. “Leulam lo nihie od Habima.” [We’ll never be another Habima]. *Tel Aviv*, 22 October 1993.

Mundy, Yosef. “Gesher leshum makom.” [Bridge to nowhere]. *Davar*, 4 October 1991.

Nagid, Haim. “Gesher bearmon.” [Bridge in the palace]. *Maariv*, 3 May 1991.

———. “Lamrot haskandalim: hayeled holem veyesh heisegim.” [Despite the scandals: the child is dreaming and there are achievements]. *Davar*, 15 September 1993a.

———. “Veet haadam shachachu.” [And forgot about Adam]. *Davar*, 31 October 1993b.

———. “Mishakei baboa niflaim.” [Wonderful play of reflections]. *Davar*, 24 April 1994a.

———. “Teatron.” [Theatre]. *Davar*, 28 July 1994b.

———. “Opera bli sabon.” [Opera without soap]. *Davar*, 29 December 1994c.

———. “Ulam yashan nivnah, spasibo.” [The old world is built, thanks]. *Davar*, 20 February 1996.

Ohed, Michael. “Gesher velo getto.” [Bridge instead of ghetto]. *Davar*, 30 August 1991.

———. “Rosencrantz and guildenstern mesarvim lamut.” [Rosencrantz and Guildenstern refuse to die]. *Shishi*, 4 March 1994.

———. “Tartif hu molière meturaf, lulyani veim zot otenti.” [*Tartuffe* is a crazy Molière, clownesque, and yet, authentic]. *Globes*, 4 August 1995.

———. “Halom kasum shemistaem babeit kvarot.” [Magical dream ending at the cemetery]. *Globes*, 9 February 1996.

Oren, Amos. “Sobol hozer lekfar.” [Sobol returns to village]. *Yediot Ahronot*, 30 January 1996.

Orian, Yehudit. “Lehayi haam haze.” [To the life of this nation]. *Yediot Ahronot*, 25 October 1995.

———. “Mea shanim aharei, ‘shalosh ahayot’ adayin betokef.” [After a hundred years, *Three Sisters* are still relevant]. *Yediot Ahronot*, 18 March 1998.

Orion, Amir. “Mitragshim besignon yashan.” [Moved in an old fashion]. *Hair*, 15 January 1993a.

———. “Elohim rotze schmaltz.” [God wants schmaltz]. *Hair*, 9 November 1993b.

Pinto, Goel. “Hamelech yevgeny harishon.” [The King Yevgeny the First]. *Anashim*, 20 January 1999.

Raisman, Shosh. “Shoah bli yatzurei matzpun.” [The Holocaust with the clear conscience]. *Tel Aviv*, 9 November 1993.

Reinecke, Stefan. “Adam Hundesohn.” [Adam Resurrected]. *Frankfurter Rundshau*, 20 October 1994.

Richard, Christine. “Das Ewige Publicum Schaut Sich die Totale Hölle.” [An eternal audience watches total hell]. *Basler Zeitung*, 2 September 1993.

Robinson, Mark. “Fears of a Clown.” *The Village Voice*, 28 July 1998.

Rose, Lloyd. “Lost Odessa, Alive Again.” *The Washington Post*, 27 March 1998.

Ross, Dina. "Death Comes to Life in a Snapshot of Israel's Birth." *The Age*, 17 October 1998.

Russo, Francine. "On the Town." *The Village Voice*, 21 July 1998.

Shachar, Aelet. "Yafe kmo kevin costner, kochav kmo whitney houston." [Handsome like Kevin Kostner, star like Whitney Houston]. *Hair*, 1 January 1993.

Shahal, Yuval. "Haalma vehamavet." [The maiden and the death]. *Zman Tel Aviv*, 24 December 1999.

"Shalosh ahayot." [Three sisters]. *Maariv*, 5 December 1997.

Shapiro, Ruth. "Meuhevet beidiot." [In love with the idiot]. *Maariv*, 5 January 1993a.

———. "Lo stam bahur yafeh." [Not just a handsome guy]. *Maariv*, 3 November 1993b.

———. "Adam ben-kelev–lefestival vienna." [Adam Resurrected–to Vienna Festival]. *Maariv*, 30 March 1993c.

———. "Hapninim vehahavrakot hen shel mark." [The pearls and the brilliance came from Mark]. *Maariv*, 9 December 1996.

———. "Yevgeny arye. Sipur hatzlaha." [Yevgeny Arye. A success story]. *Maariv*, 29 April 1997.

Shiffman, Yosi. "Nes!" [Miracle!]. *Davar*, 8 January 1993.

"Shlomo lahat: bubah shel ziva." [Shlomo Lahat: Ziva's doll]. *Yediot Ahronot*, 28 October 1993.

Shohat, Tzipi. "Latzet mehaghetto harusi." [To get out of the Russian ghetto]. *Haaretz*, 13 May 1992.

———. "Harbeh mihzur vemeat mahazot makorioit." [Lots of recycling and few original plays]. *Haaretz*, 20 October 1993a.

———. "Ktzin haeses hofech leelohim." [SS officer turns into god]. *Haaretz*, 21 October 1993b.

———. "Oskim kan beyatzur hatzagot velo be-omanut." [They deal here with showbiz, and not with art]. *Haaretz*, 20 April 1994a.

———. "Berusia ze betach haya skandal." [In Russia it would definitely be a scandal]. *Haaretz*, 28 December 1994b.

———. "Mashber beteatron gesher ekev hiluke deot bein mankal lemenahel omanuti." [Crisis in the Gesher theatre due to the disagreement between the manager and the artistic director]. *Haaretz*, 10 April 1995a.

———. "Gesher likrat shinui." [Gesher before the changes]. *Haaretz*, 11 April 1995b.

———. "Sahkan hacameri ori levy nivhar lemankal teatron gesher." [Cameri's actor Ori Levy was chosen to be a manager of the Gesher theatre]. *Haaretz*, 15 May 1995c.

———. "Achsav ani tzarich lehiot kan." [Now I have to be here]. *Haaretz*, 19 July 1995d.

———. "Teatron gesher yeftah et haona im mahazeh she katav lo sobol bemiuhad." [The Gesher theatre will open a season with a play that Sobol wrote for it especially]. *Haaretz*, 19 October 1995e.

———. "Ani margish beineihem babait." [I feel at home among them]. *Haaretz*, 10 December 1996.

———. "Yesahaku hanaarim." [The youth will play]. *Haaretz*, 6 April 1997a.

———. "Teatron gesher makim bama lesahkanim tzeirim." [Gesher theatre creates stage for the young actors]. *Haaretz*, 7 October 1997b.

———. "Hitmasrut gdola." [The Big Devotion]. *Haaretz*, 4 December 1997c.

———. "Kama mistakrim menahalei hatiatronim." [How much do theatre directors earn]. *Haaretz*, 30 March 2000a.

———. "Hamemshala taavir letiatron gesher million shekel ketmicha nosefet." [The government will transfer to Gesher a million NIS as an additional support]. *Haaretz*, 20 June 2000b.

Shrir, Dorit. "Mankal misrad hatarbut: legesher lo magiah tosefet taktziv." [Director general of Ministry of Culture: Gesher does not deserve an additional budget]. *Yediot Ahronot*, 28 March 2000.

Sofer, Ilan. "Rosencrantz and guildenstern metim bepaam hashniya." [Rosencrantz and Guildenstern are dead for the second time]. *Globes*, 30 March 1994.

Solomon, Alisa. "Do Look Back." *The Village Voice*, 14 July 1998.

"Stutzim." [Escapades]. *Tzfon Hair*, 29 September 2000.

"Teatron Gesher." [Gesher theatre]. *Hair*, 27 September 1991.

Wardle, Irving. "Theatre." *The Independent*, 6 November 1994.

Weitz, Shoshana. "Matzav hateatron bechi ra." [Theatre situation–bad crying]. *Tel Aviv*, 6 June 1992.

———. "Sipur hatzlacha." [Success story]. *Yediot Ahronot*, 18 January 1993a.

———. "Hagigat hamavet." [Celebration of death]. *Yediot Ahronot*, 2 November 1993b.

———. "Ovrim et hagesher." [Crossing the bridge]. *Yediot Ahronot*, 24 April 1994a.

———. "Yoter tov mehanifla." [Better than superb]. *Yediot Ahronot*, 29 December 1994b.

———. "Hotzim et hagesher." [Crossing the bridge]. *Yediot Ahronot*, 1 August 1995.

———. "Hagiga bekfar." [Celebration in the village]. *Yediot Ahronot*, 20 February 1996a.

———. "Kfar." [Village]. *Yediot Ahronot*, 13 September 1996b.

———. "Yir beteatron gesher. Hatmunot yafot, aval hasignon hateatrali amus vemeyagea." [City in the Gesher theatre. The pictures are beautiful, but the theatrical style is busy and tiring]. *Yediot Ahronot*, 12 December 1996c.

———. "Yotzet dofen vemarshima." [Exceptional and impressive]. *Yediot Ahronot*, 25 December 1997.

———. "Parshanut muzara." [Weird interpretation]. *Yediot Ahronot*, 23 April 1998.

———. "Ein kesher bein tohen letzura." [No connection between form and content]. *Yediot Ahronot*, 7 January 1999a.

———. "Lema mehubar hagesher?" [What is Gesher attached to?]. *Yediot Ahronot*, 22 January 1999b.

———. "Ketzer be tikshoret." [Misunderstanding]. *Yediot Ahronot*, 31 August 1999c.

Winer, Linda. "A Little Jewish Village in Palestine." *Newsday*, 9 July 1998.

Yahalom-Rimshon, Giora. "Mushchatim, nimastem." [Corrupted, sick of you]. *Yerushalaim*, 26 February 1999.

Yahil-Wax, Miriam. "Kvar zanahnu et hayiddish." [We already abandoned Yiddish]. *Haaretz*, 22 January 1992.

———. "Universali ze hahefeh miisraeli?" [Is universal an opposite of Israeli]. *Yediot Ahronot*, 29 January 1999a.

Yaron, Eliakim. "Litush miktzoi–nituk svivati." [Professional polish–detachment from the environment]. *Maariv*, 20 October 1991.

———. "Molière betzelo shel stalin." [Molière in Stalin's shadow]. *Maariv*, 13 January 1992.

———. "Lo rak bezchut dostoevsky." [Not only because of Dostoevsky]. *Maariv*, 11 January 1993a.

——. "Havayah totalit." [Total experience]. *Maariv*, 2 November 1993b.

——. "Sikum beinaim nifla." [Wonderful interim conclusion]. *Maariv*, 21 April 1994a.

——. "Haim bazevel." [Life sucks]. *Maariv*, 29 December 1994b.

——. "Molière shoneh, niflah." [Different wonderful Molière]. *Maariv*, 1 August 1995.

——. "Niflah, malhiv, sohef." [Wonderful, inspiring, moving]. *Maariv*, 20 February 1996a.

——. "Ah eizu yir." [Ah, what a city]. *Maariv*, 12 December 1996b.

——. "Ein rega shel sheket." [No a quiet moment]. *Maariv*, 25 December 1997.

——. "Gadol aleihem." [Over their heads]. *Maariv*, 22 April 1998.

——. "Shlosha kvasim be-halal." [Three sheep in the space]. *Maariv*, 7 January 1999a.

——. "Klasika hyperactivit." [Hyper-active classics]. *Maariv*, 31 August 1999b.

——. "Yafe leain, rahok mihalev." [Indulgent to the eyes, but far from the heart]. *Maariv*, 9 November 1999c.

Yaron, Eliakim; M. Aizenshtadt; D. Alter; and D. Ronen. "Pras Meir Margalit leomanut teatron tashnag." [Meir Margalit theatre prize 1993]. *Bamah* 132 (1993): 75–77.

Zaltzman, Aviva. "Derech ioter kzara vepahot koevet." [A shorter and less painful way]. *Davar*, 5 May 1992a.

——. "Neshama chachama haita lo leidiot." [An idiot had a wise soul]. *Davar*, 28 December 1992b.

——. "Soeret al habamah." [Wild on stage]. *Davar*, 22 October 1993.

——. "Meyatzgim et atzmam veet ulamam haprati bilvad." [They represent only themselves and their private world]. *Davar*, 19 December 1994.

——. "Yoter veyoter israeli." [More and more Israeli]. *Davar*, 19 October 1995a.

——. "Haisraelim, mabat min hatzad." [The Israelis, a glance from aside]. *Davar*, 6 February 1995b.

Zohar, Yuval. "Shover levavot." [The heartbreaker]. *Yerushalaim*, 10 April 1998.

Filmography

Ais, Arye. (Executive Producer). *Gesher*. Jerusalem: First Channel, Israeli Public Television, 1991.

——. (Executive Producer). *Skala: teatron gesher–retrospectiva*. [Stage: Gesher Theatre's retrospective]. Jerusalem: Thirty Third Channel, Israeli Public Television, 1999.

Hanoch, Lihi (Director). *Adam Circus*. [Film], 1993.

Mafzir, Boris (Director). Mafzir, Boris; Altman, Shmuel (Producers). *Mishpahat gesher*. [Gesher Family] [Film], 1993.

Interviews

Arye, Yevgeny. Interview. Tel Aviv, June 2003.

Ben-Zur, Efrat. Interview. July 1999.

Binder, Zvia. Interview. August 2000.

Demidov, Israel (Sasha). Interview. July 1999.

Dodina, Yevgenya. Interview. June 2001.

Gesher-2 Actor. Interview. July 1999.

Levy, Ori. Interview. June 2001.

Loevsky, Alik. E-mail Interview. November 1999.

Maltzev, Slava. Interview. June 2001.

Riskin, Victor. Interview. June 2001.

Savel, Michal. Interviews. June 1999a; August 2000; June 2001; June 2003.

Suchanova, Tatiana. Interviews. June 2001; June 2003.

Vigger, Andrea. Interview. July 1999.

Voitulevich-Manor, Natalya. Interview. June 1999.

Yahil-Wax, Miriam. Interview. July 1999b.

Yahil-Wax, Miriam and Mark Ivanir. *Russian/Jewish Workshop.* Talk presented at the BITE-99: Barbican International Theatre Event, London, UK, June 1999.

Archival Materials

Gesher Theatre [Brochure]. Tel Aviv, 1996.

Gesher Theatre [Brochure]. Tel Aviv, 1999.

Rosencrantz i Guildenstern Mertvy [Rosencrantz and Guildenstern Are Dead]. [Playbill]. Tel Aviv, 1991.

Savel, Michal. *Ona shel ahava vemavet: shtei hatzagot hadashot begesher* [The season of love and death: two new shows at Gesher]. [Press-release]. Tel Aviv, 1999b.

Scheflan, Michal. *Beshefel miet Maxim Gorky* [*The Lower Depths* by Maxim Gorky]. [Press-release]. Tel Aviv, 1994.

Scheflan, Michal. *Gesher-2–Don Juan miet Molière.* [Gesher-2–*Don Juan* by *Molière*]. [Press-release]. Tel Aviv, 1997.

Schlosser, Tibi. "Gesher–sikum." [Gesher–conclusions]. Report No. 1221820. Israeli Ministry of Foreign Affairs, 31 October 1994.

Index

Studies on Themes and Motifs in Literature

The series is designed to advance the publication of research pertaining to themes and motifs in literature. The studies cover cross-cultural patterns as well as the entire range of national literatures. They trace the development and use of themes and motifs over extended periods, elucidate the significance of specific themes or motifs for the formation of period styles, and analyze the unique structural function of themes and motifs. By examining themes or motifs in the work of an author or period, the studies point to the impulses authors received from literary tradition, the choices made, and the creative transformation of the cultural heritage. The series will include publications of colloquia and theoretical studies that contribute to a greater understanding of literature.

For additional information about this series or for the submission of manuscripts, please contact:

Dr. Heidi Burns
Peter Lang Publishing
P.O. Box 1246
Bel Air, MD 21014-1246

To order other books in this series, please contact our Customer Service Department:

800-770-LANG (within the U.S.)
212-647-7706 (outside the U.S.)
212-647-7707 FAX

Or browse online by series at:

www.peterlangusa.com